Educating Evangelicalism

The origins, development and impact of London Bible College

Educating Evangelicalism

The origins, development and impact of London Bible College

Ian M. Randall

paternoster
press

First published in 2000 by Paternoster Press

06 05 04 03 02 01 00   7 6 5 4 3 2 1

Paternoster Press is an imprint of Paternoster Publishing,
P.O. Box 300, Carlisle, Cumbria, CA3 0QS, UK
and
P.O. Box 1047, Waynesboro, GA 30830-2047, USA
Website: www.paternoster-publishing.com

British Library Cataloguing in Publication Data
A catalogue record for this book is available from the British Library

ISBN 0-85364-873-5

Cover Design by Mephisto, Glasgow
Typeset by WestKey Ltd, Falmouth, Cornwall
Printed in Great Britain by Bell & Bain Ltd, Glasgow

To Harold Rowdon –
with much appreciation.

Contents

Preface and Acknowledgements

It was a very pleasant surprise when Derek Tidball, the current principal of London Bible College, approached me about writing a history of LBC that would place it in the context of the evangelical developments of the post-war period. As we discussed the project Derek made it clear that all the college's records would be open to me and that he believed it was important for all aspects of the story – the tensions as well as the triumphs – to be told. This is what I have tried to do. Exploring, assessing and describing this remarkable story has proved to be one of the most rewarding tasks I have ever undertaken. In the first chapter I note the way in which a history of Fuller Theological Seminary, USA, by George Marsden, offered me a model.

To a large extent, my perspective on LBC is that of an outsider who has in fact been on the staff of another theological institution in London. But prior to commencing teaching at Spurgeon's College I was a part-time external student at LBC and completed an MPhil under Harold Rowdon, then the LBC church history lecturer and also known for his work as general editor of Partnership Publications. I am most grateful to Harold – who wrote the story of LBC in 1968 to mark twenty-five years of the life of the college – for his warm interest in this new history. He has carefully read all my material and has commented most helpfully on it. This book is dedicated to him. I am sorry that friends such as Harold are referred to in the book by their surnames, but I decided to follow this convention.

Most of the people about whom I am writing here are still alive and I have conducted interviews with many of those who have played a central part in LBC's life. My thanks go to each person who participated in this way. I am particularly grateful to Gilbert Kirby, Michael Griffiths, Peter Cotterell and Derek Tidball, as past and present principals of LBC, and to Dermot McDonald, a former vice-principal, for their willingness to spend time replying to my questions. Derek Tidball has made a point of encouraging me throughout. A number of other LBC staff and previous members of the faculty have talked to me about the college and offered their own perspectives on its development. Tony Lane, as a long-standing member of the LBC teaching staff, has enabled me to nuance the way I have handled issues in a number of chapters.

Others have also been kind enough to read parts (and in some cases the whole) of my manuscript and have responded with detailed comments. I am especially indebted to Leslie Allen, Ralph Martin and Ian Macnair, former lecturers at LBC, for their help. I am also grateful to Michael Eastman, Alan Gibson, Neil Hudson, Douglas McBain and David Wheaton, former LBC students who are involved in leadership within different areas of evangelical life in this country. I extend my thanks as well to Derek Warren, a former LBC board chairman; John Colwell, my colleague in the adjoining office at Spurgeon's College; David Bebbington, whose work on evangelicalism has been my guide; and Martin Light and Denise Jones who have proof-read the whole book.

Several librarians and custodians of manuscript holdings have also assisted me – especially at LBC itself, but also at Spurgeon's College, the Evangelical Alliance's offices and the Evangelical Library, London. Jenny Aston, Derek Tidball's secretary, has located several papers for me. In my overall research into evangelicalism and also in this particular project I have made extensive use of weekly and monthly Christian periodicals housed in the archives associated with these and other libraries. Such newspapers and journals provide a rich resource for students looking at any of the various strands of twentieth-century evangelicalism. For the 'inner' LBC story my main sources of information have been LBC records.

At all the stages of writing and production Paternoster Publishing has offered every possible assistance. People there have put much effort into enhancing the book through, for example, photographs, helpful appendices and reader-friendly explanations. It was no surprise to find that Tony Graham, the Production Editor at Paternoster who has been my closest contact, is a former student of LBC. This was yet another confirmation of the conclusion I had reached long before completing this book – that the influence of LBC within the evangelical world is extremely pervasive. Tara Smith, as copy editor, has offered many insightful comments.

Having acknowledged the generous help I have received, it is important to say that the interpretation given here of LBC's context and its contribution to theological education is my own. Inevitably, a great deal more could have been said about the richly diverse ways in which former LBC students have contributed to Christian life, mission and theological reflection. Additional work remains to be done, for example, on the interplay between the evangelical theological enterprise in the non-western and western worlds. In addition, LBC relates to the wider sphere of scholarship. As such, its links stretch beyond the evangelical scene. Although I have dealt to an extent with such issues, my focus has been on educating evangelicalism.

The final revisions to this book were done in Prague. Since moving here I have begun to understand a little more clearly the challenges that are involved in theological education in the new Europe. In this period of transition I have also come to a greater appreciation of the invaluable support I receive through the companionship of my wife, Janice. It is appropriate to mention that in the 1980s she studied through distance learning courses offered by LBC.

Ian M. Randall
Prague, Czech Republic
Advent 1999

Foreword

Speaking at the annual prizegiving of London Bible College in 1966, Dr Dermot McDonald, then vice-principal, spoke of the challenges facing evangelicals and how LBC was equipping people to meet them. 'The College's aim,' he said, 'is to produce men and women who could out-think as well as outlive their contemporaries. They were not to be men and women of frothy spirituality or of frothy scholarship, but well founded in devotion to God and his word.' In saying this, 'Derrie Mc' neatly summed up the vision of LBC. Spirituality and scholarship, the word and the world, thinking and living have always gone hand in hand at LBC.

That particular prizegiving took place at a significant time in the story of LBC. The year before Dr E.F. Kevan, the college's first principal, who had done so much to establish and mould the college, had died unexpectedly. Gilbert Kirby had been elected to succeed him but had not yet taken up office. Holding true to the original vision of the founders, Gilbert was not only to relocate the college from central London to Northwood, but develop it to meet the new challenges of the world church in the 1960s and 1970s. Each principal, together with his colleagues on the staff, has reengineered the college to meet contemporary needs. Throughout its history LBC has shown a creative dynamism which is the envy of many. It has never been a static institution. And it is time that its story was told.

Histories come in all shapes and sizes. Former students may have welcomed a history which focused with a narrow lens on the life of the college. It is always great fun for those who have been on the inside to read of the oral traditions, the college myths and humorous stories that get recycled from generation to generation. But such a history is not of great interest to those who have not been a part of the institution. Other histories can record the formal development of an institution and, poring over the records, provide a blow-by-blow account of official decisions and precise details. They are often not only laborious to read but also miss the wood for the trees.

Our decision was to ask for a different type of account to be written. We wanted someone to write a history which would uncover the role of LBC in the history of post-war evangelicalism. The stories of the college and of evangelicalism are closely intertwined. The traffic has been two-way. LBC has made a tremendous contribution to evangelicalism both in Britain and around the world, and the changing contours of wider evangelicalism have been appreciably impacted by LBC graduates. Equally, however, LBC's own ethos and story has been shaped by the changes in wider evangelicalism. A history of the college, therefore, serves as a window onto a wider story and much can be gleaned about post-war evangelicalism by reading the record of this one evangelical institution. It is true to say, too, that those who write about evangelicalism have too often ignored the role of LBC and we trust that in telling its story the record of evangelicalism will be balanced and corrected.

We approached Dr Ian Randall, then of Spurgeon's College, now of Spurgeon's and the International Baptist Theological Seminary, Prague, to see if he would be interested in undertaking to write such a history. Given the history of relations between LBC and Spurgeon's, at least on the football field over the years, it was, as a mutual friend said, 'an act of grace on our part to make such an approach'. But equally, as Ian pointed out, it was also an act of faith on our part. I am sure that you will conclude that grace and faith have once again been amply rewarded.

Ian Randall has established himself recently as one of the best historians of modern evangelicalism and he has brought a wide range of understanding, scholarship and skill to his task. He was given complete freedom and access to any records he wished to see. He has taken care to speak, as far as possible, to all the principal participants in the story and to check the accuracy of his record. The end result combines objectivity with sensitivity. We are deeply grateful for Ian's willingness to undertake this task and to do so with such efficiency and distinction.

As the present principal of London Bible College I find the story which is recorded in this book awesome. From nothing, and outside the main denominational structures and educational boundaries, LBC quickly became an established college with a much respected position within the evangelical world and with an enviable academic record. The diversity and significance of the contribution made by its graduates is formidable. On the day I sat down to write this foreword a senior Indian evangelical leader paid us the unsolicited compliment of saying that much of evangelical theological education in Asia owed its development and achievement to date to LBC graduates. Many names are mentioned here but not by any means all. To do so would have been impossible. Furthermore, we are acutely conscious that in 'Kingdom terms' it is often the unknown names who make the greatest contribution.

My vision would be that LBC remain a place known for its reliable evangelical commitment and for its high academic standards, but equally for its training of the whole person and its concern to develop people of spiritual maturity. Not all LBC students will end up in 'full-time' Christian work. That was never the vision of the college. The college's vision, from the beginning, was to train men and women for Christian leadership alongside one another whether they were to enter the ministry, serve overseas on the mission field or to return to the marketplace. LBC believed that there was value not in isolating one stream from another but in overcoming the introversion evident in some narrower colleges and training different people alongside one another. I believe the adaptability of LBC graduates over the years provides ample evidence that such a policy was justified. But whatever the vocational outcome of its graduates, the college has always sought to produce mature and committed disciples of Jesus Christ who for his sake will, as the current LBC advertising slogan has it, 'make a difference in an indifferent world'.

As we read this history our first response must be one of gratitude to God. We are thankful to those who had the original vision, provided so many resources and served the college in so many capacities over the years. We are also grateful to God for the tremendous impact LBC graduates have had for the sake of the gospel. Our second response must be of rededication for the future.

LBC must never fossilize the patterns of the past. Our task is to take the original vision and translate it so that we can continue to equip people for the twenty-first century for Christian leadership of all sorts. But I trust that, in the midst of a fluid evangelicalism and a rapidly changing world, LBC will remain a place where scholarship and spirituality, the word and the world, thinking and living will go hand in hand to the glory of God.

Derek J. Tidball, Principal
London Bible College
July 1999

Periodical Abbreviations

AW	*Advent Witness*
BLQ	*Bible Life Quarterly*
BT	*The Banner of Truth*
BQ	*Baptist Quarterly*
Baptist T	*The Baptist Times*
Bul	*Bulletin*
Chr	*The Christian*
Chr Grad	*Christian Graduate*
Chr Path	*The Christian's Pathway*
Chr T	*Christianity Today*
Chr W	*The Christian World*
The Churchman	*Churchman*
Ch E News	*The Church of England Newspaper*
C Rev	*College Review*
C W	*Christian World*
Ev B Evangelical	*Broadsheet*
Ev Chr	*Evangelical Christendom*
Ev Q	*Evangelical Quaterly*
Ev T	*Evangelical Times*
Expos T	*Expository Times*
JN	*Joyful News*
Kes Conv	*The Keswick Convention*
Kes Wk	*Keswick Week*
LBC Rev	*LBC Review (formerly College Review)*
Leadership T	*Leadership Today*
LF	*Life of Faith*

Min	*The Ministry*
MM	*Moody Monthly*
New Chr H	*New Christian Herald*
Pneuma	*Pnuema*
RT	*Redemption Tidings*
Ref T	*Reformation Today*
SCM	*Spurgeon's College Magazine*
SC Rec	*Spurgeon's College Record*
St Ch Hist	Studies in Church History
Th	*Theology*
Today	*Today*
Vox Ev	*Vox Evangelica*

Organization Abbreviations

ACUTE	Alliance Commission on Unity and Truth among Evangelicals
AEGM	Anglican Evangelical Group Movement
AIM	Africa Inland Mission
ANCC	All Nations Christian College
AOG	Assemblies of God
ATPM	Advent Testimony and Preparation Movement
BCC	British Council of Churches
BEC	British Evangelical Council
BGC	Billy Graham Center
BMS	Baptist Missionary Society
BRF	Baptist Revival Fellowship
BTI	Bible Training Institute
BU	Baptist Union
BYFC	British Youth for Christ
CAFOD	Catholic Fund for Overseas Development
CARE	Christian Action, Research and Education
CICCU	Cambridge Inter-Collegiate Christian Union
CIM	China Inland Mission
CLAM	Christian Life and Ministry
CMS	Church Missionary Service
CNAA	Council for National Academic Awards
CRK	London University Certificate of Proficiency in Religious Knowledge
CPAS	Church Pastoral Aid Society
CSSM	Children's Special Service Mission
CU	Christian Union

CWR	Crusade for World Revival
EA	Evangelical Alliance
ECONI	The Evangelical Contribution on Northern Ireland
ECUM	Evangelical Coalition for Urban Mission
ECM	European Christian Mission
EMA	Evangelical Missionary Alliance
EUSA	Evangelical Union of South America (now Latin Link)
FIEC	Fellowship of Independent Evangelical Churches
FYT	Frontier Youth Trust
HTB	Holy Trinity, Brompton
IFES	International Fellowship of Evangelical Students
ICC	International Christian College
ISCF	Inter-Schools Christian Fellowship
IVF	Inter-Varsity Fellowship
LBC	London Bible College
LCD	London College of Divinity
MWE	Movement for World Evangelisation
NAE	National Assembly of Evangelicals
NEAC	National Evangelical Anglican Congress
NOS	Nine O'Clock Service
OM	Operation Mobilisation
OMF	Overseas Missionary Fellowship
RE	Religious Education
SCM	Student Christian Movement
SDP	Social Democratic Party
SU	Scripture Union
TEAR Fund	The Evangelical Alliance Relief Fund
TF	Tyndale Fellowship
TSF	Theological Students Fellowship
UCCF	Universities and Colleges Christian Fellowship
WCC	World Council of Churches
WEF	World Evangelical Fellowship
YFC	Youth for Christ

1

'A Central Bible Institute in London'

What do the following have in common? George Carey (the Arch-bishop of Canterbury), Baroness Cox (the Deputy Speaker of the House of Lords), Anthony Thiselton (professor of Christian Theology at the University of Nottingham), Douglas McBain (president of the Baptist Union, 1998–99), Kwame Bediako (one of Africa's leading theologians), Judith Rose (archdeacon of Tonbridge), Clive Calver (president of World Relief), David Pickard (general director of the Overseas Missionary Fellowship), Graham Dale (director of the Christian Socialist Movement), Mary Evans (joint editor of *The Study Bible for Women*), Joel Edwards (general director of the Evangelical Alliance), and Michael Baughen (the former bishop of Chester) all have associa-tions with London Bible College, and most of them studied theology there. George Carey undertook postgraduate research through LBC. Baroness Cox, whose story is told in *A Voice for the Voiceless* (1998), is LBC president. Mary Evans is a current member of LBC staff. The list of former students of LBC who are prominent – in Britain and in many other countries – in the fields of biblical and theological scholarship, church leadership, over-seas mission, education, public life and socio-political action, is an extensive one. This book attempts to chart and evaluate some of the ways in which LBC has made a contribution to these fields through the men and women who have served on its staff and studied there as students.

The significance of LBC deserves to be better appreciated than is presently the case. Harold Rowdon, LBC's lecturer in church history, wrote a history in 1968 to mark the first twenty-five years of the life of the college. It is an informative and still-valuable study, which will be referred to quite frequently in the pages that follow.[1] Three decades later, however, a fresh perspective on that era is appropriate. Harold Rowdon's work was to a large extent an internal, institutional history. The present volume, as its title suggests, concentrates on the way in which the college has provided pan-evangelical theological education, and seeks to place LBC in the context of the wider evangelical movements of the post-war period and to examine its role within those movements. Chapters 2 to 7, covering the period up to the end of the 1960s, include some detailed coverage of the evangelical background. It is clear that by the late 1960s LBC had become an important influence within evangelicalism. Ernest Kevan, the first principal, died in 1965. The principals who followed him – Gilbert Kirby, Michael Griffiths, Peter Cotterell and Derek Tidball – were to develop the college in new ways. Chapters 8 to 10 give greater attention to the college itself, but they continue with the attempt to show the college's wider impact.

Post-War Evangelicalism

The work of David Bebbington has profoundly affected the study of evangelicalism – in particular his seminal study *Evangelicalism in Modern Britain: A History from the 1730s to the 1980s* (1989). His definition of evangelicalism as a movement comprising all those who stress the Bible, the cross, conversion and activism has been used by most books on the subject published in the past decade.[2] One of these books, *Who are the Evangelicals?* by Derek Tidball, principal of LBC from 1995 onwards, examines evangelical approaches not only to the Bible, the cross and conversion, but also to eschatology, the church, social action and

---

[1] H.H. Rowdon, *London Bible College: The First Twenty-Five Years.*
[2] D.W. Bebbington, *Evangelicalism in Modern Britain: A History from the 1730s to the 1980s*, 2–17.

spirituality.[3] In *Evangelicalism in Modern Britain* Bebbington refers once to LBC, 'an interdenominational body for training graduates in Christian work that commenced classes in 1943'.[4] The innovative and ambitious vision of the founders of LBC was, as it was expressed at the time, for 'a central Bible institute in London' which would operate with the standards of 'a fully recognized college of a British University'.[5] This was a pioneering concept for post-war evangelicalism.

The evangelicals who set up LBC were clearly not anti-intellectual fundamentalists. A recent important book by Harriet Harris, *Fundamentalism and Evangelicals*, properly highlights the interest in serious evangelical scholarship that was emerging in the 1930s and 1940s. Although she does mention LBC, she seems to see other ventures, such as the work emanating from the Theological Students Fellowship (TSF), founded in 1933, as more significant.[6] Further historical work remains to be done to show the way in which other bodies ensured that what emerged as mainstream evangelicalism in Britain in the post-war years was not fundamentalist in its ethos. There is an increasing number of books that show the broadening influence of LBC on individuals who studied there. For example, 1999 saw the publication of two books by former LBC students telling their own stories. Joel Edwards has reflected on the way in which many LBC students in the 1970s experienced 'important paradigm shifts' through their studies.[7] George Mitchell, who went on to school and college teaching and pastoral ministry, speaks of his time there in the early 1960s. He recalls the way in which Ralph Martin's lectures on theology at LBC 'ravished my mind with the range and possibilities of study he presented and modelled'.[8] The influences here were undoubtedly not fundamentalist.

---

[3] D.J. Tidball, *Who are the Evangelicals?*
[4] Bebbington, *Evangelicalism*, 260.
[5] Rowdon, *London Bible College*, 11–13.
[6] H.A. Harris *Fundamentalism and Evangelicals*, 51.
[7] J. Edwards, *Lord, Make us One – But not all the Same!* 26.
[8] G. Mitchell, *Comfy Glasgow*, 101–2.

From the 1940s, LBC has functioned as a vital connecting agent between a number of post-war evangelical bodies. Those who began in the later 1930s to talk about the possibility of a college in London were, as we will see in Chapter 2, associated mainly with interdenominational conservative evangelical organizations. The most important of these was the Inter-Varsity Fellowship of Evangelical Unions (IVF), formed in 1928, which drew together groups – frequently small groups – of students in the universities and colleges, and which spawned the TSF. One observer, Oliver Barclay, who was actively involved in the IVF from 1938 (and was its general secretary from 1964 to 1980), has written that in the inter-war period it was almost universally assumed that a conservative evangelical view of the supreme authority of the Bible was dead. Those who held this position, he comments, 'were regarded as theological dinosaurs on their way to extinction'.[9] Adrian Hastings, in *A History of English Christianity, 1920–1990*, notes that the evangelical movement had been linked with the Victorian empire and with simplistic attitudes that could not survive the complexities, ambiguities and cynicism of the 1920s. Indeed, in his section on the 1930s Hastings sees nothing worthy of mention taking place within English conservative evangelicalism.[10]

There were broader or 'liberal' evangelicals in the inter-war period who tended to reject conservative evangelical views about, for example, the verbal inspiration of Scripture or the substitutionary nature of the atonement. They espoused ideas found in more progressive Christian thinking – about the inspiration of Scripture, the nature of the atonement and worship. Within the Church of England, the Anglican Evangelical Group Movement (AEGM) was, for a time, a self-confident expression of such liberal evangelicalism. At least five thousand evangelicals of a more conservative hue met each year at the Keswick Convention in the Lake District. As an alternative, in 1928 the

---

[9] O. Barclay, *Evangelicalism in Britain, 1935–1995*, 16.
[10] A. Hastings, *A History of English Christianity, 1920–1990*, 77; chs. 13–23.

AEGM set up its own Church Convention at Cromer, Norfolk. A parallel development in Methodism was the Fellowship of the Kingdom, and within Congregationalism there was a movement of broader Reformed thinking.[11] The spirit within some sections of these movements, however, was rather uncritically optimistic. This outlook did not seem so convincing in a world confronted, during the Holocaust, by evil on a horrific scale. On the other hand, the Second World War, as David Smith argues in his book on evangelicals and social action, can be seen as having finally severed evangelicalism from the memory of its Victorian phase, 'and thus liberated it from the burden of that past ascendancy, enabling it to confront the challenge of evangelizing a non-Christian society'.[12]

Certainly, as Chapters 3 and 4 of this book show, the decade following the end of the war saw a massive upsurge in evangelistic activity. It was this new evangelistic impetus, rather than complete doctrinal unanimity, that drew evangelicals from different denominations together. At the same time, emerging evangelical leaders such as John Stott were determined to promote a reasoned evangelical faith. Stott was approached in 1947 about joining the LBC staff, but he remained at All Souls, Langham Place, London.[13] For some, the over-riding commitment which they had to conservative evangelical convictions meant that denominational ties were relatively unimportant. Douglas Johnson, for example, the first general secretary of the IVF, was brought up in the lay-led Brethren movement. He later looked for any church where he felt the preaching of the Bible was taken seriously, and for a time he regularly attended a London Presbyterian church.[14] Within this kind of environment, LBC,

---

[11] For these movements see I.M. Randall, *Evangelical Experiences: A Study in the Spirituality of English Evangelicalism, 1918–1939*.

[12] D.W. Smith, *Transforming the World?* 82.

[13] For the invitation to John Stott see T. Dudley-Smith, *John Stott: The Making of a Leader*, 239–40.

[14] I am indebted to Roger Shuff, who is undertaking doctoral research on the Brethren, for this information.

with its strongly evangelical position and also its interdenominational stance, was an attractive option for those seeking theological education. The later 1950s, as Chapter 5 shows, saw LBC grow rapidly.

Evangelicals, LBC and Society

Because the focus of this book is mainly on the place of LBC within evangelical Christianity, it makes only occasional references to the wider social and political background. But LBC's development cannot be understood without some reference to the social context. The college grew at a time when there was much talk of post-war reconstruction. The first full-time students, who started in 1946, were almost all reasonably mature students. Many who had returned from the Second World War had become used to extreme hardship and even those who had not been in the war were quite ready to put up with the very basic living conditions pertaining at the college. Not many of this initial intake were academically qualified. One among the first group of students, Donald Guthrie, was a shy person with a stammer whose academic ability and teaching potential were nonetheless recognized by Ernest Kevan, the first principal. Guthrie, who was later asked by Kevan to become a member of staff, vividly described the early days at LBC. All the lectures took place in one room of a house in Marylebone Road, London, that was due for demolition. Textbooks were balanced on knees, as there was no room for tables. There was a minute library which also served as a space for lectures.[15]

The facilities as a whole were spartan. When resident in the college, Guthrie was asked to bring his own chair for his bedroom, but when he arrived he found he was sharing the bedroom with three others and that there was no room for the chair. A willingness to overcome such obstacles during their training shaped the future direction of many of those early

---

[15] D. Guthrie, *I Stand for Truth*, 38.

students. The college's determinedly disciplined regime, put in place and maintained by Ernest Kevan ('If the Holy Spirit brought you here, He means you to obey the rules') also had an effect. Considerable numbers of the early students were to go overseas in mission, while others would become involved in teaching in secondary schools in difficult areas in Britain. Something of the feeling of hopeful idealism that characterized British society at large had its effect on LBC. Visions of a better future were tempered in the years immediately after the war by austerity and affected in the later 1950s by increasing affluence. But idealism was consistent with and encouraged the spirit of active evangelical endeavour.

In the 1960s the optimism that had been found in society would begin to fade. As Hastings puts it, the prosperity and sense of release of the 1950s were of a fairly conservative and controlled type, whereas the secular hopefulness of the 1960s became something 'ever more shapelessly radical' – 'anti-elitist, easy going, even ecstatic, self-satisfied, libertarian'.[16] Among the crucial conduits for the spread of this new outlook were a number of television programmes, including the BBC's highly satirical and controversial *Not so Much a Programme, More a Way of Life*. Within the churches, and especially within Anglicanism, the new mood was epitomized by calls from the more liberal for a new image of God.[17] Evangelical anti-institutionalism found its expression in the charismatic movement that also emerged in this period. For many evangelicals, however, the freedom of the 1960s represented a serious threat. Their response to the generally more relaxed atmosphere in society was to draw the boundary lines of belief and practice more emphatically than before. Within LBC, as is outlined in Chapters 6 and 7, this decade – when the college moved on from the Ernest Kevan era to the 15-year leadership of its second principal, Gilbert Kirby – mirrored the unease present within wider evangelicalism. Kirby was a naturally inclusive and

---

[16] Hastings, *History of English Christianity*, 516.

[17] See the discussion in ch. 6 of this book, as well as J.A.T. Robinson's *Honest to God*.

conciliatory evangelical, which meant that he felt deeply some of the polarizing tendencies of the period.

By the 1970s, evangelicals were waking up increasingly to their individual and corporate responsibilities for society. Some more radical evangelicals, as Chapter 8 describes, were calling for social justice to be seen as integral to mission. LBC was also reaching a more confident position in the evangelical world. It was always sensitive to the views of the wider evangelical constituency, and criticisms of the theological positions of members of its faculty were on occasions the cause of considerable tension. But from the 1970s the college (through its staff and former students) increasingly reached a new maturity. It was, from this point on, to be as much a significant shaper of the wider scene as a body influenced by those outside its ranks. Throughout the 1970s and 1980s LBC would send out people who would affect not only the theological world but also the world of socio-political action. For example, at the end of the 1990s David Porter, who left LBC in 1981, was the director of ECONI, the Evangelical Contribution on Northern Ireland, which has sought to foster understanding in the province. David Evans, an LBC student in the later 1980s, became UK and Ireland team leader for The Evangelical Alliance Relief (TEAR) Fund, the largest British evangelical relief agency. TEAR Fund is a highly influential force for social action from within the evangelical community.

LBC and Evangelical Developments

The methodology of this book is modelled on George Marsden's *Reforming Fundamentalism: Fuller Seminary and the New Evangelicalism* (1987). Marsden has related aspects of the story of the post-war era's 'new evangelicalism' in the USA, an evangelicalism that quite deliberately moved away from more fundamentalist attitudes. In order to tell this story he has used as his lens one pivotal institution, Fuller Theological Seminary. Although the size and influence of LBC has never approached that of Fuller, LBC has played a central role within the British evangelical story. There are clear distinctions to be drawn between the evangelical communities found on either side of the Atlantic. One notable difference is the stronger tendency to militant fundamentalism and separatism that has characterized some evangelicals in the USA. Evangelicals in Britain are much more likely to be found in the mainstream denominations.[18] The denominational sectors with which LBC has had most links have been Baptist and evangelical Anglican. The analysis that follows, however, seeks to chart the evangelical movement in Britain not only in the historic denominations but also in other sectors. For instance, in recent years considerable attention has been paid to the 'new churches'. A number of the new church leaders are former LBC students, and this study explores their significance.

Although the personalities of evangelical leaders play an important part in the story of evangelicalism, it is impossible in a book like this to do justice to the range of people who have influenced the strands of the evangelical movement in Britain. Particular attention is paid, naturally, to leading figures associated with LBC – both staff and former students. But the stories of thousands of former students remain untold. Many of these are exercising important ministries in their own contexts, often using ideas absorbed at LBC. The styles of leadership of the LBC principals also made their mark. During LBC's first two decades, many of the college's students – considerable numbers of whom entered pastoral ministry – were deeply impressed by Ernest Kevan's pastoral theology.[19] In the later 1960s and especially in the 1970s, Gilbert Kirby encouraged a number of influential younger evangelical leaders. Michael Griffiths, the principal in the 1980s, operated rather like a general mobilizing the troops. His provocative comments, such as his warnings against 'pulpit prima donnas', were calculated to remain in student memories. Peter Cotterell, who followed Griffiths, was an

[18] D.W. Bebbington, 'Evangelicalism in its Settings: The British and American Movements since 1940'.
[19] George Balmer to the author, 4 Dec. 1998, speaking of his own early experiences at LBC.

iconoclast, excited by radical change, and a self-confessed autocrat, yet he was also a highly effective team builder. In 1995, Derek Tidball became the first principal who had himself trained at LBC. He had also been a lecturer at the college. A pastoral leader, he is committed to holistic training that will produce people equipped for ministry, mission and the marketplace.

This book, because it is concerned to explore the process of educating evangelicalism through a Bible College, will not examine the details of the internal workings of LBC. Many people have served the college in a variety of vital administrative and support roles, but their contributions have been, or will have to be, told elsewhere. Even the lighter side of LBC's life will, regrettably, receive little attention. For instance, the fact that Donald Guthrie, the eminent New Testament scholar and senior member of staff, was the star of many faculty drama productions, was of great importance to the life of the college. But to do justice to many similar facets of staff and student life and leisure would require a different kind of book. For those wishing to write in that vein, an excellent place to start research would be the LBC student magazine, *Areopagus*. The following one-liner gives a flavour of the many gems to be found in the pages of a magazine which, naturally, showed an interest in male-female relationships. J.F. (concerning F.W.'s missionary call): 'She may not convert the heathen, but they'll die happy.' The LBC minute books also yield some fascinating insights, but the records have been used with restraint. Those wishing an entertaining description of the less public side of some leading evangelicals in Britain can turn to Michael Saward's *A Faint Streak of Humility* (1999). It is right to recognize that theological education in the evangelical tradition, while a serious business, can be fun.

The final chapter of the book blends historical analysis with some questions for LBC as it enters the next millennium. Evangelicalism has seen its place within wider church life transformed since the 1940s and 1950s. Donald Guthrie, looking back over this period, noted that there was still 'a stronghold of critical orthodoxy in many of the theological departments of the Universities and in many theological Colleges'. At the same time, it was clear to him 'that there had been a resurgence of traditional orthodoxy', with many more lecturers and professors prepared to uphold the authority of the Bible than had been the case forty years before. Donald Guthrie's concern, as he looked into the future, was to ensure that a new generation of Christians was informed about the faith and that the challenges of the world – conflict, violent crime, sex offences, family breakdown – were addressed. Guthrie's vision was to bring a Christian viewpoint to bear on contemporary issues.[20] Evangelicalism since the eighteenth century has regarded loyalty to the core of the Christian message as of great importance, but the way in which the message has been communicated has been adapted to meet the changing culture. LBC, as 'a central Bible institute in London', has had a crucial part in that developing process over the past half century and seems set to continue to play that role.

---

[20] Guthrie, *I Stand for Truth*, 65–6.

2

'A High Standard of Scholastic Attainment'
1939–44

On 5 May 1939, four people met to discuss possibilities for a 'Bible training institute' in London. These four were W.H. Aldis, home director of the China Inland Mission (CIM), G.T. Manley, known for his service with the Church Missionary Society, A.J. Vereker, secretary of the Crusaders' Union, and Douglas Johnson, a medical doctor who was the creative general secretary of the IVF. The meeting was held at the IVF offices in Bedford Square, London. A slightly larger group met on 25 May 1939 to discuss the formation of a Bible Institute in London, 'which would give instruction courses which were in keeping with the best education standards'. It was agreed at this second meeting that the aim should be to achieve a 'high standard of scholastic attainment such as was required for Institutes affiliated to Universities for the purpose of examinations for Diplomas in Religious Education'.[1] The nine people at the meeting represented evangelicals who were keen to see a new initiative in the field of theological education at a time when, as we have seen, the evangelical sector of British Christianity lacked much of the strength it had enjoyed in the nineteenth century. It was agreed on 25 May to form a sub-committee to explore new possibilities. This brought together Aldis, D. Martyn Lloyd-Jones, who in the previous year had joined G. Campbell Morgan in ministry at the

---

[1] Minutes of meeting held on 25 May 1939.

Congregationalist Westminster Chapel, London, and two members of the Brethren (the section known as the Open Brethren) – Montague Goodman and John Laing. This exploratory committee met three times in June and July 1939.

As the Second World War began it seemed that further progress towards a Bible institute would be unlikely, but informal discussions continued. Vereker had been concerned since the mid-1930s about the lack of training for Crusader leaders, and because he and Johnson lived near one another in Surrey – in Banstead and Epsom Downs respectively – they were able to meet regularly. According to Johnson, Vereker used to waylay him after church or come over for coffee to press his ideas for a college.[2] In the later part of 1941 Vereker and Johnson, together with Hugh Evan Hopkins (a travelling secretary of the IVF, 1937–39, and vicar of Holy Trinity, Redhill, 1940–44), met at the Drift Bridge Hotel, Tattenham Corner, Surrey. After discussion, which Johnson described as taking place 'in the smoky atmosphere . . . over a miserable sandwich', they resolved to go forward.[3] As a result, a meeting was held on 26 February 1942 at the Caxton Hall, London, when details of the ideas for a London college were put before invited evangelical leaders. Although discussions among those present at the meeting brought disagreements to the fore, there was sufficient support for a formal council – 'The Bible College Council' – to be constituted on 26 November 1942. From the council a board of directors was appointed. The evening classes of London Bible College began in 1943 and were held in Eccleston Hall (loaned by the Scripture Gift Mission) and then in St Andrew's Church Hall, Holborn. A faculty was brought together in the following year. This chapter examines the developments from 1939 to 1944 against the background of the evangelicalism of the period.

---

[2] D. Johnson to T.J. Buckley, 15 Sept. 1965. I am indebted to Tim Buckley for this correspondence. At one point in 1937–38 Johnson spoke to his wife about Vereker and 'that *wretched* Bible College'.
[3] D. Johnson to T.J. Buckley, 15 Sept. 1965.

Evangelical Influences

David Bebbington puts the nadir of twentieth-century British evangelicalism at about 1940.[4] Within Anglicanism, the inter-war years saw a strong Anglo-Catholic drift. This movement also affected Free Church life. With evangelicals on the defensive, the discussions being held from 1939 about a new educational venture seemed quite unrelated to wider Christian events. There were signs even at that early stage, however, of what was to be a post-war conservative evangelical resurgence. One of the nine present at the meeting on 25 May 1939 was Hugh Gough, later to be Bishop of Barking and then Archbishop of Sydney, Australia. Writing in the May–June 1939 issue of *Evangelical Christendom*, the journal of the Evangelical Alliance (EA), Hugh Gough out-lined the possibility of a new evangelicalism which would avoid the extremes of either the fundamentalist or liberal wings of the movement. For Gough, the problem in the recent inter-war years had been that the term 'evangelical' had been used to cover 'a multitude of variegated and hyphenated Evangelicals'. The reference was primarily to inter-war 'liberal-evangelicals'. Many of these, Hugh Gough believed, should drop the label 'evangelical' altogether. He argued that the task for those evangelicals who – by contrast with the liberals – believed in the 'atoning and substitutionary death of Christ', was to combine to enunciate the 'full gospel' of the cross of Christ.[5]

The motivation of the members of the groups that met at the IVF offices in 1939 was a determination to unite in order to equip a new generation of Christians espousing such evangelical distinctives. Their agenda seemed to offer important possibilities for the future of evangelicalism. Denominational allegiance was not, for these evangelicals, a major issue. Anglican clergy such as Gough made common cause with leaders of the Open Brethren. One member of the group which met on 25 May, J. Chalmers

---

[4] Bebbington, *Evangelicalism*, 252; cf. Bebbington, 'Evangelicalism in its Settings', 367.
[5] *Ev Chr* (May–June 1939), 112.

Lyon, was an English Presbyterian minister whose preaching Douglas Johnson appreciated. Two of the most significant individuals, A.J. Vereker and Douglas Johnson, represented inter-denominational agencies. Such bodies, which were a common feature of British and American evangelical life, contributed to the relativizing of denominational distinctives. This was a process that would gather pace after the Second World War and aided the development of inter-denominational colleges such as LBC. The highly energetic Vereker, who was the chief innovator at that stage, had in mind a college providing, among other services, training for Crusader leaders. Lay people led the Crusader groups that met throughout the country and the move-ment had as its aim 'the advancement of Christ's Kingdom amongst private and public schoolboys, with the promotion of all that tends towards a true Christian manliness'. In the post-war period the Crusaders' Union opened its membership to boys from state schools.[6]

A.J. Vereker's view, which was shared by Douglas Johnson and was to be crucial in all the future development of LBC, was that a new evangelical educational institution must operate at a credible academic level. The Bible Training Institute (BTI) in Glasgow, which dated from 1892, was seen as having given a lead through the pan-denominational training it offered people hoping to enter full-time Christian service. In the London area, however, there seemed to be little inter-denominational evangelical theological training available. Colleges such as All Nations Bible College, the (rather spartan) Pioneer Missionary Colony run by the Worldwide Evangelization Crusade, Redcliffe College, and Mount Hermon and Ridgelands colleges for women, were primarily for missionary training. As he pursued his vision of a different kind of institution, Vereker enlisted the support of Montague Goodman and John (later Sir John) Laing, who was expanding his building firm while also promoting many evangelical ventures. Johnson's contribution was as a strategic thinker and behind-the-scenes facilitator. Under Johnson's

---

[6] J.D. Walford, *Yesterday and Today*, 11.

leadership the IVF, as a network of conservative evangelical student groups, had a crucial role in nurturing younger leaders. Hugh Gough, for example, was one of its early travelling secretaries. The evangelicalism of the 1930s was shaped by a number of different strands, and this mixture of influences would create tensions as the identity of LBC was shaped in the 1940s. But those within the inner circle at the beginning were united in their opinion that a new initiative in the education of evangelicals was vital for the future.

Tensions Over Policies

Several tensions had to be resolved straight away. Missionary idesls strongly influenced one important school of thought regarding a new college. In keeping with the stress on missionary activity in the evangelical tradition, it was expected that a new Bible college would contribute to the furtherance of this vision. Thus candidates for foreign missionary societies wishing training comprised an important group for which the college would seek to cater. It is almost certain that faith missions such as the CIM, established by Hudson Taylor in 1865, were in mind. Indeed CIM's home director, W.H. Aldis, who would also steer subsequent gatherings, chaired the first informal meeting in 1939 about a London institute. Aldis was an evangelical Anglican clergyman with Open Brethren roots. He was ordained in 1902 and served as curate at St Paul's, Portman Square, under Stuart Holden, a Keswick Convention leader. Aldis then served as a missionary in China and in 1919 he became youth secretary of the CIM. Ten years later he became its home director. With this background, Aldis was personally keen to see a college set up which would educate and equip missionaries for service and which would offer existing missionaries 'refresher' courses. He played a vital role in early meetings and he became the first chairman of the council, formed on 26 November 1942, of the embryonic London Bible College.

An increasing number of evangelicals in Britain were convinced that concentration on the spread of the gospel at home or overseas, although vital, would not in itself solve all the problems of evangelical weakness. Raising such issues could potentially produce a degree of tension between those dedicating immense energy to mission, often through evangelical inter-denominational agencies, and those who believed that evangelicalism had – as an urgent priority – to engage with theological and apologetic issues. This tension was not eased by the fact that theology was regarded warily in certain evangelical circles. Although a Brethren lawyer such as Montague Goodman could operate as a convincing Christian apologist, the Brethren as a whole did not tend to encourage their emerging leaders to attend theological colleges for training.[7] Even among Anglican evangelicals there was some wariness about the place of theology. A case in point was Eric Nash, a highly individualistic Church of England clergyman and Scripture Union (SU) worker who organized very effective evangelistic camps for boys ('Bash' camps, as they were popularly called) from the leading public schools. Nash was frightened of the dangers of going 'intellectual'.[8] This kind of attitude was in marked contrast to the vision for an educated evangelicalism that led to LBC's foundation.

A number of those whom Eric Nash initially influenced during their camp days did not embrace his perspective on intellectual activity. Some adopted the outlook of the IVF, which encouraged theological rigour. Nash regarded one of his ex-campers, John Wenham (who joined the staff of the London College of Divinity in 1938 and was at Tyndale Hall, Bristol, from 1953) as having been 'spoiled' through his IVF involvement.[9] Wenham owed a great deal to Douglas Johnson's integration of 'the intellectual and the spiritual'.[10] John Stott, later rector of All Souls, Langham

---

[7] F.F. Bruce, *In Retrospect: Remembrance of Things Past*, 71.

[8] Barclay, *Evangelicalism*, 27.

[9] Barclay, *Evangelicalism*, 27.

[10] J. Wenham, *Facing Hell: An Autobiography, 1913–1996*, 76.

Place, London, and post-war Anglican evangelicalism's most formative leader, was converted through the Bash camps and expressed his indebtedness to Nash's encouragement,[11] but Stott was to give enormous energy to promoting a thinking evangelicalism and was to be an important supporter of LBC. Douglas Johnson, John Wenham and Alan Stibbs of Oak Hill Theological College were involved from 1938 in an IVF Biblical Research Committee, and the role of the IVF in this period cannot be underestimated. According to F.F. Bruce, one of its leaders, the committee was set up to roll away 'the reproach of anti-intellectualism, if not outright obscurantism, which had for too long been attached to English evangelicalism'.[12] LBC's backers were all convinced of the need to offer thorough training for Christian ministry at home and overseas, and a number saw lack of thoughtful theological reflection as a source of particular vulnerability.

There was some tension over the place of women in the proposed college. Women clearly played a vital role in world mission. Two women, Mildred Cable and Amy Miller, were invited to one meeting in 1939 to explore possibilities for the new institute. Mildred Cable was very highly regarded for her almost forty years of remarkable pioneering missionary service with the CIM, most famously in the remote Gobi Desert in the 1920s and 1930s.[13] Cable suggested that since Ridgelands College was looking for a different site, some aspects of its work might be arranged in conjunction with the new institute. She had in mind especially evening classes in biblical and theological subjects. It was agreed that the London college would welcome women on its courses. Consensus was not, however, complete. The intrepid Cable, who was by then in her sixties, asked a question that was later seen as having to some extent 'scuppered the ship'. She enquired whether there would be 'equal opportunities', not only

[11] J. Eddison, *A Study in Spiritual Power*, ch. 6.

[12] Bruce, *In Retrospect*, 122.

[13] I am indebted to Valerie Griffiths of Guildford for her unpublished paper, 'The Teacher of Righteousness', on Mildred Cable.

for female students, but also for 'women members of staff'. One member of the college planning group, Martyn Lloyd-Jones of Westminster Chapel (where Cable was a member), 'expressed himself definitely that men only should form the main teaching staff, and that this would seem to be the Scriptural requirement in the teaching of these particular subjects, especially in the matter of Christian doctrine'.[14] Lloyd-Jones, according to Douglas Johnson, was later 'set on' by Cable.[15] For the time being, the view of Lloyd-Jones would prevail.

A Sharpened Strategy

Given these tensions, it was vital that those backing the new college should be able to attract a level of support that would make the college viable. It became clearer in 1942–43 that such support was forthcoming. Plans in 1939 had envisaged between fifty and sixty day students, with commensurate residential accommodation, and between two and three hundred evening students. It was recognized that, to achieve these numbers, missionary societies and youth movements would need to direct students to the college.[16] The college was aiming for a higher level of theological education than was common in the world of interdenominational evangelicalism. It was therefore encouraging when a letter sent to the Christian press by Hugh Evan Hopkins in December 1941 produced over thirty replies, mainly from leaders of mission societies interested in the provision of training.[17] A conference was then held on 26 February 1942 in the Caxton Hall, London, to

---

[14] Meeting of the exploratory committee on 6 July 1939; there is a note on file regarding a further meeting scheduled for 28 July 1939 but this was not sent to the female members.

[15] D. Johnson to T.J. Buckley, 15 Sept. 1965. Mildred Cable felt that the whole enterprise was becoming 'too theological and doctrinal'. Lloyd-Jones disagreed.

[16] Minutes of a meeting held on 25 May 1939.

[17] *Chr* (11 Dec. 1941), 7.

submit details of the scheme for a college to invited evangelical leaders. Subsequent plans took into account the views expressed on this occasion.[18] In his introductory remarks Aldis, as chairman, emphasized that the proposed college would not be used for training for ordination in 'known denominations'. He initially stressed what was clearly acceptable: a training college for missionary candidates, for 'whole-time workers at home and abroad', and for those wishing a deeper knowledge of Scripture.[19]

Aldis and his inner group did not intend to set out their vision in detail at this February 1942 consultation. Rather, it emerged through discussion and debate. The first issue was a location for the proposed college. Montague Goodman reported that a generous offer had been made of an ideal site in London. John Laing, who was the person making the offer and who would give enormous financial help to LBC in the coming years, explained that the site was in Marylebone Road near Baker Street tube station. Aldis was clearly embarrassed that the impression might be given that the whole scheme was cut and dried. In fact, the possibility of using 19 Marylebone Road had been discussed since 1939. The land, which had on it an almost derelict building belonging to the Metropolitan Water Board, had been bought by Laing's firm for development and Laing was now prepared to offer it for the new college at cost price. Aldis wished, however, to dampen expectations about rapid progress. He was also sensitive to the possibility of adverse publicity about finance. Francis Harding, formerly secretary of the Scripture Gift Mission, suggested that another college that had sold its premises (almost certainly All Nations) had funds in hand that could be used to meet the cost of the proposed London college. Aldis did not wish to encourage the idea of seeking to acquire money from another college, although in the event a gift from All Nations was received.

A second issue discussed at the consultation was the support the proposed college could offer to missionary society candidates.

---

[18]   Although full minutes of this conference were retained, there is no list of those who attended.

[19]   Minutes of conference at Caxton Hall, London, 26 Feb. 1942.

For some, this aspect of the planning was a priority. H.D. Hooper, of the Church Missionary Society (CMS), spoke from experience of having dealt with several hundred missionary candidates and suggested that they suffered increasingly from lack of biblical knowledge. He hoped, therefore, that the college would have Bible teaching as its main purpose and would in this way complement missionary training. It was evident, however, that some interdenominational faith missions had very different aspirations. Stuart McNairn, of the Evangelical Union of South America, was outspoken, noting that the word 'missionary' did not appear in the brochure about the proposed college. It was, he complained, 'all very well to say that the candidates can be passed on from the College to the Society to give them their specialised training. Societies like the C.M.S. have got training Colleges, but the bulk of the Interdenominational Societies have no Colleges.' He continued: 'I think I am voicing the disappointment that will be felt by these Societies in seeing their dreams of a Central Training College going west.' Aldis, with his experience of the CIM, knew the problem McNairn had identified. As far as Aldis was concerned, there was no reason why the college could not offer training that would be relevant to missionaries. 'Why should there not', he asked, 'be a special department for the special needs of missionary candidates?'

Another group of leaders at the consultation wanted to create a training school of a much more practical nature. Frederick Wood of the National Young Life Campaign could not be present, but he relayed through his wife his view that there should be room for students who could not achieve matriculation level study. Wood had seen colleges in North America that trained a wide range of young people, including those who had 'less educational facilities'. He also offered the suggestion, based on his American experience, that students should be required to undertake practical tasks. Aldis diplomatically replied that it would not be possible to reproduce the North American environment. Others at the consultation, however, were in sympathy with Wood and suggested that Aldis had misled them. It was alleged that Aldis had discouraged moves towards setting up a practically orientated Bible school in Birmingham on the grounds that it would duplicate effort. Now it seemed as if there was to be a higher level college in London that would not necessarily provide for those Christians who wished basic training. Nor would it readily service the Midlands.[20] In response to what was clearly an issue generating feelings of grievance, Aldis acknowledged that one college for the whole of England might be inadequate. But other modes of study could be employed. Charles Cook, editor of *The Christian*, and J.A.G. Ainley, rector of Morden, were strongly in favour of appealing to a wider group of evangelicals through evening classes and correspondence courses.

Speakers at the consultation also drew attention to the need for education and training to be offered to women. This was not simply to train women for overseas mission, although that was needed. Alice Hoare, from Hampstead, commented that the place of women was changing as a result of the Second World War. 'Women', she insisted, 'are taking a vast share in the national cause, and many of us who are engaged in Christian work among women and girls are hoping that they will come back from their national service eager for training in the service of the King of kings.' Hoare's view, which she believed was shared by others, was that the proposed college 'would be completely inadequate if it did not meet the needs of the many girls of education and keen spirituality'. A representative from the Girl Crusaders' Union asked that there be a meeting of women – she was probably aware of the way that women had been marginalized in the earlier stages of discussion – and Aldis replied that it was intended to have women on the college's committee. Newer views about the role of women, which would in time affect evangelical thinking, were clearly being shaped by the changing social context. When the council of the college was formed, on 26 November 1942, three women involved in missionary training were included – Mrs Howard Hooker, Irene Crocker and Amy Miller.

---

[20] Minutes of conference at Caxton Hall, 26 Feb. 1942. It was John Batstone, a clergyman from Birmingham, who noted that the college in London would not service the Midlands.

Those at the heart of establishing the vision for the college saw that there was scope for the new venture to offer training which was international and open to young people's workers and to women. They felt it was important, however, that the groups lobbying for missionary, youth or women's interests should not dominate proceedings. Aldis was pleased that some of the younger representatives who were present at the February 1942 consultation were fully supportive of the idea that there should be university-level education at the new college. Colin Kerr, vicar of St Paul's, Portman Square and founder of the Campaigners youth movement, indicated that he could commend the proposed college only if it aimed for and achieved a high educational standard. Thus Kerr was not happy about the references made to North American training institutions as examples. Although the Moody Bible Institute in Chicago was cited as an acceptable model, that did not fulfil the aspirations of the IVF constituency. More forward-thinking Anglican clergymen such as Colin Kerr were important voices. 'We need', Kerr stated, 'to be a little careful in the way we associate this scheme with the Canadian and American Bible Schools, inasmuch as the type of students attending these Schools do not reach the same educational standard that I think we should stand for. This is equally true of the educational standard of the lecturers.'

The position adopted by Kerr attracted the heavyweight support of Campbell Morgan, the senior minister of Westminster Chapel. He had, he explained, considered starting such a college in London thirty years before but that proved not to be possible. Morgan opposed the idea that the college should cater for missionary training. 'Keep it a Bible College', he urged, 'and then you will be assisting the Missionary Societies and the theological Colleges . . . Above all else, keep the educational standard at a high level.'[21] It had always been the view of Vereker and Johnson

---

[21] Minutes of conference at Caxton Hall, 26 Feb. 1942. Bible schools of the American sort held no attraction for Morgan, partly because of his own experiences when he was in the USA of the deleterious effects of their narrowness.

that the new college must be adequately staffed by well-qualified teachers, and that teaching should be conducted in accordance with the very best educational standards. It was recognized at this stage, in the 1940s, that the college could not expect to gain recognition as a place for ordination training (although many evangelicals were far from happy about the dismissive attitude to evangelical theology found in some denominational training colleges). A memorandum from June 1939 noted agreement that 'the Institute should aim at qualifying its students for Diplomas and Certificates recognised by London University'.[22] A high standard of scholastic attainment was thus central within the vision.

Spiritual Priorities

A number of those behind the beginnings of LBC were concerned that a new college should offer biblical instruction but also that it should be committed to spiritual formation. The Keswick Convention, held annually since 1875 in Keswick, had on its platform many leading evangelicals and also spawned many mini-Keswicks in other parts of Britain and of the world. It was Keswick's call to 'full surrender' to Christ that shaped much of the evangelical piety in Britain in the first half of the twentieth century. In its early period Keswick had made it clear that its main aim was to bring people to an encounter with God rather than to be a Bible teaching conference. It had also initially resisted the introduction of a missionary element into convention meetings (on the grounds that it was a distraction from its main task). By the 1920s Keswick's Bible readings became touchstones of evangelical orthodoxy. In addition – especially through the influence of the CIM – world mission had become a central part of Keswick's identity.[23] Aldis, who was chairman of the Keswick

---

[22] Memo of a meeting of 6 June 1939.

[23] I.M. Randall, 'Spiritual Renewal and Social Reform: Attempts to Develop Social Awareness in the Early Keswick Movement', 70.

council from 1936, was committed to maintaining the focus on the practical and missiological implications of Keswick's biblical teaching on holiness. Many young people offered themselves for missionary service each year at the convention. Another of Aldis' goals was to ensure that overseas missionaries attended the convention.[24] The spiritual priorities Aldis urged at the convention were to influence his thinking about LBC.

Others intimately involved in the genesis of the college, however, had no links with Keswick. Indeed, at the initial meeting on 5 May 1939 Aldis was the only Keswick participant. G.T. Manley was not enthusiastic about the idea of a new college and played no further part in discussions. It was Vereker and Johnson who took matters further. Johnson felt a close affinity with Martyn Lloyd-Jones. Both he and Lloyd-Jones had given up highly promising medical careers, and in the 1930s both were becoming significant younger leaders within British evangelicalism – Lloyd-Jones as an outstanding preacher and Johnson as an organizer. Lloyd-Jones, and others who followed him, subjected the Keswick stress on personal consecration to fairly scathing critique. In 1939, addressing an international conference of evangelical students in Cambridge, Lloyd-Jones portrayed holiness movements as passive, smug and psychologically unhealthy. He proposed instead standard Reformed views of sanctification as a life-long process of active spiritual growth.[25] At a conference arranged by Johnson at Kingham Hill School, near Oxford, in 1942, Lloyd-Jones spoke to an audience which included Manley (then vicar of St Luke's, Hampstead), F.F. Bruce (at that time lecturer in classics at Leeds University) and Alan Stibbs (vice-principal of Oak Hill). In a wide-ranging address on 'The Causes of the Present Weakness' Lloyd-Jones spoke of Keswick as having contributed to the reduction of interest in biblical theology.[26]

---

[24] *Kes Wk* (1925), 104.
[25] D.M. Lloyd-Jones, 'Christ our Sanctification'.
[26] I.H. Murray, *D. Martyn Lloyd-Jones: The Fight of Faith, 1939–1981*, 73–4.

It is clear that in 1942 Lloyd-Jones was willing to risk a theological fight with the Keswick strand of evangelicalism. Yet his attack contained a measure of caricature. Lloyd-Jones must have been aware that his allegations about Keswick teaching did not reflect the perspective of such a typical Keswick speaker as J. Russell Howden. During the debates between conservative and liberal evangelicals in the 1920s Howden had been one of those who took up the theological cudgels over contentious issues. For example, in a crucial article in *The Life of Faith* entitled 'Evangelicalism at the Cross Roads', Howden argued that the theology of the liberal evangelicals was fatally flawed. He asserted that they accepted destructive biblical criticism, promoted ritual and denied Christ's substitutionary atonement. Keswick, for Howden, meant 'a trustworthy Bible and an infallible Christ'.[27] Neither did the criticisms by Lloyd-Jones appear to take note of Graham Scroggie, a Baptist minister who was the dominant mind at Keswick by the 1930s. As early as 1921, *The Life of Faith* vividly described Russell Howden and Graham Scroggie, as 'among the most capable and trusted men of the Keswick platform' and 'far removed from the realm of religious cranks or long-haired visionaries'.[28] The Keswick of the 1930s and 1940s was deeply concerned for evangelical orthodoxy.

Doctrinal Beliefs

In line with this concern, key players within the embryonic college were involved in formulating a doctrinal statement. On 6 June 1939 it had been agreed that 'there should be a basis of evangelical belief for the Institute based on the Word of God'. Recognizing that evangelicals differed from each other on certain points, they also stated that 'points of theology and doctrine on which evangelical Christian opinion differs widely,

---

[27] *LF* (10 Feb. 1926), 143.
[28] *LF* (19 Oct. 1921), 1191.

should not be stressed and taught at the expense of other viewpoints'. It is probable that most of those wishing to see a college established wanted to avoid the rigid position associated with American fundamentalism. A doctrinal basis was unanimously approved in October 1942 as a summary of what the college would both stand for and teach. Lloyd-Jones, Montague Goodman and Alan Stibbs had drawn up the basis. The college became committed to what were termed the 'Fundamental Truths of Christianity', including:

1. The unity of the Father, the Son, and the Holy Spirit in the Godhead.
2. The divine inspiration and supreme authority of the Holy Scriptures.
3. The guilt and depravity of human nature in consequence of the Fall.
4. The substitutionary death of our Lord Jesus Christ, and His resurrection, as the only way of salvation from sin through faith.
5. The necessity of the work of the Holy Spirit in the new birth, and His indwelling in the believer for sanctification.
6. The personal return of the Lord Jesus Christ.[29]

It is significant that the statement on Scripture avoided the use of the word 'inerrancy'. The doctrine of biblical inerrancy was promoted by pressure groups such as the Bible League, but would not attract the support in Britain that it would in America.[30] Nonetheless, the Bible League, responding to a call for 'closer cohesion among those who cleave to the teaching of the Word', had brought together 162 bodies for an inter-war

---

[29] See Appendix 1 for LBC's current Doctrinal Basis (adopted in Feb. 1998).

[30] G.M. Marsden, *Fundamentalism and American Culture: The Shaping of Twentieth-Century Evangelicalism, 1870–1925*, 3–8.

protest against Protestant 'religious rationalism'.[31] Some British fundamentalists believed there was a need to engage in militant protest against doctrinal 'shilly-shallying'.[32] Linked to some extent with this outlook was a 'separatist' stream within British evangelicalism, represented by E.J. Poole-Connor. In 1922 Poole-Connor had formed an undenominational union, later the Fellowship of Independent Evangelical Churches (FIEC). The FIEC attracted congregations wishing no part in what they saw as doctrinally mixed denominations. In *The Apostasy of English Non-Conformity* (1933), Poole-Connor pronounced that 'all separated Conservative Evangelicals should draw together'.[33] Poole-Connor became a member of LBC's council in 1943 and two years later was put in charge of All Nations' college training.

There were some links between LBC and earlier fundamentalist thinking. The Bible League and the Bible Testimony Fellowship had offered a platform in the 1920s to Johnson and Stibbs, then student leaders. A. Rendle Short, a distinguished Brethren surgeon (professor of surgery at Bristol University, 1933–46), who supported the IVF and LBC, had also been a speaker in such circles. *The Bible League Quarterly* carried pleas for robust defence of the faith,[34] and these fuelled concern for a distinctive evangelical apologetic. But there were major evangelical leaders associated with LBC who took a determined stand against narrowing tendencies. *Evangelical Christendom*, for the Evangelical Alliance, carried a statement from Graham Scroggie, a leading Keswick figure who was

---

[31] *BLQ* (Jan.–March 1919), 3; *LF* (18 April 1923), 449–50; *BLQ* (July–Sept. 1922), D.W. Bebbington, 'Missionary Controversy and the Polarising Tendency in Twentieth-Century British Protestantism', *Anvil* 13.2 (1996), 141–3.

[32] *BLQ* (Oct.–Dec. 1926), 180, quoted by D.W. Bebbington, 'Martyrs for the Truth: Fundamentalists in Britain', in *St Ch Hist* 30 (Oxford, 1993), 425.

[33] E.J. Poole-Connor, *The Apostasy of English Non-Conformity*, 74.

[34] *BLQ* (Oct.–Dec. 1926), 185.

director of LBC for a period in 1943, saying that subscription to a particular definition of biblical inspiration was not a true test of doctrinal orthodoxy. 'If you demand', Scroggie said, 'that I subscribe to your theory of inspiration, I shall decline, but I am not on that account a Modernist.'[35] Scroggie and other British evangelicals had been unimpressed by bellicose American fundamentalism. Speaking at Keswick, Scroggie argued that given the conflicts over theological modernism it was preferable to have the Apostles' Creed as a basis of faith than for groups to construct their own bases and splinter from the wider church.[36] LBC continued to avoid being identified with a fundamentalist position.

Another issue for the college was premillennialism. A common view among conservative evangelicals was that the return of Christ would inaugurate a thousand years of Christ's reign. In 1917 a manifesto had been published in the British Christian press affirming that Jesus might return 'at any moment' and that Israel would be territorially restored and converted by Christ's appearing.[37] The Advent Testimony and Preparation Movement (ATPM) was a body formed to propagate these beliefs. It was sponsored by such household names among British evangelicals as F.B. Meyer, H.W. Webb-Peploe, Campbell Morgan and Dinsdale Young, minister of the Methodist Westminster Central Hall.[38] The present world situation seemed to discredit the postmillennial view, that Christ's return would follow a golden age for Christianity. *The Advent Witness*, the monthly mouthpiece of the ATPM, carried denunciations of modern trends in society. Many premillennialists adhered to the pre-tribulation prophetic teaching of the Brethren leader J.N. Darby, that through a 'secret rapture' the church would be caught up out of

---

[35] *Ev Chr* (Nov.–Dec. 1924), 188.

[36] *Kes Conv* (London, 1929), 139.

[37] For the full manifesto, see, e.g., *Chr W* (8 Nov. 1917), 7.

[38] W.Y. Fullerton, *F.B. Meyer: A Biography* (London: Marshall, Morgan & Scott, 1929), 157–9; Bebbington, *Evangelicalism*, 192–3; *Chr W* (22 Nov. 1917), 10; (29 Nov. 1917), 7.

the world and would escape from the 'great tribulation'.[39] Lloyd-Jones did not subscribe to the premillennial position. He believed that the second advent would usher in the eternal age.[40] When Ernest Kevan, who took the same view as Lloyd-Jones, was asked to teach at LBC, he sought assurances that he would be free to set out opposing views on the interpretation of prophecy.[41]

Despite the fact that the new college did not wish to be constrained by the narrowness of fundamentalism, separatism or a particular view of eschatology, it drew clear theological boundary lines. It was agreed that appointments to the staff were to be carefully vetted with a view not only to teaching ability and technical qualifications but also loyalty to Scripture. In practice this meant that there was no place for the liberal evangelicals of the Anglican Evangelical Group Movement (which was formed following the liberal-conservative storm in 1922 in the Church Missionary Society)[42] or for those from the Methodist Fellowship of the Kingdom. Both the AEGM and the Fellowship of the Kingdom had been seeking to enunciate a more scholarly and, as they saw it, more relevant evangelicalism. Martyn Lloyd-Jones, wary of so-called experts (e.g. in biblical criticism), suggested in 1939 that the church had too readily accepted the authority of 'men of knowledge'.[43] Yet Lloyd-Jones had been present at the planning meeting at which it was decided that the new institute should aim at qualifying its students for diplomas and certificates recognized by London University and other authorities. Given this understanding, it was inevitable that wider theological thinking would be studied at LBC.

---

[39] See F.R. Coad, *Prophetic Developments with Particular Reference to the Early Brethren Movement* (Pinner, Middlesex: Christian Brethren Research Fellowship, 1966), 22, 27, 28.

[40] T. Sargent, *The Sacred Anointing: The Preaching of Dr Martyn Lloyd-Jones*, 251.

[41] G.W. Kirby, *Ernest Kevan: Pastor and Principal*, 29.

[42] K. Hylson-Smith, *Evangelicals in the Church of England, 1734–1984*, ch. 16.

[43] *Ev Chr* (March–April 1939), 77.

Leadership Strands

Almost from the beginning of discussions about a new college it had been hoped that Lloyd-Jones would serve as principal. The formative period in the history of the college cannot be understood without an analysis of the place of Lloyd-Jones. At the meeting of Aldis, Manley, Vereker and Johnson on 5 May 1939 they recognized the need for 'an outstanding personality as first Principal' and at that point Lloyd-Jones was an obvious choice. Johnson, who was close to Lloyd-Jones, was to 'sound him out', while Aldis, whose role was as an elder statesman, would reinforce the initial approach.[44] At a subsequent meeting in June 1939, when Aldis, Goodman and Hopkins as well as Lloyd-Jones himself were present, it was minuted that Lloyd-Jones should be invited to become principal.[45] No response from Lloyd-Jones was recorded. It is likely that over the next two years he gave consideration to the matter. His conviction, expressed at the 1941 Kingham Hill School conference, was that to answer liberals there was 'the need for highly trained persons of the academic type'.[46] At a meeting on 2 February 1942 Lloyd-Jones consented to have his name put forward, and Alan Stibbs was suggested as a member of staff.[47] But on 25 June 1942 the college's backers were given disappointing news. Aldis read out a letter from Lloyd-Jones stating that he 'had no light about undertaking the Principalship, and could not promise to do so, as things are at present'.[48]

There was continued discussion in 1942–43 about a principal for the college, and Graham Scroggie, who had experience of running his own Bible correspondence course, was invited in March 1943 to become director of LBC. Scroggie had been

---

[44] Memo regarding the meeting of 5 May 1939 to consider the founding of a London Bible Institute; Rowdon, *London Bible College*, 27.
[45] Memo of a meeting of 6 June 1939.
[46] Murray, *Fight of Faith*, 71.
[47] Minutes of a meeting of the standing committee, 2 Feb. 1942.
[48] Minutes of a meeting of the standing committee, 25 June 1942.

awarded an honorary DD from Edinburgh University in 1927 in recognition of his ministry at Charlotte Chapel, Edinburgh, his place at Keswick, and especially his contribution to the scholarly study and teaching of the Bible through both preaching and writing.[49] It seems that, having turned down the principalship, Lloyd-Jones was supportive of Graham Scroggie's appointment. Iain Murray notes that Hugh Evan Hopkins asked Lloyd-Jones personally to propose Scroggie's name when the matter of his appointment came to the college council. Hopkins apparently felt that support from Lloyd-Jones would counter possible opposition to Scroggie from the Brethren element on the council.[50] This seems rather odd, since the Brethren were hardly represented on the council and since Goodman, who was the key Brethren representative, was also a 'Keswickite' and a friend of Scroggie. In the event, Lloyd-Jones did not attend the council meeting in March 1943 when the matter was discussed, and Graham Scroggie's name was proposed by Harold Earnshaw Smith, a Keswick speaker who was rector of All Souls, Langham Place, London. It is probable that Hopkins was less concerned about the position of the Brethren over Scroggie than he was about that of Lloyd-Jones himself.

As it turned out, Scroggie served as director of the college for only a few months. The need to refer to others over college matters meant that the job did not give the rather autocratic Scroggie sufficient freedom. Nonetheless, Scroggie's appointment suggests that the college's backers shared his vision of a ministry that offered solid biblical exposition and spiritual application. Yet there were marked differences between Scroggie and Lloyd-Jones over certain issues. For Scroggie, Bible teaching which was applied to life was paramount, while for Lloyd-Jones a clear theological system was essential as a foundation. In terms of spirituality, Lloyd-Jones would have had little sympathy with

---

[49] W. White, *Revival in Rose Street: A History of Charlotte Baptist Chapel, Edinburgh* (Edinburgh, n.d.), 48–9.
[50] Murray, *Fight of Faith*, 92, citing Hugh Evan Hopkins to Lloyd-Jones, 16 Feb. 1942.

some of the messages which Scroggie delivered at Keswick. On one occasion Scroggie stated that although Christ had redeemed the world, only those who accepted Christ as Saviour were saved, and of these not all had accepted his Lordship. It was this step of total consecration that Scroggie pressed upon his audience.[51] Yet Scroggie was very far from being simplistic or naïve in his approach to the application of the Bible and to evangelical piety. As Scroggie saw it, lack of biblical instruction at Keswick meant that any uplift gained through the convention's traditional call to consecration was transient.[52] Scroggie represented something of the evangelical centre-ground which LBC would seek to occupy.

Although Lloyd-Jones indicated in June 1942 that he was not prepared to take on the principalship of the college, his interest in its work continued for a number of years. So also did the dependence by the inner group of planners on Lloyd-Jones' advice. It was regarded as important, for example, that Lloyd-Jones should frame the college's basis of faith.[53] Lloyd-Jones himself was keen to ensure that the college had an adequate theological library. There was initial interest in the Beddington Free Grace Library, built up by a Strict Baptist, Geoffrey Williams. After hearing a report on this collection of twenty-five thousand books, however, the college committee decided in November 1942 that the conditions laid down by Williams and the price he wanted for the books 'were quite beyond the power of the present Committee to consider'.[54] Williams was in any case pursuing Lloyd-Jones, at first through Douglas Johnson and then directly, regarding the future of this collection, and his efforts were to result in the establishment of the Evangelical Library in 1943. In parallel with this development, Lloyd-Jones suggested that the college consider the library of the late Henry Atherton, who had been minister of

---

[51] *Kes Conv* (1929), 29–31.

[52] W.G. Scroggie to W. Sloan, 10 Nov. 1920, in Donald Gee Centre, Mattersey Hall, Mattersey, Nr. Doncaster.

[53] Minutes of a meeting of the standing committee, 19 Oct. 1942.

[54] Minutes of a meeting of the standing committee, 12 Nov. 1942.

Grove Chapel, Camberwell, and secretary of the Sovereign Grace Union, but this did not materialize.[55]

Both the first board of directors and members of the teaching staff were appointed in 1943 and evening classes began. Overseas mission interests were represented on the board, especially by Aldis and D.M. Miller, secretary of the Africa Inland Mission (AIM). Members such as Frederick P. Wood, co-founder in 1911 of the National Young Life Campaign, and Montague Goodman, with his wide experience of Crusaders and student missions, represented other evangelistic activity. Thus four of the six board members had clear missionary and evangelistic priorities. Goodman stated: 'We want our young men and women to be able to preach and teach Christ, not only in this land, but throughout the world.'[56] But it was scholarship that would be repeatedly emphasized. In 1943, when Aldis gave a report on LBC to a conference of the Interdenominational Missionary Fellowship (which drew together a number of the faith missions), he spoke of the new college as 'definitely conservative, Evangelical, scholarly and thorough'. The thirty delegates present were supportive, although some wondered if LBC lacked the missionary zeal 'so urgently needed'.[57] In 1944, All Nations Missionary College (as it then was) proposed that it should function in co-operation with LBC. The council of LBC expressed a welcome for any students from All Nations wishing to attend lectures, but did not see the need for liaison between the two college councils.[58] The vision of LBC would be wider than the area of overseas mission, although it would seek to integrate the academic and the practical for missionary candidates.

It was hoped that the teaching staff appointed would be both scholars and practitioners. Those initially suggested by Vereker and Johnson as possible lecturers were Anglican clergymen – Alan

---

[55] Minutes of a meeting of the standing committee, 20 Jan. 1943.

[56] Minutes of a conference at Caxton Hall, 26 Feb. 1942.

[57] Minutes of a conference of the Interdenominational Missionary Fellowship, 24 Feb. 1943.

[58] Minutes of a council meeting, 28 Dec. 1944.

Stibbs, Harold Earnshaw Smith and Colin Kerr – and of these only Stibbs had academic standing. Another contender, however, Ernest Kevan (1903–65), came from a different ecclesiastical stable. From 1924 Kevan was minister of Church Hill Baptist Church, Walthamstow, which was part of the Metropolitan Association of Strict Baptist Churches and which was regarded as London's oldest Baptist church. Many Strict Baptists espoused the high Calvinist view that faith should not be demanded of unbelievers as a 'duty' since that would imply human ability to respond. They were also strict communionists, welcoming only baptized believers to the Lord's Table. In his early ministry Kevan adhered to these positions.[59] In 1934 he became pastor of Zion Chapel, New Cross, London, and later expressed his excitement that people were joining Strict Baptist churches because they wanted the 'strong meat' of doctrinal ministry.[60] But his connections were broad. He was, for example, twice chairman of the Deptford Ministers' Fraternal. In 1943 he became minister of a Baptist Union (BU) church – Trinity Road Chapel, Upper Tooting, London. A year before he had obtained an MTh from London University. As a competent evangelical thinker with a Calvinistic doctrinal framework, Ernest Kevan fitted Lloyd-Jones' picture of a suitable college lecturer, and it was Lloyd-Jones who was behind the proposal, in the summer of 1943, that Kevan join the college staff.[61]

In 1944, a college teaching faculty began to operate. L.F.E. Wilkinson, then assistant secretary of the (Anglican) Church Pastoral Aid Society and later principal of Oak Hill College, was asked to be chairman. His two colleagues were Ernest Kevan, a Baptist, and another Anglican, Frank Colquhoun, who was then vicar of St Michael and All Angels, Blackheath Park, London and later became chancellor of Southwark Cathedral. On 4 February 1944 the first formal meeting of the faculty was held. An

---

[59] *Chr Path* (June 1928), 119; (Jan. 1929), 16.
[60] Kirby, *Ernest Kevan*, 21; *The Gospel Herald and Earthen Vessel* (April 1938), 70–71; (May 1938), 93.
[61] Murray, *Fight of Faith*, 93.

ambitious programme of lectures and correspondence courses was set out. Certificates were to be awarded to those who passed examinations. The influence of the Reformed thinking of Ernest Kevan was seen in the titles of lectures planned for delivery – in the Scripture Gift Mission's Eccleston Hall – in the autumn of 1944. It was Kevan who planned the college curriculum,[62] and he proposed that Lloyd-Jones should lecture on grace, Howden on election, George Beasley-Murray (later principal of Spurgeon's College, London) on condemnation, Stibbs on repentance, Wilkinson on faith and Colquhoun on justification. Russell Howden was also assigned the subject of sanctification, giving him the opportunity to expound the Keswick teaching on holiness so despised by Lloyd-Jones. The launch of a pan-denominational teaching programme of this theological quality was a milestone for the evangelicalism of the period.

Conclusion

It is clear that in the period 1939–44 there were competing ideas as to what a Bible college in London might provide. The stress on overseas mission within evangelicalism meant that the picture in the minds of some was of a missionary training college. Links with the CIM were close, and many missionaries were to be trained at LBC, but the focus on the needs overseas was not to be primary. Nor was the new college to be simply a Bible school to train evangelists. The need for practical training was stressed, however, and Keswick spirituality was influential. A number of these issues created tensions. Mission agencies were often to be rather critical of LBC. The Keswick approach, in the eyes of some, was insufficiently rigorous in the area of theological reflection. F.F. Bruce, who was to become Rylands Professor of Biblical Criticism and Exegesis at Manchester University, was unimpressed by evangelical students (no doubt 'Keswickites') in

---

[62] E.F. Kevan to J. Russell Howden, 23 Nov. 1944.

Cambridge who were 'more developed in brawn than in brain'.[63] A new and persuasive line of thinking, heavily influenced by the IVF, produced a vision of a Bible college with high academic standards. Aldis noted that the IVF was constantly receiving applications from those wanting scriptural teaching 'who would be prepared to attend a College for two, or even three years in order to secure that knowledge'.[64] At the heart of the vision in this period was the need to prepare a new generation of evangelical leaders. To fulfil its task of educating a developing post-war evangelicalism LBC was convinced that its goal must be a high level of scholastic attainment.

[63] Bruce, *In Retrospect*, 70–1; J.C. Pollock, *A Cambridge Movement*, 242.

[64] Minutes of a conference at Caxton Hall, 26 Feb. 1942.

3

'Ecumenical Activity Within an Evangelical Framework' 1944–49

The period from 1944 to 1949 saw the shape of LBC emerging much more clearly. Ernest Kevan, initially appointed on a part-time basis, was the first person appointed to the full-time staff. Fred Mitchell, known for his ministry at Keswick and his leadership within the China Inland Mission, acted as director. In October 1945, Ernest Kevan became resident tutor and soon he was offered the post of college principal. He remained principal for 20 years and his leadership left a firm impression on the college. In 1946 there were seven full-time students, with others seconded to the college from mission agencies. Three years later one student, Donald Guthrie, was appointed to the teaching staff. Guthrie's abilities in the field of New Testament studies would serve to enhance the college's academic prestige and would make a significant contribution to the development of evangelical biblical scholarship. Guthrie's background was, like Kevan's, Strict Baptist, but Kevan made determined efforts to ensure that the college would represent wider evangelicalism.[1] This chapter examines ways in which the college engaged in the theological education of those who it was hoped would be future leaders. It also looks at the relationship of the enterprise to the wider Christian world. Harold Rowdon suggests that the conservative evangelical basis of the college was crucial to its identity. 'This,

---

[1]   Kirby, *Ernest Kevan*, 31.

rather than any denominational basis,' he stated, 'was to be its distinguishing feature and was to make it an outstanding example of ecumenical activity within an evangelical framework.'[2] It was not to prove easy, however, to maintain theological unity within the conservative evangelical camp.

Teaching Resources

It was essential that LBC should seek to match the kind of coverage of biblical and theological material offered by recognized theological institutions. Kevan himself specialized in dogmatic theology. He was also a preacher and pastor, deeply committed to church life and ministry. His insightful lectures in homiletics and pastoral theology embodied his belief that LBC courses fitted students for pastoral work. Aware of the importance of appropriate qualifications for teaching staff, Kevan added to his MTh a PhD through London University. His subject, as befitted someone from his Reformed theological background, was the teaching of the Puritans about the moral law. The thesis was published by the Baptist Carey Kingsgate Press as *The Grace of Law*.[3] Although it was a detailed and solid study, Kevan never established himself as an expert in seventeenth-century Puritan literature, whereas Geoffrey Nuttall, to whom Kevan acknowledged his indebtedness, and J.I. Packer, whose doctoral thesis on Richard Baxter Ernest Kevan cited, were to be widely regarded as authorities. Kevan's attention to college administration no doubt militated against academic productivity. In addition, he was determined to remain in touch with the needs of congregations and much of his writing and speaking addressed a broader Christian audience. He was outstandingly gifted at communicating with children.

Nonetheless, it was important to Kevan to ensure that the LBC teaching staff made contributions to scholarship. George

---

[2] Rowdon, *London Bible College*, 50.
[3] E.F. Kevan, The *Grace of Law: A Study in Puritan Theology*.

Beasley-Murray, who would later establish himself as the leading
Baptist New Testament scholar in Britain,[4] joined the LBC faculty
on a part-time basis (he was also in pastoral ministry at the time)
in the autumn of 1944. He taught until January 1948 when he
took the pastorate of Zion Baptist Church, Cambridge. Other
part-time staff helped to raise LBC's profile in the missionary and
evangelistic sectors of the evangelical world. H.L. Ellison, a
former Anglican clergyman who had joined the Brethren in 1939,
taught at LBC from an early stage. He had been a missionary to
Jews in Romania. L.F.E. Wilkinson became principal of Oak Hill
College in 1945, while still remaining an active LBC adviser. In
November 1945 Gilbert Kirby, who in 1966 would follow Kevan
as principal, became a part-time tutor. He had recently accepted
the pastorate of Ashford Congregational Church, Middlesex, but
was never confined to local church ministry and his contacts
within evangelicalism were unusually broad. From the beginning
of his involvement with LBC, Kirby was a member of
Lloyd-Jones' Westminster Fellowship, a monthly meeting of
evangelical ministers. In the immediate post-war period the
fellowship comprised about a dozen ministers, including Kevan,
Stibbs, Beasley-Murray and Morgan Derham, then editorial
secretary of SU.[5]

Ernest Kevan himself established the tone of LBC during its
first two decades. In his leadership Kevan set the highest standards for himself and others. His workload was astonishing. All
communications he received were answered immediately. As an
aid to his administration, he developed an elaborate index system,
which he was known to take on holiday with him.[6] He meticu-
lously prepared his lectures and delivered them with conviction
and lucidity. The college atmosphere was rather severe and
formal – for example, students were never addressed by their first

---

[4] See, for example, his seminal work, *Baptism in the New Testament*
(London: Macmillan, 1962).
[5] S. Brady, 'Gilbert Kirby, an Evangelical Statesman: A Tribute and a
Profile', 7–8.
[6] Guthrie, *I Stand for Truth*, 42.

names – but Kevan had a personal, almost paternal, involvement with each student.[7] He saw those who left LBC in this period to begin ministry as important early ambassadors for the college. These included, for instance, Edmund Heddle, who finished his training in 1949 and became a Baptist pastor. Kevan built up an extensive LBC network through his care for former students and their work. One of Kevan's determining values was, as he put it: 'Once a member of the College, always a member of the College.' Nor was this concern limited to those students whom Kevan found amenable. The perception of one observer was that Kevan was 'patient with obtuse and unintelligent students; deeply sympathetic with those in trouble and sorrow; and very gracious towards his theological opponents'.[8]

The first full-time appointment to the LBC staff after Kevan was E.W. Hadwen, vicar of St Silas's, Liverpool, who had experience as principal of a diocesan theological college. Ill health meant, however, that he had to resign after two years. H. Dermot McDonald, an energetic Irishman recruited to the staff by Kevan in 1948, was to remain for almost three decades and would contribute enormously to LBC and to wider evangelical theological thought. McDonald had been trained at the Irish Baptist College, had a BA in philosophy from London University, and had held pastorates in Stockton-on-Tees and at the Woolwich Tabernacle, London, where Kevan had met him. 'Derrie Mc,' as he was known, continued to study and graduated with a London University BD in 1953. He followed this with a doctoral thesis, published in 1959 as *Ideas of Revelation*. Part of McDonald's intention was to show that evangelicals could engage intelligently with prevailing liberal theological thinking.[9] H.L. Ellison became a full-time lecturer in 1949. His speciality was the Old Testament, and in 1952 his book on the Old Testament prophets, *Men Spake from God* (some of which first appeared in serial form in *The Life of Faith*), was published. In

---

[7] *L F* (2 Sept. 1965), 860.
[8] Kirby, *Ernest Kevan*, 31, quoting John Stott.
[9] Conversation with H.D. McDonald, 5 Aug. 1998.

1957 the IVF's Tyndale Press published Donald Guthrie's commentary on the pastoral epistles as part of the Tyndale commentary series – a series that was to play a vital role in encouraging
evangelical scholarship.

Members of the LBC faculty and the directors of the college
were also keen to engage well-known and well-respected authors
for LBC's popular correspondence courses. It was suggested at an
early stage that Campbell Morgan should be approached.
Considerations about payment, it appears, entered into the
discussions. 'The Faculty felt,' at a meeting in 1944, 'that if he
were willing even at a more advanced fee than had been agreed for
the other Course, it would be well to proceed with this, as his
name would be a very real asset to the list of courses.'[10] Other
names suggested at that point included two Church of Scotland
ministers, Donald Davidson and Thomas Torrance. Campbell
Morgan, in response to a request to write on the poetic books of
the Old Testament, replied to say that he had already produced
articles for *The Life of Faith* on the subject. The faculty, nothing
daunted, recommended to the directors that they approach *The
Life of Faith* to purchase the course, but negotiations foundered.[11]
There were difficulties, too, with other names. Torrance, later
professor of Christian dogmatics at New College, Edinburgh, was
unavailable. It was agreed to contact Stafford Wright,
vice-principal of the Bible Churchmen's Missionary Society
College, Bristol, and J. Clement Connell, who had studied at
Regent's Park College and Balliol College, Oxford, and was then
pastor of the Baptist Church at Rayners Lane, Middlesex.

Inevitably there were differences of theological perspective
among those LBC approached. E.J. Poole-Connor, who was
asked to produce a course on non-Christian religions, was well
known for his conservative views. The college was also willing,
however, to engage Ernest Payne, a tutor at Regent's Park
College, Oxford, to write a course on the history of Christian
missions. Payne, later general secretary of the BU, was

---

[10] Minutes of faculty meeting, 25 Feb. 1944.
[11] Minutes of faculty meeting, 10 March 1944.

sympathetic to the more theologically diverse Student Christian Movement (SCM) and did not forge links with the IVF.[12] In the event, Payne did not take up LBC's offer. On other occasions there was concern about how to deal with less conservative thinking. There was, for instance, discussion in 1944 of the content of recommended book lists. It was pointed out that in some areas of study the best textbooks frequently included unorthodox statements. The question facing the faculty was whether these were to be kept out of the courses 'for fear of some criticisms'. The faculty members favoured the policy of including them, 'but with brief annotations added which would indicate the valuable parts of the book and also include a caution'.[13] Later, however, the faculty felt that Russell Howden should be advised not to present material on 'the Holy Spirit in the Apocrypha'.[14] Doctrinal sensitivities were integral to evangelical education.

Equipping the Church

The teaching staff worked in tandem with those who had wider responsibility for the college. Here, too, there was a denominational mix and also a combination of ordained and lay people. The board of directors had as its chairman from 1948 to 1951 J. Russell Howden. He was succeeded by Montague Goodman, who was already chairman of the college council. Philip Henman, the founder and chairman of two public companies, was the honorary treasurer. In a way that was typical of some of the evangelical businessmen of the period, Henman was also honorary pastor for twenty-five years of a church in Surbiton, and was chairman or vice-chairman of several missionary societies, as well as being involved in Keswick affairs. A.J. Vereker, whose original vision for a college had been so crucial, joined the board

---

[12] W.M.S. West, *To be a Pilgrim: A Memoir of Ernest A. Payne*, 27–8.
[13] Minutes of faculty meeting, 25 Feb. 1944.
[14] Minutes of faculty meeting, 8 Sept. 1944.

in 1944, but ill health and pressure in other areas of his work meant that he resigned two years later. The influence of Keswick and of Christian youth organizations was still strong. Colin Kerr, of St Paul's, Portman Square, a Keswick and young people's speaker, was an LBC director in the late 1940s. Kevan was a supporter of Kerr's Campaigners youth organization. Another director in this period with strong Keswick links was Theo Bamber, minister of the 900-member Rye Lane Chapel, Peckham, who joined the board in 1947. Clarence Foster, a Keswick trustee and co-secretary of the Children's Special Service Mission (CSSM), was a board member from 1949 until 1958. Overseas missionary interests were less evident, but D.M. Miller, secretary of the AIM, remained on the board for nearly twenty years.

It was agreed that the education offered by the college should give priority to certain core subjects. In addition, a limited number of specialized options could be offered. The faculty agreed the foundational curriculum in December 1944. First, there was to be study of the biblical text. It was felt to be vital that the college should offer an alternative to the highly critical approach to the Bible that characterized much of the theological curriculum in British universities. The second area was doctrine. One evening class student, describing the effect that Kevan's teaching had on her, said: 'I could almost feel my brain expanding to grasp the expounding of the wonderful Divine Plan.' The third area was less clearly defined, but covered church history, Christian ethics and worship. Homiletics, pastoral theology, evangelism and mission studies were also offered. Although New Testament Greek was not a core subject, it was given strong backing. From 1945 H. Carey Oakley, senior classics master at the City of London School and a deacon of Trinity Road Baptist Church, Wandsworth, conducted evening classes in New Testament Greek. There were further courses for those proceeding to a BD.

Considerable attention was devoted to the potential of the college as a training institution for schoolteachers. In October 1942 Vereker, Douglas Johnson and Hugh Evan Hopkins argued that LBC should provide courses for training schoolteachers. This conviction was entirely consistent with the drive within the IVF for evangelicals working in professions such as teaching to be articulate exponents of evangelical convictions. The Education Act of 1944 made religious education the one compulsory subject in schools. This gave added impetus to the task of training teachers for religious education. Addressing the college board as its chairman in September 1946, Russell Howden stated that 'it must be apparent to all of us today that there is an urgent need in our country for a steady flow of convinced conservative and evangelical Christians into the ranks of the teaching profession'.[15] Here was specific reference to the idea of influencing the next generation and putting evangelical views on the map. Negotiations were to take place with the Ministry of Education to see if an LBC diploma or degree might be a sufficient qualification for teaching,[16] and for a time subjects such as English, French and classics were added to the LBC curriculum.

In fact, few students at LBC in this period had degree-level theological aspirations. Many of those taking correspondence courses or evening classes were Sunday school or Bible class teachers. It had been part of Vereker's aim to help such leaders. Growth in these areas was so rapid that, by October 1944, over 300 students had commenced correspondence courses and the number of those studying by this mode was doubling roughly every six months. In 1945 LBC appeared on the University of London Pass List for the Certificate of Religious Knowledge. It was reported with considerable satisfaction at the college council in September of that year that, as far as could be discovered, LBC was the only evangelical centre providing correspondence tuition for this examination. The faculty members were intent on going on to provide study material for the Diploma in Theology and also for London University degrees.[17] New enrolments for

---

[15] Minutes of the college council, 27 Sept. 1946.
[16] Rowdon, *London Bible College*, 52. These negotiations were not successful.
[17] Minutes of the college council, 27 Sept. 1945.

correspondence courses were averaging about forty per month in the mid-1940s, and in March 1946 total enrolments numbered 1,400. Later that year, evening classes in preparation for a University of London examination commenced. It is clear that the college was making a significant impact on evangelical lay training.

Some schemes that initially seemed to have the potential to increase the effectiveness of distance learning proved ultimately abortive. One of these was the attempt to set up a network of local study groups. Correspondence course material was to be used, but a local tutor approved by LBC was to be the facilitator. It was a framework that was later to prove successful when used by the Open University. But in the 1940s, although some local groups flourished, it was difficult to find suitable leaders. A second idea that failed was to launch overseas versions of the correspondence courses. Meetings were held with representatives of missionary societies and the board of directors approved a recommendation in August 1947 that basic courses should be supplemented by material written by missionaries to be used in the main mission areas of the world. Despite being publicized in the Christian press, the idea did not attract support. It seems likely that it was too ambitious. Also, the relationship between the college and some of the interdenominational missionary bodies was not strong at this point. A refresher course for missionaries was being planned in 1947, but the response from missionary societies was not encouraging.

What did prove highly successful, however, were evening classes run in London and branch centres. These classes offered a wide range of subjects, although they were usually connected with the main LBC syllabus. Evening class students heard high-quality lectures by Ernest Kevan, Graham Scroggie and Martyn Lloyd-Jones. In 1944, day study classes and evening classes, which had initially been housed in the Scripture Gift Mission's premises, were being held in St Andrew's Church, Holborn, where Russell Howden was rector. John Laing's offer of 19 Marylebone Road had been accepted. He made the building available rent-free, which opened up huge possibilities for the college.[18] As with correspondence courses, numbers enrolling for evening classes grew dramatically. In autumn 1948, twelve classes were held. One of these had 98 people attending, although the largest room in 19 Marylebone Road could only hold 80. An evening class student who gained high marks, Percy Eyers, attracted the attention of Kevan, who was always keen to appoint able people to the faculty. Eyers, a schoolteacher from Watford, had a BA in theology and philosophy, and joined the staff in 1948 to lecture in ethics, philosophy and New Testament.[19] In the same period, LBC branched out to Bristol, Newcastle, Bournemouth and Belfast. Evening lectures were offered, and in 1949 the average attendance in Newcastle was thirty-seven. Awareness of LBC's training was spreading.

Education for Ministry

Although the correspondence courses and evening classes had a significant impact on the evangelical community, the college was strongly committed to full-time theological training. Such training began in 1946, and on 31 October 1946 there was a service of dedication of the Marylebone premises at which Lloyd-Jones preached. Those who came to the college for full-time training were seen as being prepared for Christian service at home or overseas or for teaching religious knowledge. In autumn 1946, the beginning of the first full academic year of LBC's story, 23 full-time students, four of them women, commenced studies. The intention was that they would proceed to obtain certificates, diplomas and degrees. On 25 February 1944 the faculty had set out quite baldly its ambition to achieve academic credibility. Preparation for the Certificate of Proficiency in Religious Knowledge (CRK) 'would give the College recognition in the scholastic field, and the holding of this

---

[18] F.R. Coad, *Laing: The Biography of Sir John W. Laing, C.B.E. (1879–1978)*, 191.

[19] Percy Eyers died in 1953 at the age of forty-seven.

Certificate would enable those who secured it to obtain various posts'. What was undefined was the exact nature of the posts. In this immediate post-war period about half of the students had in mind overseas missionary service. One of them, Joyce Baldwin, was to serve briefly with the CIM but was later to become an outstanding biblical scholar, the author of several commentaries and the first female head of an Anglican theological college. She also became a supporter of the ordination of women in the Church of England.[20] In the 1940s the concept of 'ministry' was not strictly defined by LBC, since the college had indicated that it did not see itself as providing full-orbed training for ministry in the denominations.

Tensions were apparent, however, over the position of those who wished to enter ordained ministry in Britain. On 9 November 1944 the directors had decided, in what was a momentous shift from earlier policy, that students should be prepared not only for lay evangelism and overseas mission but also for home ministry. Commenting on this decision, Harold Rowdon suggested in 1968 that the initial fears of denominational colleges about LBC entering this field had proved 'largely groundless'. The interdenominational ethos of the college had indirectly served to undergird denominational convictions.[21] Within Anglicanism, many conservative evangelicals in the 1940s chose either the Bible Churchmen's Missionary Society College in Bristol (which from 1952 was Tyndale Hall), or Clifton Theological College, also in Bristol, or Oak Hill College, London. Joint arrangements for preparation for Anglican ministry were formally set up between Oak Hill and LBC, partly because of Oak Hill's position in Southgate, north London, and partly because of the involvement of L.F.E. Wilkinson in both colleges. It was helpful to Oak Hill students that they could attend LBC for classes preparing them for the University of London BD. There was no question, however, of training for Anglican ministry through LBC alone.

---

[20] I am indebted to Valerie Griffiths of Guildford for a yet-to-be-published manuscript on Joyce Baldwin.

[21] Rowdon, *London Bible College*, 51.

It is possible that the sensitivity of denominational colleges to which Rowdon referred was not due primarily to the possibility of convictions being undermined. A more immediate issue was overall ministerial student numbers. If students chose LBC for basic theological training, the viability of smaller denominational colleges could be threatened. Baptist colleges in particular could have lost out since students wishing to enter Baptist ministry could choose LBC for their training and later obtain ministerial recognition. But Kevan, who was keen to see LBC engaged in ministry formation, suggested on 19 December 1944 that in the post-war period, when it was anticipated that many ex-servicemen would be applying for ministerial training, colleges would probably be over-crowded. Kevan believed that LBC could offer help. The faculty followed Kevan's lead, recommending to the directors that LBC should publicize the availability of training for those unable to gain admission to other evangelical theological colleges for one or two years. George Beasley-Murray considered that Percy Evans, principal of Spurgeon's College, the largest of the Baptist colleges, would welcome such assistance. L.F.E. Wilkinson said he would contact Dodgson Sykes, who was then principal of the Bible Churchmen's Missionary Society College.[22]

If the denominational colleges had in fact been unable to cope with an influx of students then Kevan's ideas about LBC's minisrerial training might have been more acceptable in denominational circles. Percy Evans' response to Kevan's approach was reported at a meeting of the LBC faculty in February 1945 under an item 'Help for Ministerial Training Colleges'. As Beasley-Murray had predicted, Evans welcomed in principle the idea of assistance but considered that the situation could not be assessed until after general demobilization.[23] Three months later, what seemed to have been an amicable relationship between the two colleges could have turned sour. George Beasley-Murray reported to the LBC faculty that Percy Evans had received a complaint that LBC was advertising itself as providing training

[22] Minutes of faculty meeting, 19 Dec. 1944.
[23] Minutes of faculty meeting, 13 Feb. 1945.

for Baptist ministry. The details of the origin of this statement were unclear, but it was clearly acutely embarrassing. It was agreed that a forthcoming article on LBC should say that it did not prepare for denominational ministry – a shift back to the position before November 1944 – but that LBC's certificates in religious knowledge and diplomas in theology helped towards that end.[24] For its part, Spurgeon's College was eager to welcome new students and put in place plans for an overflow following the end of the war. Percy Evans spoke enthusiastically in 1946 about the extra numbers 'arriving from the Forces, from bomb disposal units, and from coal mining' with 'an experience of God and of men'.[25]

The place of LBC in relation to Baptist ministerial training continued to be a matter of debate. Autumn 1948 saw one hundred full-time students at LBC – a figure that was to be maintained over the next decade – compared with 50 students at Spurgeon's College and similar (or lower) numbers at the Anglican evangelical colleges. LBC saw itself, however, as distinctively pan-denominational. Oliver Barclay suggests that Martyn Lloyd-Jones sounded an alarm when LBC started preparing students for the London University BD but that the college had adopted the view that the BD was necessary to get its graduates into BU churches.[26] Spurgeon's College was increasingly using the London BD. Yet academic commitment was present from the genesis of LBC and was not a response to denominational affairs. Russell Howden, whose interests as an Anglican did not lie in the direction of Baptist life, spoke in 1946 about the commitment of the college 'to a policy of aiming at the very highest educational standards'.[27] John Laing, who gave such substantial support to LBC, would not have been interested in a venture directed towards producing Baptist ministers. Rather, it was expected that LBC students who obtained a qualification from London

[24] Minutes of faculty meeting, 16 May 1945.
[25] Percy Evans, 'Rain after Drought', *SCM* (Spring 1946), 18.
[26] Barclay, *Evangelicalism*, 130.
[27] Minutes of the college council, 27 Sept. 1946.

University would take up a range of positions. The university link was consonant with the academic aspirations of the college, rather than being designed to gain access to BU churches. LBC's backers wished to support the training of those who would be evangelical opinion-makers.

Evangelicals, Theology and Ecumenism

In undertaking the task of theological education, LBC had to adopt a philosophy regarding the degree of freedom offered to those who were teaching. It was the policy that 'on points where there is legitimate difference of opinion among Evangelicals a tutor will have perfect liberty in his teaching – such liberty, of course, being freedom only within the bounds of the Doctrinal Basis of the College'. The later 1940s saw, however, differences of opinion emerging within the evangelical community that would cause severe strain – although this tension was not readily apparent at the time. There were conflicting views about the current state of evangelicalism and about the relationship of evangelicals to the broader Christian world. Hugh Gough warned evangelicals in 1947 against unthinking loyalty to the 'old paths', saying that he had discovered during the war that evangelicals were not necessarily preachers of the evangel.[28] Gilbert Kirby, who was working closely with Gough in this period in seeking to revitalize the EA (Gough was then a clerical secretary of the EA), was optimistic. At the annual meeting of the EA in 1948 Kirby made the statement that 'modernism is dead; it is no longer a thing to worry about'.[29] This was in marked contrast to the view expressed by Max Warren, secretary of the Church Missionary Society, that evangelicals in the Church of England often had a sense of frustration, discouragement and inferiority.[30]

---

[28] *Ev Chr* (Jan.–March 1947), 1–2.

[29] *Ev Chr* (April–June 1948), 96.

[30] Max Warren, *What is an Evangelical? An Enquiry* (London: Church Book Room Press, 1944), 7.

Gilbert Kirby may have been overly optimistic. It was certainly not the case that liberal theology was dead. Nor, as Kirby knew, was evangelicalism replete with qualified theologians. Indeed, LBC found it rather difficult to find suitable people to help with teaching when it was decided to run refresher courses for ministers which would deal with theological subjects. Trusted figures such as Graham Scroggie and Harold Earnshaw Smith were often too busy to fit in extra lecturing. There were signs, however, of the emergence of a new generation of Anglicans and Free Church leaders who would be prepared to study theological movements from a position of increasing confidence rather than being dogged by the inferiority complex of which Warren spoke. For example, in 1944 it was agreed to ask Stephen Winward, trained at Regent's Park College, Oxford, to undertake a series of lectures on 'Contemporary Trends of Theology'. The subjects suggested were 'The Revolt from Liberalism', 'Dialectical Theology', 'Orthodox Theology', 'Neo-Thomism', 'The Personal Relationships School', and 'Eschatological Schools'.[31] It was recognized that younger ministers such as Winward were prepared to grapple with trends in theology.

But some evangelicals in the 1940s argued that it was better to oppose contemporary trends rather than to engage constructively with them. The formation of the World Council of Churches in 1948 raised a fear of the implications of the ecumenical movement. For a number of conservative evangelicals in Britain ecumenism became a major issue. Ecumenical leaders were seen as inevitably downgrading doctrine.[32] Within the British anti-ecumenical camp there were those who looked for support from North America. A new evangelical body, the National Association of Evangelicals, was formed in 1942 in North America.[33] But the National Association of Evangelicals, although it had emerged from within separatist American fundamentalism, was to take a somewhat broader path. Leading figures

---

[31] Minutes of faculty meeting, 19 Dec. 1944.
[32] Barclay, *Evangelicalism*, 74.
[33] D.M. Howard, *The Dream That Would Not Die*, 26–7.

in the organization, such as Harold J. Ockenga, would contribute to a more progressive 'new evangelicalism'.[34] When Ockenga, as president of the National Association of Evangelicals, spoke at a meeting in Westminster Chapel in 1946, the opportunity was taken to encourage the National Association of Evangelicals to foster dialogue with British EA leaders. Some British evangelical leaders were, however, keen to pursue a more separatist line. The FIEC, which took an anti-ecumenical position, was critical of the more open policy of the EA.[35] In 1949 Kevan reported that he had been approached by the FIEC with a view to LBC preparing their candidates for ministry, and the faculty, although not necessarily endorsing all aspects of FIEC thinking, agreed that this should be done.[36]

LBC had no intention, however, of adopting theological perspectives that were shaped by American or British evangelicals with a narrowly conservative or explicitly separatist agenda. American influence on the college was limited. Adrian Hastings, in *A History of English Christianity, 1920–1990*, while accepting that the revival of evangelicalism in Britain in the 1940s and 1950s was not an American importation, suggested that it owed much to America.[37] His survey does not, however, mention indigenous British bodies such as the IVF or LBC, nor does he refer to Martyn Lloyd-Jones. David Bebbington has shown that there were contrasting approaches to denominational involvement within American and British evangelicalism in this period. The differences, he argues, were rooted in ecclesiastical, cultural and geographical factors. America had, for example, far more parachurch bodies than had Britain, and as a consequence evangelical organizations in Britain were much more dependent than in America on support

---

[34] G.M. Marsden, *Reforming Fundamentalism: Fuller Seminary and the New Evangelicalism*.
[35] Minutes of the executive committee of the EA, 25 April 1946; 25 July 1946; 1 July 1948; 22 July 1948; 23 Sept. 1948; 25 Nov. 1948.
[36] Minutes of faculty meeting, 28 Jan. 1949.
[37] Hastings, *History of English Christianity*, 454.

from mainline denominations.[38] By the later 1960s about one-third of the students who had been at LBC were Baptists and about one-fifth were Anglicans, followed by Free Evangelicals and Brethren. Ninety-three former students were ministers of Baptist congregations.[39]

Nor was there heavy dependence within British evangelical-ism on theological changes happening in Europe. British evangelicals were certainly aware of the powerful figure of Karl Barth, and in the inter-war years the EA's *Evangelical Christendom* relied heavily for its German news items on state-ments by Barth, who, it was said, was teaching a 'revived Calvinism'.[40] The EA accepted Barth's contention that the cause of the Confessing Church in Germany was 'the cause of all Evangelical Christendom', and when Barth was in London in 1937 the Alliance sponsored a meeting to pay tribute to him.[41] But Lloyd-Jones, the most formidable theological protagonist within LBC's orbit in the 1940s, was unimpressed by the 'neo-orthodoxy' of Barth and of Emil Brunner. In typical style he gave advice to Paul Tucker, who became minister at the East London Tabernacle: 'Don't waste time reading Barth and Brunner. You will get nothing from them to aid you with preaching.'[42] Although Barth was to change the face of theology in Europe through waging war on the older liberal hegemony, many conservative evangelicals in this period were suspicious of his doctrine of Scripture. Edinburgh University Christian Union was disaffiliated by the IVF because of its sympathies, under the influence of Thomas Torrance, with Barthian theology.[43] It was an issue that would also affect LBC.

The British conservative evangelical theological advance, then, had its own story. In 1945 the IVF opened Tyndale House

---

[38] Bebbington, 'Evangelicalism in its Settings,' 370–6.

[39] Rowdon, *London Bible College*, 109–12.

[40] *Ev Chr* (Jan.–Feb. 1930), 35.

[41] *Ev Chr* (Jan.–Feb. 1936), 24; (March–April 1937), 44.

[42] Murray, *Fight of Faith*, 137.

[43] Bebbington, *Evangelicalism*, 255.

in Cambridge and launched the Tyndale Fellowship for Biblical Research and LBC was similarly seeking to establish evangelical scholarship. The aim was to avoid the trap of obscurantism while refusing to take the path of liberalism. In 1947 the college was pleased to report that twenty-five students were working towards the London BD. The same year saw the publication of the *New Bible Handbook*, edited by G.T. Manley and published by the IVF. In an equally significant development in 1947, R.V.G. Tasker, professor of New Testament exegesis at King's College, London, made public the fact that three years earlier he had attended a meeting in King's College addressed by Martyn Lloyd-Jones which had been decisive in his spiritual experience and theological outlook. Tasker had first heard of Lloyd-Jones through essays by LBC students.[44] From the later 1940s Tasker, whose theological position had originally been moderately liberal, committed himself to promoting evangelical scholarship. At the same time, the IVF's TSF was making an impact through its annual conferences. In 1948, one-fifth of the successful candidates for the CRK had been prepared by LBC. The college was both in tune with and a strategic contributor to the development of a more informed evangelicalism.

Preaching the Gospel

The college also reflected the commitment to evangelism that was evident in America and Britain immediately after the Second World War. The Church of England's report *Towards the Conversion of England* was produced in 1945. It received considerable acclaim, but it was evident, as Hastings put it, that the Church of England as an institution was tied by venerable customs and pastoral amateurishness.[45] Within explicitly evangelical circles, the National Young Life Campaign claimed

---

[44] M. Griffiths to the author, 18 Jan. 1999.
[45] Hastings, *History of English Christianity*, 437.

thirteen thousand members in 1947.[46] New initiatives were taken by Tom Rees, a younger evangelist who had been inspired by Frederick and Arthur Wood and had worked for the CSSM. Immediately after the war Rees took advantage of the sense of psychological relief felt at the ending of the bombing to launch large-scale meetings in the Westminster Central Hall and the Royal Albert Hall. He used well-known thinkers like C.S. Lewis, leading preachers such as Martyn Lloyd-Jones and W.E. Sangster of Westminster Central Hall, and titled individuals such as Viscount Hailsham to draw capacity crowds.[47] Despite the obvious enthusiasm that Tom Rees generated, he found that his initiatives attracted limited support from London ministers.[48] Gilbert Kirby, however, forged close links with Rees, and Kirby became a regular speaker at Hildenborough Hall in Kent, a training and conference centre that Rees opened in 1945.

Ernest Kevan saw the potential of Harry Stringer, a Methodist minister in Middlesbrough who had considerable experience in evangelism, to contribute to LBC's work. Kevan's initiative proved fruitful and Stringer was welcomed to the faculty in October 1948, at the same time as Dermot McDonald. Stringer, who taught church history, had a BD from London University and had been a tutor at the Methodist Cliff College, Derbyshire, as well as having undertaken wider evangelistic ministry in Methodism. In his approach to evangelism, Stringer drew almost entirely from the thinking of Samuel Chadwick, the principal of Cliff College until 1932. In the 1920s Chadwick, exhibiting traits of the romantic medievalism of the time, had wanted a band of 'Evangelistic Friars' to engage in itinerant mission.[49] In 1925 he had a vision of the nation stretched out

---

[46] *Chr* (24 April 1947), 1. For the Wood brothers, see F.P. and M.S. Wood, *Youth Advancing* (London: National Young Life Campaign, 1961).

[47] J. Rees, *Putting Ten Thousand to Flight* (London, 1952), 95, 102, 108; *Chr* (14 Feb. 1946), 9.

[48] J. Rees, *Stranger than Fiction* (Frinton-on-Sea, 1957), 24–5.

[49] *JN* (30 Dec. 1920), 2.

like a map with bands of young men on the road.[50] He announced his determination to enlist Methodist Friars to evangelize England, and from 1926 these uniformed 'Cliff Trekkers' (as they were also called) went out in bands each year to attempt the task. Chadwick conceived of his Friars as in the tradition of Francis of Assisi.[51] One leading Methodist, J.E. Rattenbury, described them as probably the most distinctive example of old-fashioned evangelism in Methodism.[52]

It was this kind of approach to evangelism that LBC adopted, under Stringer's direction, in the 1940s. The 'treks' that were arranged by Stringer came to be seen as part of college training. Two walking treks were organized for the summer of 1949: one of 180 miles in Kent, Surrey and Middlesex; the other in the Cambridgeshire area, which took five weeks. As with the Cliff College trekkers, teams travelled round with trek carts and wore a uniform of shorts and shirts. Stringer echoed the concern that Kevan had 'not for crowded meetings, but for finding out needy, difficult places'.[53] Kevan himself had been a supporter of the Strict Baptist Open Air Mission.[54] His strongly evangelistic instincts, encapsulated by his much-quoted statement, 'I love to preach the gospel,' were strong and were in tune with the times. In 1952 the Methodist Revival Fellowship, centred on the Cliff network, was formed. Indeed, evangelism of the Cliff variety was often linked with the concept of revival. LBC, through Gilbert Kirby, was in touch with the Congregational Revival Fellowship, which dated from 1947. The Baptist Revival Fellowship (BRF) was also growing in this period. A number of BRF Baptist ministers within the LBC orbit, such as John Caiger, minister from 1942 of Gunnersby Baptist Church, began increasingly to look to Martyn Lloyd-Jones for leadership.

---

[50] J.B. Atkinson, *To the Uttermost* (London, 1945), 38.

[51] D.W. Lambert (ed.), *The Testament of Samuel Chadwick, 1860–1932* (London: Epworth Press, 1957), 52.

[52] *JN* (12 May 1932), 2.

[53] Rowdon, *London Bible College*, 66.

[54] Kirby, *Ernest Kevan*, 21.

Alongside these indigenous movements dedicated to evangelism and revival was the new evangelistic thrust coming to Britain in the 1940s from North America. Under the leadership of Torrey Johnson, the successful pastor of the Midwest Bible Church in the Chicago area, 'Chicagoland' Youth for Christ (YFC) rallies commenced in spring 1944, attracting up to thirty thousand young people. The following year saw many North American youth leaders gathering to form Youth for Christ International, an organization which, with its vision, verve and contemporary approach, would form a key element in the growing strength of conservative Christianity in America and Britain.[55] The roots of this renewed evangelicalism were in fundamentalism, but a generation was emerging in America that had not experienced the humiliation of the damaging defeats fundamentalism had suffered in the mid-1920s.[56] The new, younger leadership, epitomized in the arena of front-line evangelism by Johnson and especially by Billy Graham, was supremely confident that 'old-time religion' was utterly relevant.[57] An enthusiastic YFC report in 1947 stated: 'News of the great YOUTH meetings in America and elsewhere in the world reached the ears of English leaders who asked for the inspiration and blessing of God from their American friends.'[58] American evangelistic confidence was spreading.

The export of a new style of mass evangelism would have profound implications for British evangelicalism. Three YFC preachers – Torrey Johnson, Billy Graham and Chuck Templeton – arrived in Britain in March 1946. Tom Rees was one of the American team's few initial contacts and he gathered about sixty clergy and lay people to meet the American group at the

---

[55] For a fuller examination of the British story see I.M. Randall, 'Conservative Constructionist: The Early Influence of Billy Graham in Britain', *Ev Q* 67.4 (1995). I have drawn on some of this material in chs. 3, 4 and 5 of this book.

[56] Marsden, *Fundamentalism and American Culture*, esp. 176–95.

[57] M. Silk, 'The Rise of the "New Evangelicalism": Shock and Adjustment', 280.

[58] *YFC Magazine* (April 1947), 4.

Bonnington Hotel in London. Evangelistic events began to be scheduled, including a meeting at Dermot McDonald's Baptist church in Woolwich. Reports back to America highlighted these initiatives.[59] This 46-day visit, followed by six months of mission which Graham conducted throughout Britain from October 1946, helped to prepare for Graham's huge impact in Britain in the 1950s. Templeton, who was later to move away from his evangelical faith, recalled: 'I don't really think we affronted people over there . . . They expected ebullience from Americans. I'm not so sure they didn't welcome it . . . We were so full of bloody energy, we were just irresistible.'[60] The YFC comment on City Hall rallies in Birmingham in 1947 was certainly triumphant: Birmingham was 'in the grip of a revival'.[61] Edwin Orr, a leading chronicler of revivals, could pinpoint few differences between the methodology of YFC and that of Tom Rees.[62] By the late 1950s, new methods would overtake Harry Stringer's humbler treks.

Billy Graham was appalled at what he saw as the lack of leadership among conservative evangelicals in Britain. When he was told in 1948 that there were only four hundred young people in all the Bible schools in Britain he considered setting up a college.[63] It was an idea he did not pursue, although he had a considerable range of theological contacts through Wheaton College, Illinois, where he had studied in the early 1940s. Wheaton had among its students in that period a remarkable collection of future evangelical leaders. Several within this connection, such as Carl Henry, Harold Lindsell, Edward J. Carnell and Graham himself, would be crucial in the founding of Fuller Theological Seminary, Los Angeles, in 1947.[64] Graham spoke at an LBC chapel service on

---

[59] Billy Graham Centre archives, Wheaton College, Illinois, for these reports.
[60] M. Frady, *Billy Graham: A Parable of American Righteousness* (Boston/Toronto: Little, Brown, 1979), 166.
[61] *YFC Magazine* (Feb. 1947), 51.
[62] *Chr* (10 April 1947), 9.
[63] Report by Billy Graham, 18 Nov. 1948, BGC archives.
[64] Marsden, *Reforming Fundamentalism*, 45–52.

one of his early visits, but his British contacts were mainly with evangelistic entrepreneurs such as Rees and Lindsay Glegg, who was to work with Gilbert Kirby on a Christian holiday week launched in Filey, Yorkshire. The inauguration of British Youth for Christ (BYFC) in 1947 was a sign of the growing transatlantic dimension. In 1948 Eric Hutchings, the first BYFC field director, staged a Graham rally in Manchester with 7,500 attending.[65] Graham's crusades were backed by the EA and would raise significantly the profile of mass evangelism in Britain. During his period as LBC principal, Kirby's position within the EA, and his support of a wide range of evangelistic efforts, would help to locate the college's place within British evangelicalism.

The Denominational Map

Although evangelism was vital to evangelical life, LBC's main purpose was to equip evangelical leaders and in particular to inform theological thinking. In this way it was hoped to affect wider denominational life. Thus denominational differences between evangelicals were played down and intellectual and spiritual training were offered within areas in which evangelicals of different denominations could agree. It was, in fact, a proviso of the college that there must be no proselytizing. Students were discouraged from changing denominational affiliation. Harold Rowdon speaks of the college as serving Anglicans, Baptists, Brethren, Methodists, Congregationalists, Independent Evangelicals, Salvationists, Pentecostals and members of the Society of Friends. In fact, students from the last three groups were scarce. Pentecostals, in particular, were regarded with considerable suspicion. Baptists were always the largest group, but in 1949, of the 16 students (12 of whom were men) who were entering the college for full-time training four were Anglicans, four Presbyterian and only three were Baptists. L.F.E. Wilkinson,

---

[65] BGC archives; *YFC Magazine* (March 1948), 47, 52.

who was concerned that the college should be an amenable environment for Anglicans, was satisfied.

The lecturers brought in to teach occasional courses reflected the concern of the college to embody and express a denominational balance. In March 1944, for instance, Alan Stibbs, a respected Anglican theologian, gave a series of lectures to ministers on ecclesiological issues, while Lloyd-Jones, a militant Free Churchman whose views on ecclesiology were to prove contentious, gave lectures on preaching. These lectures were held on Tuesday mornings and attracted 25 ministers. In the autumn of 1944 there was a series of lectures by Russell Howden, an Anglican, and Theo Bamber, a Baptist. This was followed in the spring of 1945 by another course for ministers at which there was the same denominational balance among the lecturers. Kevan spoke on the person of Christ and Colin Kerr on the devotional life of the minister. During the academic year 1946–47, lectures on biblical, theological, historical and applied topics were given by Frank Colquhoun, Harold Earnshaw Smith, John Stott (who had been appointed as curate at All Souls, Langham Place, and whom Kevan, as we have seen, attempted to recruit for LBC), Wilkinson, Kevan, Connell, Lloyd-Jones (again on homiletics), Fred Cawley of Spurgeon's College, and George Beasley-Murray. All of these, with the exception of Lloyd-Jones, were Anglicans or Baptists. These were the denominations that had the predominant influence upon the college.

In 1948 the faculty, however, had a slightly wider denominational spread. Two of the staff, Wilkinson and Hadwen, were Anglicans. Inevitably, Wilkinson's main energies were being devoted to Oak Hill, but Hadwen was senior tutor at LBC. Baptist influence within the college, through Kevan and McDonald, was considerable. Gilbert Kirby was Congregational and was available to coach students intending to enter the Congregational ministry. The Open Brethren, who played an important part in wider college life, were represented on the faculty by Percy Eyers. There were also Methodist links through Harry Stringer. In the late 1940s there was discussion about names of other potential teaching staff. Lloyd-Jones suggested

that consideration might be given to the appointment of a lady
tutor. This seems to indicate something of a change of heart on the
part of Lloyd-Jones, since he had previously expressed reservations about female teachers. The faculty members supported the
idea, but they took the view that 'very few' qualified ladies were
available. In fact, there were relatively few academically qualified
conservative evangelicals – male or female. Norman Spoor, a
member of Westminster Chapel, was regarded as a possibility but
he had other interests.[66] Godfrey Robinson, then young people's
secretary of the Baptist Missionary Society, was approached in
the same period and agreed to help the faculty in a consultative
capacity. The college leadership was keen to offer training that
made maximum use of the resources available within post-war
evangelicalism.

Conclusion

In the period 1944–49 the college reflected movement within
British evangelicalism. There was a widespread concern for more
commitment to evangelical theology. The IVF and the TSF, especially, through leaders such as Douglas Johnson and Martyn
Lloyd-Jones, played a major part in this development. LBC, however, was a growing influence, with its vision for theological
education that would provide for a future generation of
evangelical leaders. In this, the college wished to work with others
who shared that vision. There were some signs of what could have
developed into a problematic relationship between LBC and
denominational colleges over LBC's involvement in training for
ordained ministry. But the growing interdenominationalism of
the post-war era, seen especially in the area of evangelism (in
1948 a marked increase in evangelistic co-operation between
churches and Christian leaders was noted[67]), opened up new
opportunities for LBC. It was reported to the college council in

---

[66] Minutes of faculty meetings, 24 Oct. 1947; 30 Jan. 1948.
[67] Tom Rees, *Chr* (29 April 1948), 6.

1949 that, of the 26 students who had finished their training that year, nine had gone into pastoral charge in Britain. Six students, it was noted, were due to go overseas with interdenominational missions, three were engaged in evangelism, two had obtained 'high class teaching appointments' (the delight was undisguised), and one, Donald Guthrie, was joining the LBC staff.[68] Across the denominations, and in different spheres of work, the college was beginning to make its mark. This impact would increase in the early 1950s, but in that period the college would also, as we shall see, encounter its first major theological controversy.

---

[68] Minutes of the college council, 13 Oct. 1949.

4

'Both Evangelical and Intelligent' 1950–55

At the annual general meeting of London Bible College on 1 November 1955 Ernest Kevan stated: 'The results of the London University examinations are encouraging once again, and seem to provide a convincing answer to the question as to whether a man can be both evangelical and intelligent.'[1] The report also mentioned that of the 106 full-time students of the college, 24 were women. (Presumably the combination of evangelicalism and intelligence applied equally to them.) The major point being made by Kevan was an important one, signalling as it did a growing confidence that the college was achieving its objectives. The college now had a decade of experience behind it and was beginning to establish an academic track record. In 1952, for example, it was reported that LBC had secured two of the four first-class honours BDs in the London University external examination category. The period from 1950 to 1955 was one in which the evangelical scene in Britain experienced considerable change – especially, although not exclusively, through the Billy Graham crusades of 1954 and 1955. There was enormous interest in the training and development of young Christians. The opportunities for an institution such as LBC were, therefore, increasing. Although the college was eager, as this chapter will show, to embrace new challenges, it was also to discover that to aim for an evangelicalism that was intelligent in its approach to the faith created its own painful difficulties.

---

[1] Minutes of the AGM, 1 Nov. 1955.

As the 1950s Began

By 1950, compared with six years earlier when the first meeting of the teaching faculty had been held, the college's teaching resources had been significantly strengthened. L.F.E. Wilkinson still chaired the faculty meetings with considerable enthusiasm and Frank Colquhoun was also present, but Kevan now had a team of seven teaching staff whom he had picked. Gilbert Kirby speaks of Kevan's outstanding ability to choose people, and suggests that all those who joined the staff were to prove themselves over the succeeding years.[2] It was probably Kevan's intention that the early team members, appointed in the 1940s, would continue for some time, but by 1955 only Donald Guthrie, Dermot McDonald and Gilbert Kirby (part-time) remained as faculty members. Percy Eyers had died, Harry Stringer had relinquished his post due to ill health, Godfrey Robinson was concentrating on Baptist ministry in Romford, and H.L. Ellison, as we shall see, had resigned in a flurry of controversy over aspects of his doctrinal position. But Owen Thomas, Ray Ash (a former student), J. Clement Connell and Harold Rowdon had been appointed. The college's extension work was given a major boost in 1950 with the appointment of Tim Buckley, a gifted singer and violinist as well as preacher. Through, for example, his friendship with Tom Rees and his long-term involvement in Keswick, Buckley would do much to forge links between LBC and the wider evangelical constituency.

These wider relationships were also the responsibility of the directors (or the governors, from 1958) of the college. In this period the chairman was Montague Goodman, then in his seventies. Other directors included Theo Bamber, who was the leading figure in the growing BRF, E.G.A. Bartlett, an industrialist and Presbyterian layman, Clarence Foster of CSSM, Philip Henman, then college treasurer and later chairman, J. Russell Howden, D.M. Miller, W.G. Norris, who replaced Frederick Wood, and T.H. Bendor-Samuel, secretary of the FIEC.

---

[2] Kirby, *Ernest Kevan*, 32.

Ernest Kevan was also a member. The obvious omission was John
Laing, the owner of the premises at Marylebone Road, but he
joined the board in 1953. Up to this point there had been a poor
response to the appeal for funds for new college premises, and the
directors agreed to ask Laing about ways in which they could
continue to utilize the existing Marylebone Road buildings.
Laing, however, felt that 'the London Bible College was a
strategic point between the warfare of the power of darkness and
the Kingdom of God's Son'. He and his wife Beatrice therefore
decided to give up to £30,000 towards a new building.[3] Henman
offered to add £5,000 and as a consequence the directors agreed,
in 1953, to proceed towards the construction of a college building
on the Marylebone Road site.

For the students, the early 1950s constituted a period of
change. There was an influx of new students, creating greater
cultural, denominational and national diversity. Extra student
accommodation was purchased in Nottingham Place. Some
students came straight from school or university. Others had
been in employment – particularly teaching or medical work – or
came from national service. The majority of those entering the
college in 1950 were Baptists, but the 40 who began in 1951
were from more varied backgrounds. Thirteen of the students
were Baptists, five were Anglican, four belonged to Evangelical
Free churches, three were Methodists and two were members of
the Brethren. Some were 'undenominational'. Countries outside
Britain were by now well represented, with LBC keen to influence the international evangelical scene. There were students
from New Zealand, Rhodesia, America, Jamaica, Switzerland,
Germany and Denmark. The college was spreading its net
widely. Some who either entered or left LBC in this period soon
took up responsibilities in the wider evangelical world. Sandy
Gilfillan, for example, became a lecturer at the Bible Institute of
South Africa, Cape Town, in 1951. Like many others, Gilfillan
had been inspired by Ernest Kevan (a 'truly great man') and

---

[3] Extraordinary meeting of the council, 8 May 1953.

especially by his valiant leadership, given the often chaotic conditions in Marylebone Road.[4]

A Great Evangelistic Effort

Considerable attention was being paid in Britain in 1951 to new initiatives in evangelism. The EA, which by then had on its council Ernest Kevan, Gilbert Kirby and John Stott, decided to sponsor a major evangelical exhibition and public meetings during the Festival of Britain, which was being planned for 1951. This was in tune with the post-war commitment to rebuilding the country, a mood that gave impetus to LBC. An editorial in *Evangelical Christendom*, 'Evangelicalism in Action', which had all the hallmarks of the thinking of Kirby, captured the note of confidence. Meetings which featured evangelistic preachers such as Tom Rees, Alan Redpath, Stephen Olford and W.E. Sangster were held during September 1951, and on two nights 7,500 people filled the Methodist Central Hall, Westminster Abbey and Westminster Chapel. Further steps were taken in 1952. Roy Cattell, then EA's entrepreneurial secretary, had been involved in negotiations with Billy Graham, and in March 1952 Graham addressed about two hundred and fifty church leaders in Church House, Westminster, about the possibility of a British crusade. The British Council of Churches, whose representatives were present, wanted a pilot crusade, but Graham was not interested in this idea. His goal, he made clear privately, was to mount 'the greatest evangelistic effort, humanly speaking, that the Church had ever committed itself to'.[5]

'Ladies and gentlemen,' said Graham in his opening remarks in March 1952, 'as I look around today, and particularly as I think of America, I am desperately afraid.' Graham went on to argue, in an address which was published and was circulated

---

[4] Sandy Gilfillan to Barbara Brown, 8 Oct. 1997.
[5] Billy Graham to Bryan Green, 5 July 1952, in BGC archives.

widely among British clergy, that America and Britain faced perils from within, the threat of communism from outside and the possibility of God's judgement. He saw the period between 1920 and 1940 as one of spiritual drought. In America the Christian community was 'prayerless and powerless'.[6] Here were themes that appealed to evangelical leaders such as Kirby, and the responsibility for arranging what became the Greater London Crusade at Harringay Arena from March to May 1954 fell, perhaps inevitably, to the EA. The crusade at Harringay served to promote conservative evangelicalism in a way that would have been unthinkable earlier in the century and which would have profound effects on LBC. The scale of the crusade was unprecedented, with an aggregate attendance of over two million at all associated meetings, including one hundred and twenty thousand at Wembley Stadium on the closing day.

What were the specific, short-term effects of the 1954 London crusade and of Graham's Scottish crusade, based in Glasgow, in the following year? Stanley High investigated the results of Harringay on behalf of the *Reader's Digest* and concluded, rather to his surprise, that large numbers of the converts were still continuing in the Christian faith. High collated many case histories of conversions that had taken place through Billy Graham's crusades.[7] One year after Harringay, 11 classes were being held at All Souls, Langham Place, to nurture new Christians. Enrolment in All Souls' training for lay leaders had doubled.[8] Many individual stories from among the thirty-six thousand who went forward at Harringay were featured in the Christian press and Hugh Gough wrote to Graham in 1956 to say that he was 'constantly meeting men and women who were

---

[6] Billy Graham, *The Work of an Evangelist* (London: WEA, 1953), 7–12.

[7] J.C. Pollock, *Billy Graham* (New York: McGraw Hill, 1966), 328. M. Rowlandson, *Life with Billy* (London: Hodder & Stoughton, 1992), 66–7.

[8] S. High, *Billy Graham: The Personal Story of the Man, his Message, and his Mission* (New York: McGraw Hill, 1956), 229.

converted through your ministry'.[9] Numbers of baptisms in Baptist churches increased from around five thousand per annum in 1954 and 1955 to around seven thousand in 1956 and 1957. Many of these new Christians would seek training through LBC, some for ministry. Townley Lord, minister of Bloomsbury Baptist Church in London (and a leading figure in the Baptist World Alliance), spoke of the changed attitude towards Christianity in England, 'from prevailing coldness and indifference to increasing warmth and growth'.[10]

At LBC, the immediate impact was felt in the areas of distance learning and evening classes. The number beginning correspondence courses in the period October 1953 to March 1954 had been 223. In the same period the following year, 482 students enrolled.[11] Evening class numbers in autumn 1954 were 'quite unprecedented'. At the start of the term, over one hundred and sixty enrolled for one lecture course.[12] This was part of a wider growth of interest in Bible study. In Scotland, sales of Bibles soared, and the readership of SU notes, which had been strongly recommended, leaped by sixty thousand in one year.[13] A new focus on the role of lay witness was also emerging. Indeed, in 1958 J.C. Pollock, editor of *The Churchman*, suggested that the most significant contribution of the crusades was the new emphasis on the part lay people (actually 'laymen'!) had to play in evangelization. Pollock was also convinced that in sharp contrast to 20 years earlier, when evangelicals were regarded as relics of a past era, the initiative now lay with them.[14] As well as catering for a general upsurge in interest in the Bible through its evening classes and correspondence courses, LBC was to be deeply involved in lay training, with many of those taking LBC courses going on to positions of leadership. The college launched an

---

[9] Gough to Graham, BGC archives.
[10] Pollock, *Billy Graham*, 201.
[11] Minutes of faculty meeting, 15 June 1955.
[12] Minutes of the AGM, 2 Nov. 1954.
[13] J. Laird, *No Mere Chance*, 165.
[14] *Chr T* 2.15 (1958), 11.

imaginative 'Christian Life' manual, and it was reported in May 1954 that the EA was printing a leaflet advertising LBC's course. The leaflet was sent to twenty-eight thousand people.[15] By November 1954, 1,842 sets of the LBC manual had been sold and it was being translated into French, Spanish and Chinese.

Many evangelical Christians were drawn into closer co-operation through the influence of Graham, a trend with which LBC was in total agreement. Graham probably overstated the extent of this co-operation when he announced that he had received the sympathy and support of 80 per cent of London's ministers and churches. Opposition, he added, came only from a few extreme modernists and exclusive fundamentalists.[16] Certainly there were criticisms from the more liberal end of the theological spectrum. The formidable Methodist preacher, Donald Soper, was quoted as commenting: 'Anyone who says we enter the knowledge of God only by accepting the Bible literally is trying to take us back 300 years – and I for one am not going.'[17] *The Bulletin* of the liberal evangelical Fellowship of the Kingdom in Methodism was worried that the 'Harringay-minded' might stimulate narrow thinking, but it took comfort from the fact that within Methodism there were 'sounder' (i.e. non-conservative) views of the Bible.[18] At the conservative end of the theological spectrum, leading American fundamentalists such as Carl McIntire hurled vituperation at Graham after he began to accept more broadly based support. In turn, Graham supported Fuller Seminary in its promotion of a more open evangelicalism in America. *Christianity Today* was a highly successful journal which Graham helped to launch as a vehicle for this purpose.[19]

Although LBC was not unduly influenced by the American scene, as has been seen, it was entirely in sympathy with Graham's

---

[15] Minutes of directors' meeting, 21 May 1954.

[16] C.T. Cook, *The Billy Graham Story: 'One Thing I Do'* (Wheaton, IL: Van Kampen Press, 1954), 50.

[17] *MM* (Oct.1954), 88.

[18] *Bul* (June 1955), 2.

[19] Marsden, *Reforming Fundamentalism*, 158, 162–7.

mission to show that what 'the Bible says' was authoritative. Martyn Lloyd-Jones, for his part, declined to take part in ministers' meetings held in conjunction with Harringay. He included in his prayer at Westminster Chapel on 1 March 1954 the 'brethren' who were 'ministering in another part of the city', but a week later, in a letter to Elizabeth and Fred Catherwood (his daughter and son-in-law), he spoke of reports from the campaign as 'most confusing'.[20] After visiting Harringay, Lloyd-Jones came away dismayed, unable to accept claims that a great spiritual harvest was being reaped, and his remarks at his Friday night meeting at the chapel made clear his unhappiness. John Stott, who had become rector of All Souls in 1950, took a different view. Like Lloyd-Jones, Stott was fully aware that evangelism could be superficial and he condemned 'ingenious stunts to attract sinners'.[21] But Stott believed that British evangelicalism had gained much benefit from Graham and he supported the EA in the launching of *Crusade*, a popular monthly designed to foster the broadly based evangelicalism represented by Harringay.[22] Stott was an LBC council member, and from 1955 onwards the college would often find itself in tune with the approach of Stott to evangelical activity in Britain.

Questions of Spirituality

The college was concerned not only that evangelical leaders should bring theological thought to bear on their activity but also that their thinking and actions should have a strong spiritual base. Given its early history, a powerful influence on the college's spirituality in the 1940s and 1950s was the Keswick Convention. It is sometimes thought that an emphasis on spirituality has been a more recent interest for evangelicals. Certainly the subject of

---

[20] Murray, *Fight of Faith*, 338.

[21] J.R.W. Stott, 'Evangelism in the Student World', 4.

[22] Minutes of the executive committee of the Billy Graham 1955 London Crusade, 22 Feb. 1955.

evangelical spirituality had come to much greater prominence by the 1990s. David Gillett, in his book *Trust and Obey* (1993), suggests that the isolation of evangelicalism from other Christian traditions has given way, through 'a sea change' within evangelicalism, to a new openness and to opportunities to examine varieties of spirituality.[23] It is true that there have been important changes, but Graham Scroggie, who in 1950 was seen as the foremost Keswick teacher,[24] said of Keswick: 'It teaches that spirituality is the key to every situation . . . the emphasis of its message is not on the Saviourship of Christ, but upon his Lordship; not upon service, but upon character; not upon organization, but upon the Holy Spirit.'[25] Many LBC students attended Keswick in the decade following the war (Philip Henman often paid their expenses) and heard this message of total submission to Christ.

Although Graham Scroggie had little direct involvement with LBC by the early 1950s, other Keswick figures did. Theo Bamber, who was known for his striking convention addresses, was an LBC director until 1952. An example of Bamber's style was a message he gave at Keswick on Tobiah, an enemy of Israel who furnished a room in God's temple. The address was remembered for its 'remarkable power'. Bamber used rather bizarre exegesis, encouraging his audience to remove from their lives radios, card tables, smoking cabinets and jewels, all of which could be 'Tobiah's furniture'.[26] Stress on separation from the world, which marked much post-war evangelical spirituality, was taken up at Keswick by Fred Mitchell, who had been an LBC director and who remained a trusted adviser on the college's council until his premature death in a plane crash in 1953. Mitchell followed W.H. Aldis in two crucial roles within evangelicalism – as

---

[23] D.K. Gillett, *Trust and Obey: Explorations in Evangelical Spirituality*, 1–3.

[24] *Kes Wk* (1950), 43.

[25] W.G. Scroggie, *What Meaneth This? A Brief Interpretation of the Keswick Movement* (London, n.d.), 9. See ch. 2 for a discussion of Lloyd-Jones' reaction to Keswick.

[26] *Kes Wk* (1939), 163–7. The story is in Neh. 12:4–9.

Keswick chairman and as home director of CIM.[27] Influenced by his Wesleyan background, Mitchell emphasized what he saw as the implications of practical holiness. Speaking at Keswick in 1946, he expressed his sadness that some conservative evangelicals were going to cocktail parties. Ten years previously, he claimed, this would never have been the case. Mitchell believed that Christians were exposed to the 'peril of worldliness' and needed to be warned.

In the 1950s Keswick spirituality affected students who attended the convention, and the college also influenced Keswick. Ernest Kevan was invited to speak at Keswick for the first time in 1953. He gave what was described as a scholarly and lucid treatment of Romans chapter 7. Although Kevan did not suggest in his message any inconsistency between Reformed theology and Keswick spirituality, he spoke of there being 'no question' of the experience of the Christian 'moving on' from Romans 7. This was a reference to the view that a Christian could move from spiritual wretchedness (acknowledged in Rom. 7) to the experience (in Rom. 8) of life in the Spirit. Instead, Kevan argued that the cry 'O wretched man that I am' was always 'the estimate that the sanctified believer makes of himself'.[28] Kevan addressed the convention again in 1955 and 1958, and his theological standpoint contributed to the convention's changing face. The Keswick council discussed criticisms from those who felt Kevan was too academic and over the heads of many in his audience. Council members defended his theological emphasis, and Kevan, especially in an article in 1957, attempted to show theologically how the spirituality of Keswick and the Puritans could be reconciled. For him, Keswick's call to accept Jesus 'as Lord' was a summons to a new spiritual awareness.[29]

Another facet of spirituality that had an impact on British evangelicalism in the 1950s was the hope of revival. This was by

---

[27] For Mitchell see P. Thompson, *Climbing on Track: A Biography of Fred Mitchell.*

[28] *Kes Wk* (1953), 32.

[29] Keswick Council, 10 Oct. 1955; *Chr Grad* (March 1957), 12–21.

no means a new theme, but in 1952 Duncan Campbell, a Scottish minister who worked with the Faith Mission, described at Keswick a revival he had experienced in the Isle of Lewis, off the west coast of Scotland. Campbell's dramatic story had an enormous impact. He pictured for his hearers one house with about 'a dozen men and women prostrate on the floor, lying there speechless. Something had happened; we knew that God had taken the field and the forces of darkness were going to be driven back, and men were going to be delivered. We left that cottage at three o'clock in the morning to discover men and women seeking after God.' The convention report for 1952 noted that many came away convinced that the convention was a prelude to revival.[30] Not everyone welcomed a revivalist emphasis: Graham Scroggie was giving studies on Romans at Keswick that year and was insisting on the importance of a *teaching* convention.[31] Nonetheless, revival became a powerful theme in the evangelicalism of the period. A number of LBC students established links with Duncan Campbell and some travelled to the Isle of Lewis. Revival prayer meetings were also convened in the college.

Under Ernest Kevan, to whom students looked as a spiritual as well as theological mentor, the emphasis was on a disciplined approach to the spiritual life, with prayer and devotional reading of the Bible being central. This was expressive of traditional evangelical spirituality. An example from Kevan's diary gives the flavour: 'Wednesday, 1st May 1946 – Up at 5.30 a.m. Prayer 6–6.30 a.m. Read II Kings chapter 9, of the unexpected divine call to Jehu. Wondered what the message was for me. O Lord, keep me humble . . . Help me to lead my students closer to Thee; give me grace as I preside at the meals. O give my mind Thy light for the lectures, and power of clear expression.'[32] Kevan was also concerned for adequate pastoral care for the students who were resident in the college. Until 1949 Ernest Kevan and his wife, Jennie, were resident themselves, but this arrangement was

---

[30] Reports are in *Kes Wk* (1952).

[31] *LF* (16 July 1952), 479.

[32] Kirby, *Ernest Kevan*, 31.

replaced by a scheme in which tutors had residential pastoral responsibilities on a rota basis. Owen Thomas, a graduate of the University of Wales, was appointed to the staff in 1951. He had trained at Tyndale Hall, Bristol, and been rector of St Silas Episcopal Church, Glasgow. At LBC he initially taught classics and biblical theology, but then became chaplain and head of practical theology.

Other moves were made to ensure that the college's spiritual base was a strong one. With his Anglican experience of wider approaches to Christian spirituality, L.F.E. Wilkinson introduced 'Quiet Days' for students and staff, although these events incorporated more teaching than they did silence. In 1950 the first college weekend was held for married students. Most students in this period were in the twenties age band and most were single, but the proportion of married students would rise. There was an increasing emphasis on the role of married couples in ministry. The programme in 1950 also covered various areas of spirituality. Godfrey Robinson addressed pastoral issues, Sister Florence Hill, a Baptist deaconess from Vernon Baptist Church, King's Cross, talked about the use of leisure, and Clark Gibson, a Methodist minister, discussed Christian attitudes to gambling. Philip Henman talked to the group on what a 'responsible layman' expected from a pastor. Angus MacMillan's wife (MacMillan, minister of Lewin Road Baptist Church, Streatham, became a college director in 1952) gave advice on the minister's wife's reading. Tydeman Chilvers, pastor of Spurgeon's Metropolitan Tabernacle, was among those leading worship.[33] In the following year, Sister Winifred Laver was the main speaker and the 1953 weekend featured John Stott, a valued LBC guest speaker, addressing the subject of 'The Minister's Care of his own Soul'.

Although Ernest Kevan's own spiritual undergirding for ministry had been shaped by the Calvinist tradition, by the mid-1950s he was beginning to find himself somewhat out of step with the ethos of what became a revival of Puritan thought. Whereas Martyn Lloyd-Jones twice declined invitations from

---

[33] Minutes of faculty meeting, 19 May 1950.

W.H. Aldis to speak at Keswick,[34] Kevan was not prepared to restrict himself to such a purist line. When F.F. Bruce was asked in 1955 whether Keswick was Arminian in theology, he pointed out that a Calvinist like Ernest Kevan spoke there.[35] Stringent criticisms of the convention had appeared in *The Evangelical Quarterly* from J.I. Packer, then on the staff of Tyndale Hall, Bristol. Packer, who was to do much to promote neo-Puritan thinking, argued that Keswick's view of sanctification was shallow and delusive, and even that it reduced deliverance from sin 'to something little better than magic'. He was surprised that one Reformed commentator, discussing a book by Stephen Barabas on Keswick, *So Great Salvation* (1952), had suggested that there was no basic discrepancy between Reformed doctrine and Keswick's message.[36] In 1955 *The Banner of Truth* magazine was launched as a vehicle to promote the Puritan theology being expounded by Lloyd-Jones and many LBC students at this point were attending Westminster Chapel.

Widening College Networks

Training of lay leaders was a vital part of LBC's ministry in the post-Harringay period. Many lay Christians had been mobilized. Gilbert Kirby gave the Brethren, who did not have ordained ministers, special praise for their evangelism. It was estimated that 28 to 30 per cent of Billy Graham counsellors in 1954 were from Brethren assemblies.[37] Roy Coad suggested that in 1959, when the Brethren probably reached their numerical peak in Britain, there were at least seventy-five thousand people in Open Brethren assemblies. This number was considerably in excess of the numbers belonging to any one of the 'house church' groups

---

[34] Murray, *Fight of Faith*, 195.

[35] *LF* (3 Nov. 1955), 755.

[36] J.I. Packer, ' "Keswick" and the Reformed Doctrine of Sanctification'.

[37] *Crusade* (July 1962), 34.

which emerged in subsequent decades.[38] Leading Brethren teachers such as Stephen Short and John Williams, whose work was mainly in Canada, studied at LBC. On the faculty, the Brethren movement was ably represented by Harold Rowdon, who joined the staff in 1954 and remained until 1991, teaching church history and also Christian ethics. Rowdon, a former schoolteacher, was concerned, as he put it, to create interest in history, a subject often dismissed as dull and irrelevant.[39] The thesis for which Harold Rowdon was awarded his PhD in 1965 was published as *The Origins of the Brethren, 1825–1850*.[40]

Missionary societies were also a crucial connection for the college. In November 1952 it was reported that the college now had 150 former students, 43 in pastoral charges, 40 engaged in missionary work and 26 in school teaching. Others were engaged in various forms of Christian service.[41] Student hostels opened in this period were named after W.H. Aldis and Fred Mitchell, two outstanding figures associated with LBC. Among those going overseas, the missions which were most popular continued to be the faith missions – the AIM, the Regions Beyond Missionary Union, the Sudan Interior Mission, the Sudan United Mission and the Worldwide Evangelization Crusade. Wycliffe Bible Translators would also attract increasing numbers of LBC students. Contacts between the CIM and the college were not quite as close, however, as they had been in the 1940s. In June 1951 a letter was received by the LBC directors from David Bentley Taylor of CIM enquiring whether the college could provide shorter and cheaper courses for CIM candidates. It was agreed that this was not practicable, but the directors were keen to meet Fred Mitchell and Bentley Taylor in order that the matter could be discussed.[42] The CIM probably had reservations about LBC's academic emphasis. In January 1953 Kevan reported that a

---

[38] F.R. Coad, *A History of the Brethren Movement*, 186.
[39] Rowdon, *London Bible College*, 37.
[40] H.H. Rowdon, *The Origins of the Brethren, 1825–1850*.
[41] Minutes of the AGM, 4 Nov. 1952.
[42] Minutes of directors' meeting, 14 June 1951.

letter had been received from CIM stating that the question of training had been reconsidered and it had been decided to revert to giving lectures at CIM headquarters. As a consequence, no further CIM students would be sent to LBC.[43]

It seems that in this period the college was devoting more effort to forging newer networks within Britain than to fostering some of the older missionary associations. This probably owed much to the priorities of Kevan. His background was not one in which the faith missions played a significant role. Nor was he closely associated with the IVF, which was still, through local Christian Unions, a vital seedbed for missionary candidates.[44] In the 1950s, too, the only person on the board of directors of the college who represented overseas mission was D.M. Miller of the AIM. Miller's presence did not mean that the AIM received any special favours. At the board meeting in November 1952 it was reported that the AIM had approached LBC, asking for the price concessions made by the college to missionaries on the field taking LBC courses to be extended to native pastors and evangelists. It was recommended that the AIM should be asked to subsidize those concerned.[45] A further factor in all of this was that overseas mission was being served by specialist interdenominational colleges. When *The Christian* published a guide to British evangelical colleges in 1952 – in which fourteen colleges appeared – LBC's entry stressed that it was a college offering preparation for service at home and abroad and also that it catered for those who would teach Scripture in schools.[46]

The new relationships that were being established were designed to ensure that LBC had a solid base of support and the kind of links that would bring it to the attention of prospective students. In 1951 an Irish council of reference was set up with James Dunlop, a Presbyterian minister and Keswick speaker, as

---

[43] Minutes of directors' meeting, 16 Jan. 1953.
[44] Barclay, *Evangelicalism*, 76. Barclay gives a figure of 10% of graduates from CUs going overseas.
[45] Minutes of directors' meeting, 21 Nov. 1952.
[46] *Chr* (25 Jan. 1952), 20.

an LBC adviser. A year later Tim Buckley, who was busy publicizing the college, had successful meetings in Scotland. As a result, Ernest Kevan suggested there might be a Scottish council. It was reported to the directors in March 1953 that advice had been sought from George Duncan, who would be the foremost Keswick speaker over the next three decades and who also became known for his ministry at St George's Tron Church, Glasgow. Duncan put forward names and suggested that the BTI in Glasgow should be informed about LBC's new initiative, although not – perhaps significantly – until after a council was formed.[47] There was bound to be some degree of sensitivity as LBC moved into territory previously associated with another college. Nine members of a Scottish council of reference were appointed. They included the redoubtable William Still, minister of Gilcomston South Church, Aberdeen, who was spearheading a conservative evangelical renaissance in the Church of Scotland. Among the Baptists was Sidlow Baxter, pastor of Charlotte Chapel, Edinburgh. The Free Church of Scotland was represented by R.A. Finlayson, a distinguished professor.[48]

LBC also put effort into building international relationships – an indication of the growth of the global evangelicalism that was to be a feature of the later twentieth century. Ernest Kevan visited the USA, and Donald Grey Barnhouse, a Presbyterian minister from Philadelphia who spoke at Keswick and created an impact with his Calvinistic theology, became an LBC supporter.[49] In 1950 it was reported that Barnhouse had forwarded his own mailing list of seven thousand to LBC and that an appeal letter, especially for LBC's building needs, would be sent to those on this list. A draft of the letter had been sent to Barnhouse for his approval and, pending his reply, a brochure was being prepared.[50] The amounts of money given to the college from North America were never large. By the mid-1950s the total figure was

---

[47] Minutes of directors' meeting, 20 March 1953.
[48] Minutes of directors' meeting, 19 June 1953.
[49] *Kes Wk* (1946), 44.
[50] Minutes of directors' meeting, 8 June 1950.

approaching £3,000. Steps were being taken to make contacts in Canada and also in Australia. By 1952, there were 81 students in the Melbourne area who were enrolled in correspondence courses. In the same year L.F.E. Wilkinson reported to the directors, on his return from a visit to Australia, that he had discovered considerable interest in LBC correspondence courses in the diocese of Sydney. He suggested that an additional branch of LBC be formed in Sydney, taking advantage of the city's strong Anglican evangelicalism and links with CSSM and the IVF.[51]

Areas of Influence

It was this kind of development that produced a glowing annual report on 3 November 1953. 'There is no continent', stated Ernest Kevan, 'in which the London Bible College Ministry is not felt, and indeed there is no major country in which there is not a representative of the work.' Ernest Kevan drew particular attention to increasing opportunities opening up on the staff of Bible colleges overseas for 'our men', a phrase intended to be gender-inclusive since one woman was mentioned. Donald Fox was principal of the Hindustan Bible College in Madras, while former LBC students staffed the Bible Institute of South Africa. At that point Gilfillan was Institute principal (to be followed by Murdo Gordon and then Clive Tyler), and Howard Green and Ruth Caplin were on the staff.[52] For Gilfillan, Ernest Kevan had provided the model of what a college principal should be. 'The man laboured like a Trojan', Gilfillan recalled, 'with an impossible schedule of lectures, and with the responsibility of administration resting upon his shoulders . . . He earned our respect both as a man and a teacher, and our affection also. He could shrivel with a cold eye suddenly fixed on us . . . his expectations of us were high, and we knew when we had disappointed him; but when we were in trouble of any kind and sought his

---

[51] Minutes of directors' meeting, 31 Oct. 1952.
[52] Minutes of the AGM, 3 Nov. 1953. Howard and Ruth later married.

counsel, he listened with understanding and sympathy, warmly human and immensely Christian.'[53]

Ernest Kevan was also keen to see LBC nurturing scholars who would take up posts in various colleges and would affect British scholarship. Donald Guthrie, who had been appointed by Kevan, was determined, in his own scholarly work, 'to avoid such adjectives as liberal or conservative or fundamentalist'.[54] Geoffrey Grogan, who started at LBC in 1949, was to help to shape the BTI in Glasgow. John Peck, who was at LBC in the same period, also went on to teach at BTI. Peck had been nurtured in an evangelicalism which had 'a deep suspicion of contemporary Christian theological academia' and which spoke derisively of those who were 'dying by degrees'. Through LBC, Peck felt that he absorbed an approach to hermeneutics that did not require an obscurantist faith. He was also enabled to look at the biblical literature as a human product as well as divine revelation.[55] By the mid-1950s Ernest Kevan was being consulted about posts in colleges in Britain that might be filled by suitable LBC graduates. He recommended Joyce Baldwin, a former LBC student, for a position as lecturer at Dalton House, Bristol, where future missionaries, female parish workers and deaconesses were undertaking training – mainly for pastoral ministries within Anglicanism. Baldwin was to have a wide-ranging impact in theological education and Anglican leadership.[56]

At LBC there had been discussions over more than a decade about having a female member of the teaching staff. About 25 per cent of the students studying in the college in the 1950s were women. Tim Buckley's wife, Doreen, who was a qualified elocutionist, was undertaking voice and speech training for students. Mildred Cable, as a visiting lecturer with vast overseas experience to offer, gave sessions on mission. In 1950 virtually all the women

---

[53] Sandy Gilfillan to Barbara Brown, 8 Oct. 1997.
[54] Guthrie, *I Stand for Truth*, 33, 55.
[55] John Peck to the author, 5 Dec. 1998.
[56] Valerie Griffiths, from a yet-to-be-published manuscript on Joyce Baldwin.

students leaving LBC after full-time study intended to go overseas, a pattern no doubt influenced in part by the lack of opportunities for women to exercise leadership in British churches. Vivienne Stacey, who left the college in 1954, became a writer and lecturer. In 1955, Rosina Parker was appointed as the first full-time female tutor at LBC. She had an MA from Glasgow University and had taught English. Of the 15 women leaving LBC in 1955, five were intending to work overseas – with the CIM, the Baptist Missionary Society (BMS) and the Regions Beyond Missionary Union. In addition, however, three of the female leavers were going on to become teachers. Two others were appointed as deaconesses (one at the East London Tabernacle and one at the Worthing Tabernacle), and two were entering the nursing profession. Marriages between students became a notable feature of LBC life, and some dubbed LBC the 'London Bridal College'. Joy and David Wheaton, for example, met and married (with the requisite permission from Kevan) while at LBC.

David Wheaton was appointed to the staff at Oak Hill, and after leaving there for parish ministry he later returned to become Oak Hill's principal. The list of students leaving LBC in 1955 showed that, of those entering ordained ministry, the largest group comprised those taking up Baptist pastorates. LBC made less impact on other Free Churches, but the college was seeking to extend its influence through its transdenominational ministerial links. Another series of refresher courses for ministers was discussed. Attendance at these courses had been small in the 1940s, but it was recognized that the college was now more widely known.[57] T.H. Bendor-Samuel consulted FIEC ministers about the idea, but the college was not yet well connected in main-stream denominational life. Indeed, the leadership of the BU regarded LBC students with some suspicion, afraid that they might lead churches out of the union. This would gradually change as LBC students took up positions of denominational leadership. For example, Edmund Heddle, who commenced

---

[57] Minutes of directors' meeting, 16 Jan. 1953.

Baptist ministry in 1949 and who was highly regarded by Kevan, would become chairman of the BU's ministry committee.[58] Douglas McBain, who entered LBC in 1951, became Baptist area superintendent for London in 1989.

LBC's attempts to integrate theology, experience and practice were to make a significant contribution to pan-evangelical advance in Britain and elsewhere. Adrian Hastings, as has been noted, fails to take account of the role of British interdenominational evangelical bodies. He suggests, with reference to the 1950s, that the Anglican evangelical 'belongs internationally on the one hand to the Anglican communion, but on the other hand to a movement dominated by the immensely rich Billy Graham Evangelization [sic] Association'. The ethos of one does not really tally with that of the other, according to Hastings.[59] For him, the alignment of a scholarly Anglican such as Stott with more fundamentalist American evangelicalism was an oddity. Both Stott and Graham, however, belonged to an international evangelical movement in which LBC, with its vision of a thoughtful evangelicalism, was an integral part. Bruce Nicholls, for example, who left LBC in 1954, was to play a crucial role in the World Evangelical Fellowship (WEF). At the WEF council in 1968, Nicholls, then with the Bible and Medical Missionary Fellowship, gave a seminal paper on 'Theological Confession in the Renewal of Asian Churches'. Nicholls was appointed as theological co-ordinator of WEF and did a great deal to develop its theological ministry in a contextual setting.[60]

Theological Conflict

The picture of steady progress, however, does not tell the full story of LBC's life in the mid-1950s. The matter that created a fissure was the doctrine of Scripture. The college's statement of

---

[58] W.C.R. Hancock to the author, 9 April 1998.
[59] Hastings, *History of English Christianity*, 456.
[60] Howard, *Dream*, 85–6.

faith simply affirmed the 'divine inspiration and supreme
authority of the Holy Scriptures', but there were pressures in the
international evangelical world to spell out what exactly supreme
authority meant. In 1951, when the WEF was formed (joining
together evangelical bodies in eleven countries), there were some
worries in Britain about WEF's use of the word 'infallible' in
relation to Scripture. It was a position that initially kept a number
of European Alliances out of the world body. The British EA,
however, although unconvinced about the need for a tighter definition of biblical authority, was prepared to join, and Gilbert
Kirby, who was able to involve himself in numerous enterprises,
subsequently became general secretary of WEF.[61] Oliver Barclay,
probably reflecting the IVF perspective, suggests that in this
period many evangelicals did not see the EA (where Kirby's influence was greatest) as having a very clear role.[62] There were some
(inconclusive) discussions between LBC and the EA about
working together.[63] Later it would become clear that there was
considerable commonality between the EA and LBC.

This broader evangelical position was to prove problematic,
however, for the college. Separatist evangelicals were not
prepared to tolerate the inclusiveness embodied in the EA. In
1952, as a consequence, the British Evangelical Council (BEC)
was formed to provide fellowship for those evangelicals who
wished to be free from all links with ecumenical bodies.[64] Hugh
Gough, a vice-president of LBC, tried, as did Kirby, to set out a
bridge position, but E.J. Poole-Connor, a determined separatist,
dismissed Gough's efforts as 'the vaguest platitudes'.[65] Most LBC
supporters took a more open stance on ecclesiastical
relationships, knowing that many British evangelicals were in
denominations that included non-evangelicals. At the same time,
the college was fully aware that it risked losing the support of the

---

[61] Minutes of the executive committee of the EA, 24 July 1952.

[62] Barclay, *Evangelicalism*, 75.

[63] Minutes of directors' meeting, 8 June 1950.

[64] H.R. Jones, *Unity in Truth*, 7–19.

[65] Murray, *Fight of Faith*, 306.

more conservative if it did not maintain a robust stance on evangelical distinctives – for example the inspiration of Scripture. Accordingly, in early 1953 LBC made a statement in relation to its position. A preamble referred to 'the fact that the doctrine of Scripture is one upon which important differences exist at the present time'. It was deemed appropriate to say that 'while not attempting to define the method of inspiration, the College believes that such inspiration results in language which is the Word of God'. Against the background of debates about the theology of Karl Barth, it stated: 'The Scriptures are thus the Word of God by virtue of their inspiration and do not merely become so in the context of human experience.'[66]

At virtually the same time, one of the most creative of LBC's faculty, H.L. Ellison, was writing an article which challenged – whether consciously or inadvertently – the adequacy of this statement. This position had fatal consequences for his place on the staff. Ellison was an unusual person. Born in Krakow, Poland (his original name was Zeckhausen), he moved to England, became an Anglican clergyman, and from 1927 to 1930 was a lecturer at the London College of Divinity. Later his views of baptism changed, and in 1936, when he was director of a mission to the Jews in Bucharest, he was baptized in the German Baptist church there.[67] He joined the Open Brethren. In October 1954, in an article in *The Evangelical Quarterly* entitled 'Some Thoughts on Inspiration', Ellison argued that 'the Bible as a record is not in itself life-giving; it is not an agent of revelation; it is never more than an instrument, the instrument used by the Holy Spirit more than any other'. His view was that the Spirit made Scripture 'the Word of God to us'. Otherwise, he believed, inherent power was attributed to the Bible. 'If we are prepared', he suggested, 'to say that the Scriptures contain, are and become the Word of God, we occupy a position which seems to cover all the facts of revelation

---

[66] Minutes of faculty meeting, 23 Jan. 1953.

[67] R. Fleischer, 'Looking for Clues: Baptists and Jews in Southeastern Europe before the Holocaust: The Jewish Baptist Missionary, Moses Richter', *BQ* 38.3 (July 1999), 139–42.

and spiritual experience.'[68] Not surprisingly, given the sensitivities about Barthian views of the Word of God, a fierce storm broke. The editor of *The Evangelical Quarterly*, F.F. Bruce, called the fallout 'the most unpleasant experience I have had in my whole literary career'. The attacks on Ellison, as Bruce put it, 'could have had no other effect than to bring Mr Ellison into serious disrepute in the eyes of the evangelical public'.[69]

In 1954 *The Evangelical Quarterly* was owned by the IVF, although two years later it became independent and was published by Paternoster Press, a publishing company founded by a member of LBC's literature committee, Howard Mudditt. Bruce noted that the IVF 'by reason of its constitution and clientele . . . had to be specially sensitive to the climate of opinion in the evangelical world'. The same was true of LBC. The minutes of the directors' meeting of 19 November 1954, a month after the appearance of Ellison's article, recorded:

> The Principal reported that his attention had been drawn to an article written by Mr Ellison and which had appeared in *The Evangelical Quarterly*. It represented views contrary to those held by the College, and it was felt by the members of the tutorial staff and by a number of friends, including Dr Martyn Lloyd-Jones, that this article was undermining the position of the College. In the circumstances the matter had been brought to the attention of the Board. The position had been explained to Mr Ellison who felt that it would be wise for him to resign and a letter to this effect had now been received.

After discussion, the board agreed to accept Ellison's resignation. He was to be permitted to continue to teach for the rest of the academic year 'on the understanding that no teaching be given by him on the lines to which objection was made'.[70]

What was the significance of this episode? For Ellison himself it was very painful. He referred to the incident in his book on Job,

---

[68] H.L. Ellison, 'Some Thoughts on Inspiration', 213–14.

[69] Bruce, *In Retrospect*, 187–8.

[70] Minutes of directors' meeting, 19 Nov. 1954.

From Tragedy to Triumph (1958), making a comment in the preface on the 'suffering and distress' that he experienced as he began the studies in Job. His own position at that time was made clear in a powerful, highly personal farewell address he gave at LBC. His theme was 'the truth shall set you free', and he spoke of being able to 'walk freely amidst all the limitations that man seeks to inflict on you and the conformities by which he would narrow your path'. Ellison dismissed 'the rather pompous edifice of orthodox theology', arguing that what was handed down in Scripture or tradition 'is not the truth for you until the Spirit of Christ has made it come to life in you and for you'. With obvious reference to his own experience, and with a passion that impressed itself on his audience, Ellison encouraged students to rise above 'the criticisms of the past-bound orthodox, the fears of the upholders of some dogmatic system that see their structure threatened and the frowns of those that would confine the truth to one tradition'. For Ellison, the 'free man' was a cause of 'offence to those who hug their chains and call them ornaments', but freedom was only possible by entering into 'a noble tradition of suffering for the truth'.[71]

In losing Ellison, LBC lost someone with a great deal to offer in the field of Old Testament studies. Michael Baughen, who studied at Oak Hill and LBC (where he met his wife, Myrtle), and who became rector of All Souls, Langham Place, and later bishop of Chester, looked back to the way Ellison's lectures restored his faith in the Old Testament.[72] As a commentator, Ellison was insightful and original. His own evangelical experience was a varied and to some extent an idiosyncratic one, and he felt that part of his calling was to challenge accepted positions. Ellison revelled in being provocative, whereas Kevan's concern was for evangelical unity. Strain was inevitable, and given the conservative climate in evangelicalism, the tension became unbearable. It is likely that Ellison had supporters within the college, such as Montague Goodman, a fellow member of the Brethren. Since

---

[71] I am grateful to Douglas McBain for the transcript of this address.

[72] Conversation with Michael Baughen, 30 Nov. 1998.

Ellison went on to teach at Moorlands Bible College, which had strong Brethren links, it seems that his standing with some Brethren leaders was not impaired. Goodman wrote to Ellison expressing the sorrow of the board about what had happened. Indeed, Ernest Kevan's instincts were probably to allow room for Ellison's views so long as they were confined to his teaching within the college. But the pressure brought to bear on LBC by Martyn Lloyd-Jones and others appears to have forced Kevan to act. The outcome of this particular doctrinal conflict was in the hands not only of the college and its principal but also of those influencing important sections of the wider evangelical world.

Conclusion

The period 1950–55 was a crucial one for post-war British evangelicalism. The event with the highest profile during this time was Harringay. Its significance, however, extended beyond its immediate evangelistic impact. LBC gained large numbers of new students, many of them new Christians, in the post-Harringay years. The college was concerned that the high level of evangelical activity should be supplemented and indeed undergirded by solid spirituality and by theological reflection. There was delight in 1950 when it was reported that 43 students from LBC had been successful in the London University CRK examination. The LBC students represented a quarter of the entire pass list.[73] The college was committed to seeking to ensure that the knowledge gained was translated into practice. Thus interest in overseas mission remained. In 1954, unusually, 11 leaving students were intending to go overseas, compared with only six settling in home pastorates. The college's debt to the CIM was enshrined in the hostels that were opened in this period – 'Aldis House' and 'Mitchell House'. By the mid-1950s, the vision of people being trained in considerable numbers through various courses was being fulfilled. Enrolments in evening classes reached one

---

[73] Minutes of directors' meeting, 13 July 1950.

thousand students, while 546 new correspondence course students enrolled in one year. In order to meet the challenge of growth, staff and students would vacate the Marylebone Road building for an extended period so that new premises could be built. Theological challenges also had to be faced. At this time of change, LBC remained committed to the view that an intelligent biblicism was vital for a healthy evangelicalism.

5

'A Big New College' 1955–60

On 10 May 1958, two thousand people packed into 19 Marylebone Road for the dedication of the new LBC building. The old building on the site had been demolished two years previously. The service was relayed into all the rooms, and excerpts were broadcast by the BBC. Despite the 'wilderness period' (as it had become known), in which LBC did not have its own building and was operating in temporary premises, the college's student body had grown dramatically to more than two hundred. The consequence was that the new building was operating at full capacity as soon as it was opened. Within a year there was talk of replacing the Marylebone Road facility with a 'big new College'.[1] The period of the later 1950s, which is the focus of this chapter, was one of considerable advance for British evangelicalism. *Crusade* magazine, launched in 1955, said in its first issue that it stood, as did the EA, 'for evangelism – and for Billy Graham'.[2] Frank Colquhoun, who had served LBC and had been editorial secretary of the EA, was an editor of *Crusade*. In 1956 Gilbert Kirby became the EA's general secretary. Ernest Kevan was, in this period, a regular contributor of articles to *Crusade* and a speaker at EA events. This chapter will examine the extent of the evangelical advance in the post-Harringay era and its impact on thinking and practice in evangelicalism in

---

[1] Minutes of the AGM, 20 Nov. 1959.
[2] *Crusade* (June 1955), 4.

Britain and elsewhere. LBC was to be at the heart of the theological spin-off from this expansion.

The evangelical renaissance caused some tensions. There were fears among some British Christian leaders that a wave of obscurantist evangelicalism of the fundamentalist type was about to engulf western Christianity. In February 1956 Michael Ramsey, then Bishop of Durham and soon to become Archbishop of York, made vague charges in the Durham diocesan magazine, *The Bishoprick*, about Billy Graham having taught unacceptable doctrines at a recent mission in Cambridge.[3] Some conservative evangelicals, especially those from the Reformed camp, also feared the buoyancy of the 1950s – but for opposite reasons. They believed that there was grave danger of a weakening of traditional evangelical doctrines and principles. Still others believed that there was a failure to achieve a balanced theological outlook. There were concerns, too, about unrealistic spiritual expectations. In 1960 Tom Rees commented that, although he wished he could share Billy Graham's convictions about coming revival, he could not do so.[4] Within this mix of perspectives, LBC, under Ernest Kevan's influential leadership and with the strong support of his colleagues, was intent on contributing to a more reasoned and reflective evangelicalism. At the same time, the college was keen to foster and channel the new spiritual impetus that was such a vital factor in LBC's rapid growth in the later 1950s.

The Growth of the College

From the mid-1950s LBC was increasingly seen as a place which offered young evangelicals a stretching theological education. A number of those who entered the college in this period would go on to make their mark in the evangelical world and beyond. One Anglican, Anthony Thiselton (Kevan's nephew), who studied at

---

[3] O. Chadwick, *Michael Ramsey: A Life*, 24–5, 92.
[4] *Crusade* (Feb. 1960), 13.

Oak Hill and LBC, went on to hold important theological posts. He taught at Tyndale Hall, Bristol, and Sheffield University, was principal of St John's College, Nottingham, and then St John's, Durham, and was subsequently appointed to a chair at Nottingham University. A contemporary of Thiselton's in the 1950s was John Balchin. Following Baptist pastorates, Balchin was to be on the staff of LBC from 1972 to 1985, teaching theology and New Testament, before returning to local church ministry. Another student in this period was Alan Gibson, later to become general secretary of the British Evangelical Council, who was a member of the London FIEC congregation led by Murdo Gordon, himself a former LBC student.[5] Whereas Gibson was one of 31 students entering LBC in 1954, the intake in 1956 had increased to 65. The college was attracting students from across the spectrum of evangelicalism and was to become an even more potent force for further evangelical advance.

How did the college become so well known in the middle and later years of the 1950s? Often students came as a result of individual recommendation. David Wheaton, when in his final year at Oxford University, investigated working in children's evangelism with the CSSM. When the subject of Wheaton's training was discussed, the CSSM's Clarence Foster, who was an LBC board member, suggested that Wheaton should attend LBC.[6] At that point few LBC students were university graduates, and Kevan was keen to attract those with Wheaton's background. Another example of the way contacts operated was the case of Douglas McBain, who left LBC in 1957 to take up Baptist ministry in Stoke Newington. After his conversion McBain joined Cheam Baptist Church, Surrey, where one of the members, a local schoolteacher, directed him to LBC to train for ministry. The teacher in question was an admirer of Lloyd-Jones.[7] Bill Hancock, who entered LBC in 1958, was – like McBain – to become a well-known figure in BU life, becoming an area superintendent in

---

[5] Alan Gibson to the author, 11 Jan. 1999.
[6] Conversation with David Wheaton, 26 Oct. 1998.
[7] Conversation with Douglas McBain, 17 Oct. 1998.

1977 and head of ministry in 1985. Before commencing at the college Hancock belonged to an independent church in Devon led by a former LBC student. Through this link Hancock entered LBC, where his own denominational convictions took shape.[8] Those commending LBC indicate the college's breadth of appeal.

The college itself also took steps to advertise its courses. In 1957 Tim Buckley was appointed as director of evangelism in addition to his role in the extension department. Tim Buckley was valued by scholars such as Donald Guthrie for the inimitable way he was able (as Guthrie put it) to 'debunk some of the theological cobwebs which tend to cling to those too deeply immersed in theological abstractions'.[9] Outside LBC, Tim Buckley was involved not only in Keswick but also in the holiday crusades at Filey, Yorkshire, and in local missions, and he found many oppor-tunities to speak about LBC's courses. The college endeavoured to ensure extra publicity for special occasions. The planning for the opening of the new building in May 1958, for example, included an effort to persuade Lord Hailsham, then Home Secre-tary, to give a speech – but he replied that he could not be present. Lloyd-Jones agreed to preach the dedicatory message, although this sermon, as will be seen, had unexpected repercussions.[10] Another well-known LBC figure was Hugh Gough, college vice-president, who became Archbishop of Sydney in 1959. The Keswick network provided opportunities for the college to be brought to the attention of potential students. Alan Redpath, a powerful advocate of the Keswick message, was secured to speak at a college prize day. It was also becoming clearer by the end of the 1950s that John Stott, who preached at several special LBC events, was to play a crucial part in the growth of the kind of educated evangelicalism LBC wished to promote.

Whereas popular platform speakers inevitably attracted attention, the board did much behind the scenes. Montague Goodman, as chairman and college president, gave LBC prestige

[8] W.C.R. Hancock to the author, 9 April 1998.
[9] Guthrie, *I Stand for Truth*, 45.
[10] Minutes of directors' meeting, 13 June 1957.

in a variety of interdenominational circles. Goodman's not untypical view of the power of board members was indicated in a famous comment he made to the CSSM board, of which he was a member. Referring to the CSSM staff, Goodman pronounced: 'But, Mr Chairman, they are our servants.'[11] For Goodman it was essential that LBC should be run on a professional basis. His statement to his fellow board members in May 1958, as he was retiring, reflected his priorities. 'The object in my view', he stated, 'should be to establish a Board composed of spiritually-minded men of varied experience and of proved worth. There should, in my judgement, be a majority of laymen who are men of affairs, of independent mind and judgment and able, from their rich experience, to assist materially in the direction of the concerns of this great and growing College.' Philip Henman, Ernest Kevan and John Laing expressed appreciation of Goodman's 'wise counsel, spiritual vision and business acumen'.[12] Henman took over the LBC chairmanship, and in 1959 Laing became president. The contributions of Laing, LBC's major financial backer, as well as that of Henman, were enormous. A Henman bursary fund enabled – among other things – suitable students to gain higher degrees. Such initiatives fostered LBC's growth.

Commitment to Evangelism

However effective the college was in its training of students and its communication with the wider constituency, it would not have increased its numbers at such a rapid pace if it had not been an integral part of an increasingly confident evangelical move-ment. Here the impact of the Billy Graham crusades was crucial. Inevitably, there was debate about the extent of the impact the crusades made. J.D. Douglas, writing in *Christianity Today* in 1961, suggested that six years after the Scottish crusade the fruit

---

[11] Laird, *No Mere Chance*, 115.
[12] Minutes of directors' meeting, 16 May 1958.

from the unchurched did not amount to much.[13] Whether or not this was the case, Robert Ferm, a Graham apologist, noted that every year for 12 years after 1954, when students entering Oak Hill College were asked how they had become Christians, the largest block of responses was 'from Harringay'.[14] Whereas in the early 1950s it was estimated that less than ten per cent of those being ordained into the Anglican ministry would have called themselves evangelicals, by 1969, as Michael Saward has shown, 31.2 per cent of those training for Church of England ministry in Anglican colleges were in evangelical colleges. By 1986 this figure had increased to over fifty per cent.[15] Baptists and Methodists also benefited. Crusade converts entered Spurgeon's College, and in 1960 five out of 50 people offering for Methodist ministry had been affected by Harringay.[16] F.P. Copland Simmons, a former moderator of the Free Church Federal Council, referred in 1959 to large numbers offering themselves for Christian service.[17]

Evangelicals in Britain did not achieve a profile in the post-war decades that was in any way comparable to that attained by American evangelicalism. Yet British Protestant churches did experience a period in the later 1950s when the steady membership decline that characterized most of the twentieth century was halted. Anglican confirmations per thousand people rose from 279 in 1950 to 315 in 1960. The Church of England was reckoned to be receiving almost fifteen thousand new adult members per year.[18] Specific evangelistic initiatives may have been effective because of increased interest

---

[13] *Chr T* 5.22 (1961), 919.

[14] R.O. Ferm with C.O. Whiting, *Billy Graham: Do the Conversions Last?* (Minneapolis, MN: World Wide Publications, 1988), 108.

[15] M. Saward, *The Anglican Church Today: Evangelicals on the Move*, 33–4.

[16] *Decision* (Nov. 1960), 6.

[17] Letter to Carl Henry, 18 Oct. 1959, BGC archives.

[18] *Official Year Book of the Church of England 1960*, 22, cited by Hastings, *History of English Christianity*, 444.

in religion.[19] Michael Eastman, who left LBC in 1958, taught religious education and then began working with the Inter-Schools Christian Fellowship (ISCF). His role was to help SU begin to reach more young people in the 'secondary modern' schools (serving pupils who had not passed 'eleven plus' examinations) as well as grammar schools. In 1958 the circulation of SU notes was three times the 1939 figure.[20] LBC's rapid growth paralleled a general trend and indicates that many new converts in this period were eager to avail themselves of training. In 1957, 629 people enrolled for LBC evening classes and within two years the figure was over one thousand. Correspondence course enrolments rose at a similar rate to over seven hundred.

Although the fresh evangelistic drive affected British churches, the most obvious indicator of mission priorities among LBC students in the later 1950s was the number going abroad. Of the 40 students who left LBC in 1956, 13 went overseas. There were fewer openings for evangelists operating in Britain, apart from among the Brethren or with youth organizations. Ian Cory, however, one of the leavers in 1956, joined Tom Rees in his evangelistic work based at Hildenborough Hall, Kent. The same year saw Gilbert Kirby become general secretary of the EA, and as someone who had a finely honed awareness of the strengths and weaknesses of the evangelical world Kirby took the view that the power of the Alliance at that stage lay in its role in encouraging evangelism.[21] A gathering of evangelists called in 1958 revealed that those who had previously felt discouraged and isolated were now revelling in the new spiritual atmosphere which was by then perceived to be prevailing in Britain.[22] On the question of co-operative activity, Kirby could point in 1959 to the examples of interdenominational missionary societies, Keswick, the IVF

---

[19] G. Parsons, 'Contrasts and Continuities: The Traditional Christian Churches in Britain since 1945', 48.
[20] J.C. Pollock, *The Good Seed*, 203.
[21] Minutes of the executive committee of the EA, 29 Jan. 1965.
[22] Rees, *Stranger*, 88.

and the EA itself, to show the effectiveness of unity.[23] This perspective was endorsed enthusiastically at LBC.

More explicit evangelistic emphases were also to be found among church leaders not previously associated with conservative evangelicalism. In 1960 the evangelical Methodist historian A. Skevington Wood, who a year previously had been invited to join the LBC staff but whom the Methodist Conference had refused to release, wrote an important survey of 'Evangelical Prospects in Britain'. Skevington Wood suggested that there was now a firmer emphasis on the Bible in mainstream denominational bodies, and he drew attention to the way this was affecting some not previously committed to the complete authority of the Bible. He enthused about new Bible teaching events. Perhaps most significantly for LBC, Skevington Wood spoke about the growing respect for conservative scholarship, instancing Clifford Rhodes, the spokesman for the theologically liberal Anglican Modern Churchmen's Union, who observed that the intellectual balance in the Church of England was weighing down on the evangelical side.[24] A similar trend was evident in Scotland. Tom Allan, who was minister (before George Duncan) of St George's Tron Church, Glasgow, even claimed of Graham's 1955 Scottish crusade that perhaps nothing since the Reformation had made such a deep impression on Scotland. Local Church of Scotland ministers became much more deeply involved in evangelism.[25]

The LBC vision included commitment to evangelism. In the wake of Harringay, the college organized campaigns in Britain and elsewhere in Europe. Owen Thomas had taken over teaching evangelism studies, replacing J.H. Stringer, and brought his Welsh enthusiasm and humour to both the evangelistic and pastoral areas of college life. He teamed up with Tim Buckley on LBC's practical training. Buckley masterminded long-distance evangelistic treks of the older style and also brought together a choir of LBC students which travelled the country in 'an evangelistic effort to present the

---

[23] *Ev B* (Winter 1959), 1.
[24] *Chr T* 4.14 (1960), 13.
[25] *Chr T* 1.7 (1957), 14–16.

gospel by song and testimony'. Thomas took teams to France, Belgium, Germany, Spain and Czechoslovakia. Through his contacts he was able, a decade later, to achieve the transfer of a Czech theological student, Jiri (George) Lukl, from the Prague Comerius Theological Faculty to LBC, and Lukl was subsequently to become general secretary of the Czech Bible Society.

The LBC leadership was keen to ensure that the college's increasingly wide-ranging activities should have a strong spiritual basis. In 1958 it was decided to strengthen spiritual oversight by appointing an LBC chaplain, a post Thomas took up.[26] Also in 1958 there was discussion of the stance to be adopted over 'participation of students in professional acting'. It was agreed that this was inconsistent with membership of LBC.[27] Older evangelical spirituality had seen separation from 'the world' – and the theatre was emphatically 'worldly' – as an essential component of godliness. Tension was increasingly evident, however, between the concern to be separate and the desire for societal involvement.

Recrudescent Fundamentalism

The Graham crusades not only stimulated evangelism; they also raised apprehensions about the rise of fundamentalism. In a letter to *The Times* on 15 August 1955, H.K. Luce, headmaster of Durham School, referred to the fact that Billy Graham was due to lead the Christian Union (CU) mission in Cambridge University. Luce called on religious leaders to make it plain that 'they cannot regard fundamentalism as likely to issue in anything but disillusionment and disaster for educated men and women in this twentieth-century world'. John Stott, who entered the ranks as the correspondence continued, was determined to repudiate the fundamentalist label.[28] It was, however, one that tended to stick.

---

[26] Minutes of interviewing subcommittee on 23 June 1958.

[27] Minutes of faculty meeting, 4 March 1958.

[28] In *Fundamentalism: A Religious Problem: Letters to the Editor of the Times and a Leading Article* (London, 1955), 15f.

Following the article by Michael Ramsey featured in *The Bishoprick* in 1956, 'The Menace of Fundamentalism', in which Ramsey described the views of Billy Graham as 'sectarian',[29] Hugh Gough wrote to Graham about his own fears of a conspiracy to frustrate evangelical initiatives.[30] Ramsey's antipathy towards evangelicalism was a throwback to his formative student days in 1926, when W.P. Nicholson, an Ulster Protestant, had been one of the speakers at a university mission in Cambridge. According to Ramsey, vulgarity and dogmatism had marked an address he heard delivered by Nicholson. Ramsey's comment was significant: 'That one evening created in me a deep and lasting dislike of the extreme evangelical style of evangelism.'[31]

Within LBC circles there was considerable support for the moderate stance adopted by Stott. There was wariness about fundamentalism's rigid insistence on 'inerrancy' as a way of defining biblical authority. Dermot McDonald, who had independent opinions which he expressed with considerable force, was sympathetic to the views of Geoffrey Bromiley, editor of the English translation of Karl Barth's *Church Dogmatics*. In 1958 Bromiley spoke about a tendency to 'give a false importance to the doctrine of inerrancy, as if the inspiration of Scripture were finally suspended upon the ability to prove it correct in every detail'.[32] Students applying to LBC were asked whether they accepted the authority of Scripture but were not required to sign a formula. Against the background of fundamentalist controversies in America, the editor of the recently launched *Christianity Today*, Carl Henry, a founding faculty member of Fuller Theological Seminary, argued that both fundamentalist and liberal attitudes were 'essentially heretical'. He continued: 'One narrowly excludes divergence of opinion, so that it becomes difficult for

---

[29] P.A. Welsby, *A History of the Church of England, 1945–1980*, 60.

[30] Hugh Gough to Billy Graham, 12 April 1956, BGC archives.

[31] Chadwick, *Michael Ramsey*, 24–5, 92.

[32] H.D. McDonald, *Theories of Revelation: An Historical Study, 1860–1960*, 214–15, citing G.W. Bromiley, 'Church Doctrine of Inspiration', in C.F.H. Henry (ed.), *Revelation and the Bible*.

some undoubted Christians to find standing room. The other is so broad and so indefinite that one cannot be sure on what ground he stands.'[33] In 1956 Stott wrote *Fundamentalism and Evangelism*, in which he distanced himself from mechanical ideas of biblical inspiration. The personalities of the Bible's authors, stated Stott, were 'fashioned, enriched and fully employed'.[34]

There was no sign in the mid-1950s, however, of the war of words over fundamentalism abating. Gabriel Hebert's *Fundamentalism and the Church of God* (1957) accepted that evangelicals did not subscribe to a 'dictation-theory' of inspiration, but Hebert attacked evangelicals for their sectarian spirit. He objected to what he saw as evangelical claims to have the whole truth. The debate, therefore, was both about the nature of Scripture and the place of evangelicalism within the historic Christian church. Hebert was clear in his focus: 'It is with the conservative evangelicals in the Church of England and other churches, and with the IVF, that this book is to be specially concerned.'[35] J.I. Packer, then the brightest luminary on the staff of Tyndale Hall, Bristol, took up the cudgels. Packer had already been using his incisive mind to address the question of the authority of Scripture, and in 1958 his *'Fundamentalism' and the Word of God* was published by the IVF. It was a book which, as Alister McGrath suggests, moulded the thinking of many evangelical students from the late 1950s.[36] Dermot McDonald, who took a close interest in the theological debates of the time, referred to Packer's work as a 'closely reasoned defence of the conservative evangelical case'.[37]

John Wenham gives a vivid picture of a debate which took place in Oxford in autumn 1958 between Packer and Christopher Evans, then dean of Corpus Christi and subsequently professor of

---

[33] J.R. Stone, *On the Boundaries of American Evangelicalism*, 108.

[34] J.R.W. Stott, *Fundamentalism and Evangelism*, 6.

[35] G. Hebert, *Fundamentalism and the Church of God*, 10.

[36] A. McGrath, *To Know and Serve God: A Biography of James I. Packer*, 80–9.

[37] McDonald, *Theories*, 172.

New Testament at King's College, London. Such was the interest aroused that over seven hundred people attended the debate, which was staged by the Student Christian Movement. Some were surprised by the power of the case for conservative evangelical views, although Wenham, a colleague of Packer's at Tyndale Hall, felt that Packer's response to questions was ineffective. To the extent that this was the case, it was due to Packer's belief that the best defence against the critical approach to the Bible was to assert the main tenets of Reformed dogmatics.[38] Although Dermot McDonald admired Packer, he suggested provocatively that Packer's writings 'on several occasions assumed the position he is out to prove'.[39] The issue of Scripture was certainly a live one in LBC in 1958. There was discussion at a faculty meeting in November of concerns raised by some students regarding the hostility of a small group of students towards the view of the Bible held by LBC. The two most prominent members of this group, one of whom had written an article on the subject, were in their final year, and it was decided to take no action.[40] There was no wish to precipitate a repeat of the Ellison crisis.

The appointment of Ralph Martin to the staff in 1959 was significant, since Martin's approach would keep alive the question of how broad or narrow was the college's evangelicalism. Martin studied for his BA at Manchester University and entered Baptist ministry in Gloucester in 1949, unaware (through an administrative error) that he had a scholarship to a Cambridge college. In 1956, by which time he was minister of West Street Baptist Church, Dunstable, he completed a (part-time) MA under T.W. Manson of the University of Manchester. Within the Tyndale Fellowship (TF) Martin, then in his thirties, had been encouraged by senior IVF figures such as Lloyd-Jones and John Wenham. Lloyd-Jones suggested that a paper by Martin on the Lord's Supper be revised for publication. The invitation to Martin

---

[38] Wenham, *Facing Hell*, 138. McGrath, in *Packer*, 87–8, suggests that Packer was more effective than Wenham indicates.
[39] McDonald, *Theories*, 213.
[40] Minutes of faculty meeting, 19 Nov. 1958.

to join LBC came about partly because of concerns about Ernest Kevan's health and the necessity of cover for classes in doctrine. Martin had a particular interest in historical theology.[41] His university theological education and his research under Manson – who was orthodox but not a conservative evangelical – had given Martin a broader framework. When, therefore, Kevan asked him to teach a course on Scripture Martin found himself somewhat torn. Kevan's own notes on the subject appeared to Martin to espouse the position advocated by B.B. Warfield, of Princeton Seminary, USA, whereas (like Ellison) Martin wished to encourage students to explore other views.[42] It was an issue that remained under the surface initially, to become public (as will be seen) in the early 1960s.

The Reformed Critique

When conflict over Ralph Martin did become apparent, the opposition to his broader sympathies came largely from those within the Calvinistic camp. While Anglican leaders such as Ramsey saw evangelicals as dogmatic and myopic, many Calvinists considered that evangelical doctrine was insufficiently robust and that it required to be rooted much more deeply in the Reformation and the English Puritan tradition. Martyn Lloyd-Jones and J.I. Packer were to be key contenders for this position. The Puritan Studies Conference, which became an important annual fixture in London, began in 1950. It was sponsored by the Puritan Studies Group of the Tyndale Fellowship for Biblical Research, with the prime movers being Packer and his close friend Raymond Johnston, who left Oxford in 1947 and spent a year at LBC. They approached Lloyd-Jones about their ideas and found that he was enthusiastic. Ten years

---

[41] L.C. Allen, 'Personal Reminiscences', 33.

[42] I am indebted to Ralph Martin for his help during an extended interview on 9 May 1998. For B.B. Warfield see I.H. Marshall, *Biblical Inspiration* (Grand Rapids: Eerdmans, 1982), ch. 3.

after its launch, over one hundred were attending what had become a two-day event at Westminster Chapel – from 1959 entitled the Puritan and Reformed Studies Conference. Lloyd-Jones was chairman and always gave the closing address. A new generation of students and ministers was being influenced by this recovery of what Packer saw as a vision uniquely embodied in the Puritans – 'a theological world-view, a God-centred ideology, a social, cultural and ecclesiastical programme'.[43]

Packer's foreword to the 1958 Puritan conference captured the mood of the time. 'After nearly a century of bitter conflict and steadily declining influence', he wrote, 'there are signs that the tide of Evangelical fortunes is turning at last. Numbers of young people are joining Evangelical communities . . . But it appears that Evangelical zeal today is not wholly according to knowledge.' Packer then went on to compare the Puritan commitment to 'order, discipline, depth and thoroughness' with contemporary evangelicalism's 'casual haphazardness and restless impatience' and craving for 'stunts, novelties and enter-tainments'. For Packer the antidote was God-centred theology, as found among the Puritans.[44] At the 1958 conference there was a discussion of what was needed by way of training in order to produce ministers of the Puritan calibre. Among those within the growing neo-Puritan circle were Humphrey Mildred and Erroll Hulse, LBC students in the 1950s who worked for the Banner of Truth. At the 1960 Puritan conference another former LBC student, Alan Gibson, gave a paper in which he asked what could ensure that 'our studies in Reformed theology lead to a different way of life'. In his closing address in 1960 Lloyd-Jones attacked purely theoretical biblical knowledge. His comments – which would have profound implications for LBC – were typically forthright. 'I have always felt it is wrong', he stated, 'to

---

[43] *A Goodly Heritage: The Puritan Conference* (London: Banner of Truth, 1959), 3.
[44] *Goodly Heritage*, 4–6.

hold examinations on Scriptural knowledge, for the reason that it tends to develop this theoretical interest.'[45]

In the later 1950s, as Iain Murray notes, there was a weakening of the previously close relationship between Lloyd-Jones and LBC. One contentious issue was denominational involvement. The college was growing rapidly, and its students were going into pastoral ministry in a variety of denominations. Ernest Kevan, as a Baptist, was aware of the relative ease with which Baptist churches could secede from the BU and he did not want his students to be associated with secession. He had been a Strict Baptist pastor in the 1930s when ministers such as Tydeman Chilvers, pastor of the Metropolitan Tabernacle, London (and a former Strict Baptist pastor), had protested that T.R. Glover, Public Orator of Cambridge University, a prominent Baptist, had departed from traditional ideas of the atonement.[46] Calls were made at that time for evangelicals who were disturbed by the situation to leave the BU.[47] In contrast to this outlook, Kevan expected those who went into the BU as pastors to be loyal to the denomination. His view was: 'When our men settle in Baptist pastorates they never cause trouble.' Lloyd-Jones did not have much truck with this position. A second issue for Lloyd-Jones was the use by LBC of the London University BD course. Murray argues that Lloyd-Jones feared that preachers were being harmed by being subjected to liberal theology.[48] When this particular ingredient was added to Lloyd-Jones' objection in principle to examinations, the mixture did not augur well for his relationship with LBC.

It was against this background that Lloyd-Jones gave what was to be regarded as something of a defining address at the opening

---

[45] *Increasing in the Knowledge of God: Papers Read at the Puritan and Reformed Studies Conference, 20th and 21st December, 1960* (Chiswick, England: Evangelical Magazine, 1961), 12, 52.

[46] K.W. Clements, *Lovers of Discord: Twentieth-Century Theological Controversies in England*, 120–3.

[47] *Watching and Waiting* (March 1932), 216.

[48] Murray, *Fight of Faith*, 309.

of the new college premises in Marylebone Road on 10 May 1958. The renowned Old Testament scholar E.J. Young, of Westminster Theological Seminary, Philadelphia, was present and viewed the address as a highlight. Indeed, Young considered that he had heard nothing like it since the death of J. Gresham Machen, the founder of Westminster Seminary. From the point of view of the college, however, the sermon seemed to raise questions about LBC's core commitment to evangelical scholarship. For Lloyd-Jones, what mattered was not BD degrees but faithfulness to the truth. 'Are the men', he asked trenchantly, 'more certain of the truth at the end of their studies than at the beginning?' The LBC faculty, according to Iain Murray, 'received the sermon coolly', and it was decided not to publish it. Nor was it mere coincidence that later that year, at the Puritan Studies conference, Packer made the highly controversial statement that evangelical colleges 'turned out anything but preachers of the Word'. Kevan, who was present, spoke in opposition to Packer, and told the conference that LBC found the BD a useful framework.[49] It is possible that Lloyd-Jones had never approved of LBC's policy in this area, yet he had not objected in the 1940s to LBC's approach. His views may have been crystallizing.

There were those who attempted to take a mediating position over both denominational involvement and theological education. The Westminster Fellowship – Martyn Lloyd-Jones' monthly meetings for ministers – was attracting about one hundred ministers by the later 1950s, and these included Ernest Kevan and Tim Buckley. Baptist figures such as Theo Bamber and Angus MacMillan, minister of Lewin Road Baptist Church, Streatham, both of whom were LBC board members, also attended. Gilbert Kirby, a founder member of the fellowship, was keen to forge closer links between Lloyd-Jones and wider evangelicalism, and as general secretary of the EA Kirby asked Lloyd-Jones to speak at Alliance meetings. Lloyd-Jones was the main speaker, for instance, at an EA day conference in 1957 at Westminster Chapel. E.J. Poole-Connor, writing to Lloyd-Jones

---

[49] Murray, *Fight of Faith*, 310–11.

to thank him for his contribution on that occasion, took exception to the fact that Hugh Gough, who had also spoken, had contemplated co-operation with the World Council of Churches (WCC).[50] Packer, however, was not a separatist; he was to remain an Anglican. Indeed, Packer had a vision of the catholicity of evangelicalism. Nor did Packer follow the line advocated by Lloyd-Jones over academic theology. Tyndale Hall, Bristol, where Packer taught, operated within a university syllabus.[51]

It is probably the case that because the neo-Puritan movement was centred in London, especially at Westminster Chapel, LBC felt the impact of its critique of contemporary evangelicalism more acutely. After 1958 Lloyd-Jones was, it seems, asked to take little part in LBC affairs, and those around Lloyd-Jones increasingly came to feel that LBC was not living up to their Reformed ideals. John Waite, who was appointed to the LBC staff in 1955 and taught Old Testament, was part of the burgeoning Reformed constituency and, as we will see, would later become a critic of the college. In 1959 there was a 70 per cent increase in the sales of Banner of Truth books over the previous year, with many of these books being bought by students. It seems that in a period of two years around fifty thousand Banner volumes were sold.[52] By 1960 Maurice Wood (who in the following year became principal of Oak Hill) warned at the Islington Clerical Conference that Calvinism was threatening Anglican evangelical unity.[53] Five years earlier Stott had founded the Eclectic Society as a forum bringing together younger evangelical clergy. At the Islington Conference in 1957 Wood had been optimistic, saying of evangelicals that 'the future is ours'.[54] In 1960 he and others felt that the future was less certain.

An article on C.H. Spurgeon's views on training for ministry in the July 1960 *Banner of Truth* magazine reflected the changed

---

[50] E.J. Poole-Connor to D.M. Lloyd-Jones, 20 June 1957, cited in Murray, *Fight of Faith*, 306.

[51] McGrath, *Packer*, 73.

[52] *B T* 18 (1959), 3.

[53] *Ch E News* (15 Jan. 1960), 3.

[54] *Ch E News* (11 Jan. 1957), 3.

climate of opinion. The article was unsigned, but it probably reflected the views of Iain Murray, the editor. The author stated:

> By Spurgeon's day, it had become fashionable for theological colleges to prepare students for London University degrees; he [Spurgeon] saw this for what it has proved to be – an invasion of the Church by the world, and an abandonment in practice of what should be the true aim of ministerial training. Once let such procedure be adopted, and it is the death of the preparation of powerful preachers.

Moving beyond historical analysis, the author took the opportunity to comment on contemporary theological education, suggesting that anyone entering Free Church ministry had to attend a liberal college. The fact that George Beasley-Murray, principal of Spurgeon's College, wanted students 'to be men of God and men of the Word' was ignored.[55] Neither did colleges such as LBC escape the *Banner's* stricture. Some evangelical students, it was noted, 'attend an inter-denominational evangelical college' where (despite some benefits) they were 'generally up against a curriculum largely governed by a non-Christian outlook'. BD courses, it was argued, were imposed to gain academic recognition and state aid and to give students 'the other side' of the theological picture.[56] This article showed the extent of the parting of the ways on the subject of educating evangelicalism.

Evangelical and Academic Constituencies

It was clear to LBC by the end of the 1950s, however, that in spite of the tensions within evangelicalism the college had a growing constituency to be served. LBC saw itself as standing within the historic Protestant tradition. In 1956 it was agreed that the faculty would write a course on Protestantism.[57] It was also emphasized in the 1950s that all the activities of the college would be in accordance with LBC's doctrinal basis. In its spirituality, the

---

[55] *S C Rec* (June 1958), 2.

[56] *B T* 21 (1960), 31–2.

[57] Minutes of directors' meeting, 20 Jan. 1956.

college was by 1960 leaving behind the Keswick influences of its past, although Tim Buckley was leading the singing at Keswick and LBC student house parties at the convention continued. Packer's merciless critique of Keswick in *The Evangelical Quarterly* in 1955 (repeated in the Strict Baptist *Free Grace Record* in the following year) was intended to strike a fatal blow. 'It is widely agreed', McGrath comments, 'that Packer's review marked the end of the dominance of the Keswick approach among younger evangelicals.'[58] The premillennialism which had been a feature of Keswick was also disappearing in LBC circles. Kevan, with his lectures on the doctrine of 'the last things', played a part in this shift. Such was Kevan's opposition to the kind of dispensational premillennialism popularized in the footnotes to the Scofield Reference Bible that he told some students: 'If you have a Scofield Bible, I have a word of advice – burn it.'[59]

By contrast with doubts being expressed about academic examinations, Kevan believed in serving the evangelical constituency by thorough academic rigour. He saw LBC as helping in this way to shape evangelical thinking and to make evangelical scholarship credible. The progress of former students with academic potential was closely followed. Thus Geoffrey Grogan, who went on from LBC to achieve his MTh in 1957 when on the staff of the BTI, Glasgow, was invited to return to LBC to teach in 1965. When *Crusade* wanted to publish a series of articles in 1958 on such subjects as 'Archaeology and higher criticism', 'The Bible and science', and 'The Eucharist', it turned to LBC staff to produce them. Ronald Inchley, the publications secretary for the IVF, was a near neighbour of Donald Guthrie and they were members of the same Baptist church. Not surprisingly, conversations between them led to Guthrie writing for the IVF's Tyndale Press. Dermot McDonald had the ability to pursue research in the LBC senior common room, which was also a study room, despite the noise around him. His concentration on theological work, as Donald Guthrie noted, 'enabled him to make many valuable contributions

---

[58] For Alister McGrath's account, see McGrath, *Packer*, 76–80.
[59] Conversation with Michael Eastman, 28 Jan. 1999.

to theological literature and helped in no small measure to establish the academic reputation of the college'.[60]

The rules of the college were intended to reflect commitment to an academic ethos. At the insistence of Ernest Kevan, who was anxious that there should be a proper sense of dignity, those entitled to be regarded as undergraduates wore academic gowns. It was agreed in 1959 that during hot weather students could divest themselves of gowns during lectures, but at the time this was exceptional. One student's gown had been missing when the 'gown check' took place and because this was interpreted as symptomatic of an insolent attitude it was suggested that he should be 'rusticated for a term'. The sense of discipline at LBC was, as has been indicated, very strong. Yet in his autobiography Donald Guthrie described a kidnapping and other escapades which lightened student life, and Ernest Kevan took a number of such bizarre episodes in his stride. But when a student received a printed card with his or her name and 'Kindly see the Principal' written on it, there was usually some apprehension. Kevan's penetrating eyes, encountered at close quarters by students in his study, were often remembered. At times he could treat very seriously issues that his colleagues regarded more lightly. Kevan and his staff shared a united commitment, however, to seeking to ensure that LBC was both a reputable academic institution and a community reflecting Christian values.

LBC was also contributing to the thinking going on in the wider world of evangelical education and training. There were discussions in this period with other Bible colleges about the possibility of an Evangelical Diploma and these conversations led to the adoption of guidelines by a number of evangelical colleges as a way of addressing 'the need to raise standards of teaching in Evangelical Training Colleges'. By the end of the 1950s, 18 ex-former LBC students were on the staff of theological colleges (three as principals) in Britain and elsewhere.[61] Henri Blocher, who left the college in 1957, became a leading French theologian.

---

[60] Guthrie, *I Stand for Truth*, 44.
[61] Minutes of the AGM, 15 Nov. 1957.

The college was, in addition, making links with local churches and involving them in partnerships, so that academic training involved reflection on practical experience in ministry. Each year, a number of students who were intending to enter pastoral ministry were given assignments as ministers' assistants. At one stage it seemed that the provision for Anglicans was being over-looked and Anglicans asked for discussion of the practice of infant baptism. In response to the concerns raised, Owen Thomas, who looked after LBC's practical theology, contacted the Church Pastoral Aid Society (CPAS) which promised to speak to London clergy about possible opportunities. Soon the CPAS provided a list of vicars through whom pastoral experience for Anglican students could be arranged.

By 1960, LBC's staff and students represented various denomi-national influences. The Baptist presence on the staff was still a strong one. Ernest Kevan, Dermot McDonald and Donald Guthrie were a formidable trio. J. Clement Connell was also a Baptist minister, as was John Waite, who had been at Mill End, Rickmansworth, Hertfordshire. Waite, however, was to move out of Baptist life. Tim Buckley, though a Methodist by back-ground, was linked with Trinity Road Baptist Church, Upper Tooting, for some time. Owen Thomas was an Anglican whose interests lay in pastoralia, evangelism and music, and who pressed, with some success, for music to be given space in the college curriculum. The only Brethren member of staff was Harold Rowdon, but the Brethren had a clear stake in the devel-opment of LBC. In 1960 Leslie Allen, a member of the Brethren, became assistant tutor in Hebrew. The denominational analysis of those students about to enter LBC in 1960 showed that members of Baptist churches were, as usual, the largest group, but that Brethren and Anglicans were present in equal numbers. Growing numbers of students at that stage were declaring them-selves to be 'undenominational', a sign of the changing values of the post-war evangelical constituency.

There were large numbers of LBC students who were not entering pastoral ministry, and evangelical leaders were increas-ingly keen to direct able younger evangelicals towards taking up positions within the 'secular' market place, especially the professional world. LBC continued to see itself as contributing especially to training people for the teaching profession. The college was, however, in some difficulty over teacher training. Grants to students were not given unless they were attending a recognized education department. But the college could not start such a department until there was recognition by the Ministry of Education. Despite the obstacles, plans were pursued in the later 1950s to establish a teacher-training department at LBC.[62] Branse Burbridge, the secretary of the ISCF, was interested in promoting this development. John Laird, who from 1956 was sole secretary of the CSSM, became an LBC board member. He played a key role in the college's thinking about educational links. Prospective teachers, some of whom already had degrees, showed considerable interest in LBC, and the faculty noted in 1959 the 'upsurge of evangelicalism and the drive for more conservative evangelicals for Scripture teachers in schools'.[63] Harry Burgess, then director of education in the Sheffield diocese, helped to draw up plans for teacher training at LBC. These were not, however, accepted by the Ministry of Education.

It was important for LBC that it should be seen by grant-awarding education committees as a reputable academic theological institution. When David Wheaton was interviewed by his Local Education Authority he was grilled by the chairman (a public school headmaster) as to why he should expect a grant if he wished to study at a college which believed Jonah was swallowed by a whale. Ralph Gower, who left LBC in 1957 and went on to become a Religious Education inspector, obtained a grant from the Middlesex local authority. Cheers from LBC student prayer groups greeted such news. While at LBC, Gower was deeply influenced by the 'bravery and honesty' of H.L. Ellison's approach to scholarship, although when he began to teach Religious Education (RE) at 'A' level Gower found that he was not acquainted with many critical views which he had to

---

[62] Minutes of directors' meeting, 14 Dec. 1956.
[63] Minutes of faculty meeting, 18 Nov. 1959.

teach.[64] Each year LBC had between 12 and 15 successes in the University of London BD examinations. At least double that number of students obtained the university's Diploma in Theology and similar numbers obtained the CRK. Indeed, the college headed the pass lists of London external theology examinations and three LBC staff became responsible for the Scripture syllabus of the Royal Society of Arts. Academic recognition was seen as adding to LBC's repute.[65]

Such advances would not have been possible but for supportive evangelicals connected with the college. The fact that in 1958 LBC moved free of debt into its new premises, which cost £215,000, was a tribute to its benefactors, particularly John Laing. The original offer by Laing, to charge for labour and materials only and to allow delayed payment, had been vetoed by the government's Treasury department, which was pursuing a severe monetary policy and restricting loans. To pay for the premises Philip Henman therefore arranged that the Times Furnishing Company would lease the top three floors. Other college governors such as F.N. Martin, a member of the Open Brethren and managing director of Scribbans-Kemp Ltd, the biscuit manufacturers, offered their guidance. In 1958 Derek Warren, also a member of the Brethren, became a board member (later chairman), and the same year saw Gilbert Kirby join the board. Warren was in the same legal firm as Montague Goodman and acted as college solicitor. In November 1959 board members discussed solutions to the crisis caused by LBC's continued growth. The new building in Marylebone Road was already full and it was thought that a college of twice the size was needed, preferably with residential accommodation. Board members felt that there was nothing in continuing growth that was 'injurious to the spiritual work of character training'. At this point there was the first mention of a dream, to be fulfilled a decade later, of a 'big new College'.[66] A number of properties were explored. The

---

[64] Ralph Gower to the author, 6 March 1998.

[65] Minutes of directors' meeting, 13 Dec. 1957.

[66] Minutes of the AGM, 20 Nov. 1959.

options seemed to be a college for two hundred and fifty students in central London or one for up to four hundred in the suburbs.[67]

International Dimensions

Several of the developments in evangelism and theological education in Britain in the 1950s mirrored what was happening elsewhere, especially in North America. On occasions there were direct links, as with the visits of Billy Graham. British evangelists followed in Graham's footsteps, notably Eric Hutchings.[68] The crusade style became the dominant model for evangelism from the 1950s to the 1980s. There was a concern, articulated by Tom Rees, for greater co-operation between evangelists and local church pastors. Rees believed that there had been 'a complete lack of co-ordination between the pastor and the evangelist', which he compared to a 'clash between the priest and the prophet'.[69] An example of someone in Britain seeking to integrate these roles was David Sheppard, who from 1958 was Warden of the Mayflower Centre in Canning Town, East London.[70] A number of those leaving LBC in this period were seeking, like Sheppard, to address issues in British society. In the area of scholarship there was two-way traffic between America and Britain. E.J. Young of Westminster Theological Seminary, USA, whose work was highly regarded in Britain, was invited by LBC to give a series of lectures on 'Old Testament Theology Today'. Dermot McDonald was asked to spend 1960–61 at the Northern Baptist Theological Seminary, Chicago, a college affiliated to the University of Chicago, as a visiting professor.[71]

---

[67] Rowdon, *London Bible College*, 82.

[68] J.E. Tuck, *Your Master Proclaim: The Story of Eric Hutchings' Evangelistic Crusades, and the Hour of Revival Association* (London: Oliphants, 1968), 29, 31.

[69] *Crusade* (Feb. 1960), 12.

[70] D. Sheppard, *Built as a City: God and the Urban World Today* (London: Hodder & Stoughton, 1974), 336–7.

[71] Minutes of faculty meeting, 18 Nov. 1959.

LBC's links were not only with North America. Arthur Cundall, who left the college in 1956 and was to return as an Old Testament tutor in 1961, had trained for ministry at the Baptist Theological College of New South Wales. He then became minister of Granville Baptist Church, New South Wales, as well as a lecturer at the NSW Baptist college. Another internationalist was Tony Wilmot, a Christian businessman with wide experience of life in West Africa. In response to suggestions from Wilmot, the LBC board set up a meeting with a number of interested parties from the faith missions with which the college had links, notably the Evangelical Union of South America, the Sudan United Mission, the AIM and the CIM.[72] During the 1950s about one-third of the students leaving the college each year went overseas. A slightly smaller, but nonetheless significant, proportion of students came from overseas to LBC. This international dimension was encouraged. David Bendor-Samuel (who left the college in 1958) and his wife, Margaret, worked for Wycliffe Bible Translators in South America. David later took responsibility for Wycliffe's academic affairs. A number of other LBC students in this period joined Wycliffe, such as John and Audrey Taylor and Kathleen and John Callow. In addition to Bible translation, several of these former students were to contribute to international research in the area of anthropology.

The part-time appointment to the college of John Savage of the Evangelical Union of South America (EUSA), who had considerable experience in Peru, gave a boost to the place of world mission at LBC. During conversations in 1959 with missionary societies, under the auspices of the newly formed Evangelical Missionary Alliance (EMA), significant points emerged. The societies considered that colleges needed to give greater attention to character training. Mission work required candidates with knowledge of the Bible, but societies were wary of 'mere academic achievements' and they were divided over the value of examinations.[73] A recommendation had already been made to the

---

[72] Minutes of faculty meeting, 28 Nov. 1956.
[73] Notes of a conference of the EMA, 6 Nov. 1959.

LBC board about the inauguration of a missionary department.[74] John Savage was invited to head this, but he was reluctant. He was willing, however, to come to LBC one day a week to talk individually to missionary candidates and to lecture on aspects of mission. It was also agreed that Savage would build up contacts with former students who were on the mission field. By the end of the 1950s Savage felt that the missionary department, as it came to be called, was functioning well. He gave weekly missionary lectures, dealing with issues such as mission and culture. Other well-known missionaries visited the college – for example Len Moules from Worldwide Evangelization Crusade. Missionary lectures attracted over ninety students.[75]

There were also wider moves happening with the development of the Evangelical Missionary Alliance. In 1959 there were 40 societies and eight training colleges in membership with the EMA. Gilbert Kirby, then acting secretary of the EMA, was keen that LBC should become affiliated. John Savage explained to the LBC faculty in June 1959 his conviction that affiliation of the college to the EMA would enable it to make a positive contribution towards the maintenance and improvement of standards of missionary training. The link would also help to promote closer contact between the college and the missionary societies. There were, of course, denominational missionary societies that were not affiliated to the EMA, but the body had good relations with these. Affiliation, Kirby believed, would not entail approval of low academic standards.[76] By the end of 1959 the college had become an associate member of the EMA, and one consequence was that a conference was convened of representatives from the various training colleges to discuss what was being taught. Kirby, in his role as EMA secretary, called the group together and a common syllabus of basic studies for missionary training colleges was produced as a standard of reference.[77]

---

[74] Minutes of faculty meeting, 20 Feb. 1957.
[75] Minutes of the AGM, 20 Nov. 1959.
[76] Minutes of faculty meeting, 1 June 1959.
[77] Rowdon, *London Bible College*, 60.

Conclusion

In the years 1955–60, the immediate post-Harringay era, LBC more than doubled in size. Student numbers on the college's main courses reached 220. Evening class enrolments approached fifteen hundred. Although many evangelicals were given fresh confidence in this period, there were also serious issues which evangelicalism had to face. LBC, in line with the British evangelical constituency as a whole, disclaimed obscurant fundamentalism. LBC's early vision, as expressed in the 1940s by Montague Goodman, who died in October 1958, was for 'a sane, informed understanding of the Scriptures'.[78] Aspects of the neo-Puritan advance in the 1950s presented new challenges for the college, but Kevan showed independence of mind and a determination to place the college firmly in the evangelical centre-ground. Kevan was always eager to add promising people to the LBC faculty. In 1959 he brought Ralph Martin onto the staff and a year later he recommended Leslie Allen to the board. Both would bring prestige to LBC's faculty. Their theological and biblical contributions were to be stimulating but also controversial. More radical evangelical thinking about gospel, church and society was to become increasingly evident in the 1960s. Having experienced rapid advance as a result of the post-war evangelical renaissance of the 1950s, LBC would play a major part in shaping the theological perspectives of a new generation of evangelical leaders.

---

[78] *Annual Report of the London Bible College, 1957–58*, 1.

6

'The Line Between Conservative and Liberal Views' 1960–65

The front page of *The Observer* of 17 March 1963 carried the headline 'Our Image of God Must Go'. John Robinson, bishop of Woolwich and the author of the article, summarized in it ideas to be found in his book *Honest to God*, which was about to be published. Reflecting on *Honest to God*, David Edwards, then editor of the SCM Press and later dean of King's College, Cambridge, suggested that no new book of serious theology had ever sold so quickly, with 350,000 copies in print within less than a year. Robinson had actually popularized the thinking of theologians such as Paul Tillich, Dietrich Bonhoeffer and Rudolf Bultmann, to whom he expressed his indebtedness.[1] No doubt the *Observer* article assisted sales, but the reception given to Robinson's writings indicated that thinking about faith was in flux. This was consistent with the rapidly changing socio-cultural patterns of the 1960s. For LBC, too, this was a period of change. In 1960 Ernest Kevan, the college's academic architect, suffered a severe coronary attack. He recovered, but was strongly advised by his consultant to reduce his workload. Kevan maintained, however, that it was better to burn out than rust out.[2] Following a further illness, Kevan died in August 1965. LBC also had to

---

[1] J.A.T. Robinson, *Honest to God*, 21–6; J.A.T. Robinson and D.L. Edwards, *The Honest to God Debate*, 7.
[2] I am indebted to Owen Thomas for this information.

address theological challenges. In 1964 the board considered questions raised as a result of reviews by Ralph Martin in *The Christian*. Martin had encouraged the reading of Bonhoeffer, one of John Robinson's mentors. Martin was writing extended book reviews and Kevan considered that Martin's open-minded approach had 'led to his reviews tending to confuse the line between conservative and liberal views'.[3] It was a line that was to prove difficult to draw.

A Theology of Grace

Those involved in the push for a distinctively Reformed evangelicalism were convinced that they knew where doctrinal boundary lines should be drawn. The stance of LBC on this front was to come under intense scrutiny. Articles on Reformed themes, some written by former LBC students, appeared in *The Christian* in 1964. Several students from this period would go on to achieve prominence within the Reformed constituency in Britain. While Colin Buchanan has suggested that in 1960 the Puritan 'revival' peaked,[4] the influence of Lloyd-Jones was in fact continuing to grow. For Brian Edwards, who studied at LBC from 1959 to 1963, Lloyd-Jones was an exemplar, 'a preacher who took his authority exclusively from the Bible' and who had also experienced revival.[5] Edwards became known both for his leadership within the FIEC and for his writing on revival and associated subjects. Another student deeply influenced by Lloyd-Jones was Peter Lewis, who entered LBC in 1963. During his LBC years Peter Lewis was a noted dissenter from certain evangelical taboos – he was, for example, a pipe-smoker. Following his LBC training Lewis began a significant ministry in Nottingham. Reflecting on the qualities that characterized his mentor's ministry, Lewis, who became one of Lloyd-Jones' close friends, spoke of how 'the

---

[3] Minutes of a meeting of governors, 29 July 1964.

[4] C. Buchanan, 'Anglican Evangelicalism: The State of the "Party" '.

[5] B. Edwards, *Revival: A People Saturated with God*, 66.

power of his evangelistic preaching . . . still thrills, impels and challenges me'.[6] Others with Reformed convictions, such as John Legg and Stuart Olyott, were also LBC students in this era. Olyott combined writing with pastoral ministry in Britain and Switzerland.

What was the line being taken over Reformed thinking within LBC as a whole in this period? Kevan's approach was unambiguous. In 1963 he made criticisms of Emil Brunner's exposition of the moral law in *The Divine Imperative* that were both stringent and scholarly. Brunner, argued Kevan, expelled the law from its high place in the mind of God.[7] A year later Carl Henry, who knew Kevan, published *Frontiers in Modern Theology* (drawing together articles from *Christianity Today*) in which he welcomed the growing interest in Puritan writings in England and the associated increase in substantial conservative writing by evangelicals.[8] Dermot McDonald, too, who from 1958 was LBC's vice-principal, gave impetus to theological endeavour within the broader Reformed tradition. Writing in 1964 on the doctrine of providence, McDonald criticized what he called the 'Deistic-Arminian' view for seeking to restrict divine sovereignty. He also offered a critique of John Robinson, asserting that the chief weakness of *Honest to God* was its reduction of theology to an analysis of experience. This removed the true ground of faith, which was a God who speaks and 'sustains and governs'. McDonald's own books introduced students to wider Reformed thinking – for example, to P.T. Forsyth and James Denney. For McDonald, Forsyth's understanding of God's action in Christ was normative.[9]

A similar debate about spiritual experience and God's activity in the world was continuing over Keswick teaching. Ralph Martin considered that J.I. Packer's severe strictures of Keswick

---

[6] P. Lewis, 'The Doctor as a Preacher', 81.
[7] E.F. Kevan, 'Legalism: An Essay on the Views of Dr Emil Brunner', 51.
[8] C.F.H. Henry, *Frontiers in Modern Theology*, 126.
[9] H.D. McDonald, 'The Changing Emphasis in the Doctrine of Providence'.

devotion, first delivered in 1955, had not been answered. In 1964 Martin indicated his own sympathies with a more Reformed spirituality when reviewing John Pollock's recently published book, *The Keswick Story*. After commending Pollock's account, he proceeded to assess the convention. Keswick's 'outstanding fault', according to Martin, was 'a tendency to be pietistic, atomistic and intra-personal, with the impression given that my individual relationship to God in Christ and my immediate neighbour is the be-all and end-all of biblical Christianity'. There could not, in Martin's view, be a true doctrine of holiness apart from a consideration of its wider social ramifications. A further criticism made by Martin of Keswick was that although he heard serious exegesis at the convention there seemed to be no systematic theology. Finally, Martin asked that the place of silence be given more prominence. 'Incessant hymn-singing, sometimes only to avoid the "awkward" silences before services, smacks too much of an Evangelical jamboree', he commented, 'instead of a resolute determination to seek quietly the face of the holy God and to attend to His awesome Word.' Martin advocated continuing reformation.[10]

The new emphases that were affecting the evangelicalism of the period included not only a stronger doctrine of God's providential rule and a concern for social ethics but also what Oliver Barclay calls 'the vision of vocation as including every useful occupation'.[11] This idea affected LBC. Of the 32 student applicants who were interviewed in early 1962, 17 indicated that they wanted to become schoolteachers. Ten of these were women and seven were men. Most would become RE specialists. Ron Aldrich, who entered LBC in 1964, later became an RE consultant. There were some worries that this high percentage of students training to be teachers might begin to undermine LBC's position as a trainer of ministers and missionaries. Of the student intake in the early 1960s – 80 to 90 per year – only about 10 per cent initially envisaged home ministry. The college secretary was

---

[10] *Chr* (31 July 1964), 14.

[11] Barclay, *Evangelicalism*, 89.

told 'to advertise the fact that the college trained men for the Home Ministry'.[12] An increasing number of younger Christians would embrace the idea that the ordained ministry was not a superior vocation. In 1964 the Inter-Varsity Press published *The Christian in Industrial Society*, by Fred Catherwood, who became the Labour government's Chief Industrial Adviser and then Director General of the National Economic Development Council. Catherwood had resisted early pressures to enter ordained ministry.[13] His concern for evangelical involvement in socio-political affairs constituted a powerful challenge to much existing evangelical thinking.

The growth of bodies such as the IVF and LBC contributed to this interest in a range of vocations. In 1938 the IVF had 37 affiliated CUs, a figure which grew to 554 over the next four decades. This was a measure of the growing strength of evangelicalism within a rapidly expanding higher education sector. Many of those graduating in this period would later fill influential positions in a range of professions. There were also considerable numbers of evangelical graduates entering ordained ministry. By 1968, the overall number of Anglican ordinands had fallen to a figure 20 per cent below the number of residential places available in Anglican colleges. By contrast, the evangelical Anglican colleges were full.[14] LBC was to benefit from these wider trends. Many evangelical school leavers wanting a degree to enter a profession – especially education – chose LBC for that purpose, whereas others – usually those who had experience after leaving school – used the college for ministerial training. In 1964, when 86 students entered the college, 24 had just taken their 'A' levels. The average age of the new students was 24.7 years. The proportions of men and women were equal, but for almost all the women ordained ministry was not at that time a realistic option.

---

[12] Minutes of a meeting of governors, 16 March 1962.

[13] H.F.R. Catherwood, *At the Cutting Edge*, chs. 5–7; 'An Interview', 107.

[14] Welsby, *History*, 144; K. Hylson-Smith, *The Churches in England from Elizabeth I to Elizabeth II*, III: *1833–1998*, 238.

Although LBC continued to stress ministerial education, the college became an attractive route into employment in teaching and other fields.

The most obvious effect of Reformed theology on LBC students in the 1960s, however, was a keen interest in doctrinal issues related to the sovereignty of God. Student discussion of Banner of Truth volumes tended to polarize opinion over Arminianism and Calvinism. J.I. Packer's *Evangelism and the Sovereignty of God*, published in 1961 by the IVF, became standard reading. The book was based on material Packer had delivered to the London Inter-Faculty Christian Union in 1959, at a time when the students were divided over whether to give appeals at evangelistic meetings. Packer spoke about the 'antinomy' (apparent contradiction) between God's sovereignty and human responsibility. Many Calvinists of that period expressed their beliefs in terms of the 'five points of Calvinism' – total depravity, unconditional election, limited atonement, irresistible grace and the perseverance of the saints. In his writings Packer affirmed John Owen and other Puritans who held these tenets.[15] Although within LBC it was generally Kevan who handled such matters, in 1965 Owen Thomas wrote in *Vox Evangelica* on the subject of irresistible grace. Thomas identified with John Calvin, encouraging those engaged in 'the cure of souls' to recognize that 'true heartfelt seeking after God is evidence of the incipient working of effectual grace'.[16] It was this theology of grace that many evangelicals were affirming.

Evangelical Scholarship

At the same time, evangelical leaders were aware that biblical scholarship required much more attention. In 1961 Guthrie was

---

[15] J.I. Packer, *Evangelism and the Sovereignty of God*, 103; cf. J.I. Packer's introductory essay in J. Owen, *The Death of Death in the Death of Christ* (London: Banner of Truth, 1959), 1–25.

[16] O. Thomas, 'Irresistible Grace', 64.

awarded a London University doctorate for his thesis on 'Early Christian Pseudepigraphy and its Antecedents'.[17] It was also decided at this point that an LBC theological journal should be launched. In the same year, the Minister of Education recognized LBC as an establishment of further education following an inspection by G.R. Driver, professor of Semitic philology at Oxford. A somewhat nervous Leslie Allen, then in his first year of teaching, was delighted to be among those who received Driver's approval.[18] Ralph Martin was asked to investigate possible articles for an LBC journal, and in February 1962 he reported that there was sufficient material to publish a single volume. The mailing list of the IVF would, it was hoped, be available for publicity purposes. Epworth Press, the Methodist publishing house, brought out the volume.[19] Undoubtedly the first issue of *Vox Evangelica*, as the volume was entitled, was a showcase for LBC. It contained scholarly contributions in the fields of Old Testament, New Testament and church history. Leslie Allen wrote on Isaiah 53, Ralph Martin on the composition of 1 Peter in recent biblical studies, Donald Guthrie on canonical pseudepigrapha in New Testament criticism (later published by SPCK) and Harold Rowdon on the Brethren teacher, B.W. Newton.[20]

The response to the first *Vox Evangelica* from some in the theological world was encouraging. LBC board members were informed in June 1962 that congratulatory messages had been received from, among others, A.M. Hunter, professor of New Testament at Aberdeen, and G.R. Driver.[21] A review of *Vox Evangelica* in *Theology*, in May 1963, said that the articles gave a valuable insight into the way theology was now being taught in conservative evangelical circles. The reviewer was encouraged

---

[17] Minutes of faculty meeting, 15 May 1961.
[18] Leslie Allen to the author, 4 Feb. 1999.
[19] Minutes of faculty meeting, 14 Feb. 1962.
[20] R.P. Martin (ed.), *Vox Evangelica: Biblical and Historical Essays by Members of the Faculty of the London Bible College* (London: Epworth Press, 1962).
[21] Minutes of a meeting of governors, 15 June 1962.

that critical scholarship was receiving proper treatment.
Attention was drawn particularly to the work of Martin and
Guthrie. 'The whole collection', noted the review, 'shows that the
students at the College are being encouraged to read widely and
think deeply. It is possible for them to come to different
conclusions from their teachers.'[22] At the time, LBC was the only
college in the UK publishing its own theological journal. Gilbert
Kirby proposed that steps should be taken to have Kevan,
McDonald and Guthrie acknowledged as 'recognized teachers' of
the University of London, and this was agreed. It was also agreed
that there would be a further issue of *Vox Evangelica*, especially
to publish scholarly work by the faculty, and that a public lecture
series should be inaugurated.

In the 1963 issue of *Vox Evangelica* Ralph Martin pursued his
interest in aspects of worship in the New Testament and Guthrie
wrote on recent literature on Acts. These were articles that
showed a high degree of acquaintance with current scholarship.
But they also made connections with contemporary spiritual
experience. 'It is to be hoped', Guthrie wrote, 'that in the next
decade scholarly work on the Acts will bring into yet clearer focus
the dynamic part that the book can play in promoting the spiritual
development of the modern Church.'[23] By this stage Guthrie had
written two of the three parts of what would become his comprehensive *New Testament Introduction*. Geoffrey Grogan, then at
the BTI, Glasgow, was talking to the popular commentator,
William Barclay, in 1960, soon after the first volume of Guthrie's
Introduction was published, and Barclay said that Guthrie's work
was the best of its kind. Admittedly there was little competition –
liberal or conservative. Barclay made a point of meeting
Guthrie.[24] Within LBC, one of Guthrie's concerns was to promote
postgraduate study. In 1962 four students were working for
higher degrees.[25] By January 1965 the department of advanced

[22] J.C. O'Neill, in *Th* 66 515 (1963), 206–7.
[23] D. Guthrie, 'Recent Literature on the Acts of the Apostles', 46–7.
[24] Geoffrey Grogan to the author, 7 May 1998.
[25] H.H. Rowdon, 'Donald Guthrie: An Appreciation', x.

studies had grown to almost twenty students pursuing research at MTh or PhD level. In 1964 George Carey, then curate at St Mary's, Islington (who moved to academic and episcopal posts, becoming Archbishop of Canterbury in 1990), was the first to obtain an MTh. He went on to study for a PhD, supervised by Dermot McDonald.

There was increasing commitment on both sides of the Atlantic in the early 1960s to the promotion of evangelical scholarship. Carl Henry, who had a significant voice through *Christianity Today*, said in 1964: 'If evangelical Christianity is again to acquire mainstream theological power, it cannot perpetuate itself by remaining in ideological isolation from dominant trends of thought.' Karl Barth and Emil Brunner were the main theological supply for evangelical students, and Henry believed the paucity of conservative theological literature had to be remedied.[26] One way in which this was addressed transatlantically was in the publication of *Revelation and the Bible*, edited by Henry. This volume grew out of conversations on Protestant theology in which Ernest Kevan took part. There were twenty-four contributors to the volume, including eight authors from Britain. These included Packer, Alan Stibbs, F.F. Bruce, Geoffrey Bromiley, then at Fuller Theological Seminary, R.A. Finlayson from Edinburgh, W.J. Martin, a senior lecturer at the University of Liverpool, and Donald Wiseman of the Department of Western Asiatic Manuscripts at the British Museum.[27] Kevan, in 'The Principles of Interpretation', argued for interpreting the Bible in its grammatical and historical sense. Augustine and Calvin were his guides. The commitment of Kevan and others to the grammatical and literal meaning of Scripture was to influence much evangelical scholarship.[28]

To many people in the period 1963–65, however, it did not seem that evangelicals were at the forefront of theological developments. *The Christian Mind* (1963) by Harry Blamires, a friend

---

[26] Henry, *Frontiers*, 111–12.

[27] Henry, *Revelation*, 7.

[28] E.F. Kevan, 'The Principles of Interpretation', 295–6.

of C.S. Lewis, was a persuasive defence of orthodoxy, commended by Eric Mascall in the *Church Times* as the most important non-technical religious book to appear in a decade. It was welcomed by a number of former LBC students, but it was written from an Anglo-Catholic rather than an evangelical stand-point. Towards the other end of the theological spectrum, John Robinson's *Honest to God* was bought by nearly a million people in the three years from 1963. J.I. Packer, in *Keep Yourselves from Idols*, while accepting that Robinson had a genuinely pastoral intent, suggested that Robinson had created a false God.[29] *Honest to God* was discussed at length in the LBC common room and in college lectures. Malcolm Goodspeed, a student at that time, appreciated the way in which Dermot McDonald, when discussing issues raised by Robinson, refused to spoon-feed students. It was vital, in McDonald's view, to engage at depth with contemporary philosophy.[30] A more questioning society, which was clearly emerging in the 1960s, was not prepared to swallow pre-packaged religious answers. Ralph Martin endorsed more open approaches. In July 1963, Martin, to acclaim within LBC, received his doctorate.[31] A few months later, however, Martin's reviews in *The Christian* would lead LBC into deepening controversy.

New Theological Tensions

Ralph Martin's articles grew out of his friendship with Tom Allan, field organizer of the 'Tell Scotland' movement. From 1 September 1963 Allan was editorial director of *The Christian*, and he asked Martin to write a regular feature, 'In the Study'. This column, which Martin began in October 1963, was intended especially to guide ministers in building a library. As such, it fitted

---

[29] J.I. Packer, *Keep Yourselves from Idols*, (London: Church Book Room Press, 1963) 14.
[30] M.N. Goodspeed to the author, 2 Dec. 1998.
[31] *Chr* (26 July 1963), 10.

LBC's aim to educate evangelicalism. A number of the volumes Martin reviewed, however, were not standard evangelical fare, and in the course of the reviews Martin also opened up areas of theological debate. On 20 December 1963 he raised the question of the human nature of Christ. 'The orthodox answer', wrote Martin, 'is that it was an unfallen nature. But Barth (most popularly in his sermons collected under the title *Christma*s [Oliver Boyd, 1959]) . . . called attention to the biblical and theological justification for holding that He took our sin-blighted nature.' Martin emphasized that this did not imperil the sinlessness of Jesus but meant that Christ's moral conflict was real.[32] In February 1964 Martin returned again to what he called the 'enigmatic genius' of Karl Barth. Martin encouraged students at LBC to engage with Barth's understanding of the threefold form of the Word of God: incarnate in Christ, witnessed in Scripture and proclaimed in preaching.

Sympathetic treatment of Barth was controversial, given the opposition to Barth from conservatives in Britain and America (for example Cornelius van Til of Westminster Theological Seminary in his book *The New Modernism*), and for LBC more acute problems were to come. In June 1964 Martin wrote on Dietrich Bonhoeffer, who had become much more widely known through John Robinson's appreciative comments in *Honest to God*. Martin's view was that Bonhoeffer's *Letters and Papers from Prison* (published by Fontana, 1959), written when he was in Tegel prison before he was put to death by the Nazis, was a classic prison document. What, asked Martin, was Bonhoeffer advocating when he spoke about 'religion-less Christianity'? For Martin, the key to Bonhoeffer's thinking was the idea that Christians were not distinguished by religious observance but by sharing in God's suffering in the world. This was consistent with Bonhoeffer's commitment to the Confessing Church in Germany. The idea of Christian involvement 'interpenetrating the whole life of man in pervasive fashion' was appealing to Martin, and he suggested that Bonhoeffer was essential reading for those trying

---

[32] *Chr* (20 Dec. 1963), 12.

to understand modern thought. Martin also recommended critiques of Bonhoeffer, since he accepted that in places Bonhoeffer might be questionable. Martin suggested that time would tell whether Bonhoeffer was a prophet, but there was no question in Martin's mind that he was a Christian martyr.[33]

Indignant responses soon appeared in the correspondence columns of *The Christian*. In July 1964, Michael Boland, who wrote for *The Banner of Truth*, queried whether Bonhoeffer taught the true gospel. Boland asserted that such was the evangelical preoccupation with scholarship that truth no longer seemed of much importance. In answer to the question about Bonhoeffer as a prophet, Boland was quite clear that Bonhoeffer was a 'false prophet'. Nor was Bonhoeffer a martyr. Although his heroism was unquestionable, he did not, Boland contended, give his life for biblical Christianity.[34] At the same time, Ernest Kevan was receiving letters of complaint about Martin's articles. It was alleged that Martin had failed to stress conservative evangelical doctrine, and at a board meeting on 29 July 1964 Philip Henman expressed his concern. Kevan, when asked to comment, stated that 'Dr Martin's reviews had attracted attention in that they were over generous to the liberal position.' Kevan made it plain that Ralph Martin's 'evangelical beliefs coincided exactly with his fellow members of the Faculty', but Kevan considered that Martin, as a young scholar, tended 'to confuse the line between conservative and liberal views'. The governors agreed that Martin should be told that as a member of the faculty his writings should not jeopardize the college's position.[35]

Further developments followed over the next three months. In August 1964 Boland returned to the attack. 'There is very good reason to believe', he stated in a letter to *The Christian*, 'that the movement represented by Karl Barth and Bonhoeffer . . . is another gospel, another religion from that in which Evangelicals believe.'[36]

---

[33] *Chr* (26 June 1964), 13.
[34] *Chr* (3 July 1964), 13.
[35] Minutes of a meeting of governors, 29 July 1964.
[36] *Chr* (14 Aug. 1964), 16.

Erroll Hulse added a more explicitly historical perspective: 'Solemn warnings in regard to the dangers of imbibing doubt through the study of modernist literature', he commented in a letter in September, 'are so uncommon that we may have to go back to Spurgeon to find them.'[37] This was a clear challenge to LBC.

Martin's last article for *The Christian* was certainly not one which ducked difficult issues or ignored dangers. He acknowledged that Barth was open to serious criticisms, and he welcomed evaluation, but whereas Martin did not hesitate to use the word 'baneful' when referring to Rudolf Bultmann's ideas, he saw Barth as rightly stressing the way the Word of God searches and judges. Because of this emphasis, Barth's commentary on Romans, as Martin put it, 'threw a bomb into the playground of the theologians' when it appeared in 1918. Quoting the Scottish theologian James Denney, that theologians should be evangelists and evangelists theologians, Ralph Martin mused: 'When scholars have forgotten that the New Testament was not written for them primarily nor to be inspected critically, but for the ongoing life and witness of the Church, they have failed and prostituted their gifts.'[38] This was a comment that reflected the ethos LBC had sought to foster.

It was reported on 16 October 1964, at a meeting of the LBC governors, that Henman and Kevan had seen Martin. As a result, Martin had agreed that he would not submit further articles to the press and that he would leave LBC on 30 September 1965, or earlier if he found another appointment. During the academic year 1964–65 he was on a previously planned sabbatical, as visiting lecturer at Bethel Seminary, St Paul, Minnesota. Kevan indicated to Martin privately that there could be a continuing place for him on the staff at LBC – but in teaching New Testament, not doctrine. Other scholars who were aware of the situation, such as George Beasley-Murray and F.F. Bruce, were supportive of Martin. Within the board, Derek Warren felt that the governors were yielding to pressure in restricting Martin and

---

[37] *Chr* (11 Sept. 1964), 6.
[38] *Chr* (28 Aug. 1964), 15.

that LBC would lose scholars if others were treated similarly. The board, however, did not agree.[39] In the event, it was reported in July 1965 that Martin had accepted an appointment at Manchester University as assistant lecturer in New Testament studies. Two years later, his PhD was published under the title *Carmen Christi* and it became a standard work on the second chapter of Philippians. Harold Rowdon has remarked that at LBC Martin 'combined academic brilliance with spiritual and pastoral concern and insight'.[40] These were qualities that were to continue to characterize his career.

Gerald Parsons comments that the 'kaleidoscope of radicalism, self-criticism and innovation within the life of the principal Protestant churches of Britain in the 1960s was exciting, vibrant and exhilarating . . . Inevitably, however, it also produced much controversy, disquiet and resistance.'[41] Although he is referring to broader Protestant theology, his analysis can be applied to evangelicals as well. Ralph Martin was not alone in his desire to provoke evangelicals to think about theological questions. In the USA Carl Henry was intent on bringing an intellectual challenge. In the articles that appeared in *Frontiers of Modern Theology*, Henry drew attention to contemporary evangelical thought, including the work of the rising American apologist, Francis Schaeffer. There was a growing awareness of the importance of providing answers to pressing questions.[42] Some evangelicals, however, believed that the answers were to be found primarily in past tradition. Writing in *The Christian* in October 1964, Humphrey Mildred, a former LBC student, asked if it was 'so outrageous to suggest that the great duty of modernists is not to write learned and scholarly books which will deceive the flock of God but to repent and believe the Gospel'.[43] LBC had, to some degree, contributed to evangelical tensions.

---

[39] Minutes of a meeting of governors, 16 Oct. 1964.

[40] Rowdon, *London Bible College*, 38.

[41] Parsons, 'Contrasts', 63.

[42] Henry, *Frontiers*, 105–6.

[43] *Chr* (2 Oct. 1964), 8.

Evangelicals and Ecumenism

Ecumenism was another area in which evangelicals of the 1960s found themselves divided. A deepening desire for visible unity among denominations worldwide had led to the founding of the WCC in 1948, and assemblies of the WCC were held at Evanston in 1954 and New Delhi in 1961. At that point, conservative evangelicals were seen as being opposed to the ecumenical movement. John Lawrence, in *The Hard Facts of Unity* (1961), identified two reasons for this stance. The first was the evangelical view that 'Christian unity is invisible'. Lawrence noted that evangelicals pointed to Keswick as 'an unsurpassed demonstration of Christian unity'. The second problem for evangelicals was unsound theology. 'They think', Lawrence observed, 'that we are tinged with modernism and at the same time they point to the fact that we seek relations with Roman Catholics.'[44] In his report on New Delhi, Kenneth Slack, general secretary of the British Council of Churches (BCC), saw that assembly as formulating a conception of unity which 'departs wholly from any idea that Christian unity is a wholly "spiritual" idea'.[45] On the question of doctrine, New Delhi's 'Report on Unity' did speak of the place of the creed, the gospel, the sacraments and ministry, although one delegate commented that the report 'did not sufficiently explain the substance of these terms'.[46]

One evangelical leader who attended the New Delhi assembly was A.T. Houghton, secretary of the Bible Churchmen's Missionary Society and chairman of the Keswick council. Houghton was not an uncritical observer of the WCC, but he believed that there was a place for ecumenism. 'The call of the

---

[44] J. Lawrence, *The Hard Facts of Unity: A Layman Looks at the Ecumenical Movement* (Naperville, IL: SCM Book Club, 1961), 65.

[45] K. Slack, *Despatch from New Delhi: The Story of the World Council of Churches, Third Assembly, New Delhi, 18 Nov.–5 Dec. 1961* (London: SCM Press, 1962), 79.

[46] W.A. Visser't Hooft, *The New Delhi Report* (New York: Association Press, 1962), 134.

Churches overseas in face of the strengthening of non-Christian and materialistic forces', he argued in 1962, 'is for a coming together of the Churches, and the getting rid of unnecessary denominational differences which have no foundation in Scripture.'[47] This missiological and international perspective, delivered by a respected evangelical statesman, carried weight. LBC's own international network was growing in this period as former students took up increasingly strategic positions. Richard Anderson, for example, would become international general secretary of the AIM. Klaus Fiedler's analysis of faith missions in Africa covers AIM's outreach in Turkana, Kenya, and the pioneering medical work of Richard Anderson in the 1960s.[48] Don Ford and Maurice Wheatley, both of whom left LBC in 1960, would become general secretaries of EUSA and AIM respectively. Interdenominational missions did not always share Houghton's enthusiasm for structural unity but, as Fiedler shows, missions such as AIM were well aware of mission/denominational complexities overseas.

For evangelical Anglicans, the views expressed by Houghton about the ecumenical movement contributed to new thinking about their place within a body that was theologically inclusive. Anglican students at LBC in the early 1960s were to address this in differing ways. Gordon Kuhrt, who came to LBC in 1960 as a Strict Baptist – a member of Zion, New Cross, where Kevan had been pastor – embraced Anglicanism while at college. After parish and other ministries Kuhrt became archdeacon of Lewisham and then chief secretary of the ministry division of the Church of England. He designated his ecclesiological position as 'principled comprehensiveness', or catholicity – the view that 'in each locality, in principle, all Christians constitute the church in that place'. Kuhrt contrasted this with separatism.[49] Tony Higton, who with his wife Patricia left LBC in 1965, had a long ministry as rector of Hawkswell Parish Church, Essex, and also founded

---

[47] A.T. Houghton, *What of New Delhi?* (London: BCMS, 1962), 59.

[48] K. Fiedler, *The Story of Faith Missions*, 370–2.

[49] G.W. Kuhrt, 'Principled Comprehensiveness', 129.

'Action for Biblical Witness to Our Nation'. One issue to which he would give considerable attention was homosexual practice in the Church of England.[50] Both Kuhrt and Higton exemplified a growing willingness among evangelicals to become involved in wider ecclesiastical affairs. In 1964, at Nottingham, 550 delegates from 15 denominations passed a resolution inviting BCC member churches to work for unity in 1980, and for the first time evangelicals were represented in some strength at such a conference.[51]

Baptists were also caught up in these issues. Ernest Payne, who from 1951 to 1967 was general secretary of the BU, became a leading ecumenical figure. The WCC, Payne pointed out in *The Christian*, was 'a fellowship of Churches which confess the Lord Jesus Christ as God and Saviour according to the Scriptures', and he asked more evangelicals to become involved in the ecumenical movement.[52] Payne was committed to the Free Churches as 'part of the one holy, catholic, apostolic Church', and Ernest Kevan commended Payne's ecclesiology.[53] At Kevan's invitation, Payne was guest preacher at one of LBC's weekly devotional services, which provoked mixed student reaction. There was tension between the ecumenical stance of Baptist leaders such as Payne and the reservations about ecumenism that characterized many local Baptist churches. More LBC students were entering Baptist Union ministry through the Union's official interviewing processes, but there was a perception that the BU was making it difficult for LBC students who came to recognition committees. Kevan reported to LBC's governors in 1963 on steps being taken to ease the path for Baptist students, which no doubt included conversations with Payne. It was agreed that LBC should accept only students of the highest calibre to train for ministry.[54]

---

[50] Tony Higton (ed.), *Sexuality and the Church*.

[51] *Chr* (25 Sept. 1964), 1.

[52] *Chr* (4 Dec. 1964), 4.

[53] West, *To be a Pilgrim*, 122–30; E.A. Payne, *The Fellowship of Believers* (London: Kingsgate Press, 1944); *LF* (6 Aug. 1952), 548.

[54] Minutes of a meeting of governors, 31 May 1963.

Evangelicals who opposed ecumenism often did so because, as they saw it, the ultimate goal of the ecumenical movement was unity with the Roman Catholic Church and because the WCC did not oppose liberal theology. Fear of the growing influence of Catholicism was considerable. *Crusade* reported in 1960 that three former LBC students associated with the Perivale Mission Church, Middlesex, had set up an 'Evangelical Enquiry Bureau'. This was a response to a 'Catholic Enquiry Centre', which had achieved a high profile and had received over one hundred thousand enquiries, many of the enquirers serious about Catholicism. An EA enquiry bureau had attracted mainly those wishing financial or social help.[55] In October 1962, LBC faculty members expressed concern that the committee of the London Theological Colleges' Association was to receive a proposal that a meeting on unity be addressed by a Catholic. It was agreed that the LBC student representative should make clear that LBC could not participate in such a meeting.[56] Six days later, Vatican II opened under the leadership of Pope John XXIII, but many Protestants were unimpressed by the pope's talk of reunion. The Banner of Truth published the widely read *Unity in the Dark*, by the Irish Presbyterian Donald Gillies, who argued that the 'soft winds of false doctrine are lulling us to sleep and carrying us slowly but surely in a Romeward direction'.[57]

Liberal theology was also a major issue. In 1963 the Billy Graham Evangelistic Association asked Martyn Lloyd-Jones to chair the first World Congress on Evangelism, which was held in Berlin in 1966. Lloyd-Jones said he would accept if Graham would no longer have liberals and Catholics on his platform, and would drop what was termed 'the invitation system'. It could not have been a surprise to Lloyd-Jones that these conditions were not acceptable.[58] Yet there were signs that liberal theology was waning. Michael Ramsey, Archbishop of Canterbury, was a

---

[55] *Crusade* (July 1960), 28.
[56] Minutes of faculty meeting, 5 Oct. 1962.
[57] D. Gillies, *Unity in the Dark*, 104.
[58] Murray, *Fight of Faith*, 440–3.

devoted Anglo-Catholic. In the 1960s and early 1970s seven Anglican theological colleges, representing on the whole the more liberal end of the Church of England, were closed. In the period from 1963 to 1965, when J.I. Packer was a member of the Anglican-Methodist Unity Commission discussing the report *Conversations between the Church of England and the Methodist Church*, Packer began to contemplate a comprehensive state church that excluded liberals but included Anglo-Catholics. Lloyd-Jones found this a disappointing development and in June 1965 stated his belief in the need for more independent evangelical churches.[59] Meanwhile Gilbert Kirby, who would take up the LBC principalship a year later, was planning a large National Assembly of Evangelicals (NAE) for September 1965. Kirby had enabled churches as well as individuals to affiliate to the EA. At a time of growing evangelical strength, however, a devastating division was looming.

Evangelical Unity

Gilbert Kirby was well aware of the way in which 'church unity' was, ironically, beginning to divide evangelicals. The older view, that ecclesiology was a 'secondary' matter, was being questioned – not least because of the neo-Puritan movement's emphasis on the church.[60] Nonetheless, the period up to the mid-1960s was one in which evangelical co-operation was widespread and the EA's slogan 'Spiritual Unity in Action', introduced by Kirby, seemed justified.[61] Keswick and the EA remained important symbols of evangelical unity. In 1964, A.T. Houghton pronounced confidently that the Alliance and Keswick had exhibited a genuinely ecumenical spirit.[62] John Stott made an enormous impact at Keswick in 1965 through his expository

---

[59] Murray, *Fight of Faith*, 498–506.
[60] C. Buchanan, *Is the Church of England Biblical?* 6–7.
[61] *Ev B* (Winter 1962/3).
[62] *Crusade* (Nov. 1964), 4.

addresses. But Keswick continued to be regarded with disfavour by Reformed separatists, not only for its view of sanctification but also because it did not take an anti-ecumenical stand. Lloyd-Jones, who continued his early opposition to Keswick, did not tend to use the name 'Keswick' when referring to the convention, speaking instead about 'a certain town in the Lake District'.[63] For many evangelicals, however, Keswick remained important. Harry Stringer, a former LBC tutor, urged that Methodist believers in entire sanctification should make common cause with Keswick teachers.[64] This concern for unity was typical of LBC's thinking.

It was no surprise, therefore, that LBC was heavily involved in an EA-sponsored united celebration of the Lord's Supper in London in January 1963. Within the college, communion was celebrated twice a term and students were asking for more frequent observance. The EA, under Kirby, affirmed that spiritual unity was expressed 'when Christians of varying traditions participate together in the Lord's Supper, unhindered by differences on secondary matters'. This affirmation was part of a broader 'Union and Communion' statement prepared by an EA theological study group and signed in 1962 by 40 evangelical leaders.[65] The preachers at the united communion service, held in the Royal Albert Hall and attended by more than three thousand, were Ernest Kevan and John Stott. Others who led the service were Houghton, Kirby, Skevington Wood, T.H. Bendor-Samuel and G.C.D. Howley, editor of *The Witness*. The report in *The Christian* by Morgan Derham, then editorial secretary of SU, suggested that the platform was 'a visible demonstration of unity in diversity, with the Anglicans in their robes, a Congregational minister in Geneva gown and bands, a Methodist in hood and gown, Baptists and an FIEC pastor in

---

[63] I am indebted to the late Morgan Derham, formerly editorial secretary of SU and then general secretary of the EA, for this information.
[64] *Chr* (13 March 1964), 17.
[65] *Crusade* (Dec. 1962), 18, 27.

suits and clerical collars, and a member of the Christian Brethren in suit, collar and tie'.[66]

In addition to the college's participation in such events there was a continuing commitment to communication between evangelical theological colleges. In 1961, a conference was held at LBC at which 60 students from 16 Bible colleges were present, representing seven European countries.[67] A new, more academic 'Bible College' identity was emerging. Leslie Allen came to LBC originally on a temporary basis, while waiting for a university appointment. While he was in the middle of his PhD work, however, he was approached about such an appointment and decided that he found teaching Bible college students committed to Christian work much more satisfying.[68] By the early 1960s, LBC's partnership with Oak Hill was proving difficult to sustain. It was noted that final-year students resident at Oak Hill were becoming increasingly absorbed in the affairs of Oak Hill, and it was agreed to continue this link for mature students only. The place of LBC within the arena of missionary training was also discussed again in this period, as it had been many times before. D.M. Miller of the AIM asked LBC's board, of which he had been a founder member, if the college was giving sufficient time to missionary training. The faculty felt that the college's basic biblical teaching was ideal for missionary preparation. John Savage, still teaching mission part-time at LBC, made the rather astounding statement that LBC 'was the only College undertaking serious missionary training'.[69]

The relationship of LBC with Spurgeon's College continued to be highly adversarial on the sports pitches. George Mitchell, a student from Glasgow who was at LBC from 1960 to 1964, found football an important means of self-expression. LBC was in the Theological Colleges' league, and Mitchell was part of a dominant LBC team. The 'needle' matches were against Spurgeon's, and

---

[66] *Chr* (18 Jan. 1963), 1.
[67] Minutes of a meeting of governors, 17 Feb. 1961.
[68] L. Allen to the author, 7 July 1999.
[69] Minutes of a meeting of governors, 13 July 1962.

Mitchell was intrigued to arrive at the Spurgeon's College gates and find five students dressed as undertakers, with top hats. A coffin with 'LBC – RIP' painted in black on both sides was marched round the pitch until kick-off. Prayer was offered by the referee before the match commenced, but then no quarter was given or received. As Mitchell put it, 'we kicked each other's lights in'.[70] Contacts between these two London colleges were, however, much more co-operative at a theological level. In 1965 Geoffrey King, president of the Spurgeon's College conference that year, took the second advent as his theme and asked Kevan to speak at the college's speech day on the subject of a millennialism ('the kingdom of Kevan' was the Spurgeon's students' title for the address) and Skevington Wood to speak on the premillennial position.[71]

LBC felt that evangelical unity could be furthered by the college's explicitly academic contribution. Donald Guthrie and Gilbert Kirby were keen to present evangelical scholarship as a distinctive and uniting factor. Guthrie believed that 'all Evangelicals' welcomed the interest in biblical theology Barth had helped to create, but Guthrie argued that if 'the Word of God can be distinguished from the documents that contain it' this left space for 'an outworn literary scepticism' which conservative scholars were challenging. Kirby saw agreement that the Bible 'as originally given' was 'the very Word of God' as the basis for unity.[72] At LBC's end-of-year celebration in 1963 (attended by nine hundred people), there were reports on colleges overseas and in Britain being staffed by former LBC students. During the previous year one thousand students had attended LBC's evening classes. Over two hundred LBC students – including distance learners – had entered for various University of London examinations, and the university's theology pass lists included many LBC students, a number having obtained honours BDs. An analysis of past students showed that 150 were in pastoral ministry, 180 were in mission overseas, 73 were schoolteachers and 23 were lecturers in

---

[70] Mitchell, *Glasgow*, 104–5.

[71] *Chr* (18 June 1965), 14. I am grateful to Ralph Martin for details.

[72] *Crusade* (Oct. 1958), 23; (Dec. 1962), 27.

theological colleges. For the first time, LBC had a female member of staff who had graduated from the college. Margaret Manton replaced Rosina Parker, and from 1964 Manton lectured in New Testament Greek.

The college also attempted to promote evangelical unity through transdenominational evangelistic involvement. Each year Owen Thomas and Tim Buckley organized evangelistic campaigns, including missions in mainland Europe. British campaigns were mainly in Baptist churches. LBC did, however, have links with Anglican missions. Colin Chapman, who entered LBC in 1960, later went on to serve with CMS in the Middle East, before returning to Britain to teach missiology. While at LBC, Chapman lived in John Stott's rectory in Weymouth Street and was one of about twenty Anglican LBC students who met with Stott to discuss Anglican issues.[73] But the college's constituency remained predominantly Free Church. At a London Baptist rally in Trafalgar Square in 1962, which attracted four thousand people, the prominent participants all had connections with LBC. The event was organized by Geoffrey King and featured Theo Bamber's preaching, with Tim Buckley singing a solo.[74] Although British church-going was in decline, evangelical confidence was high: in 1964 the EA estimated an evangelical constituency in the UK of a quarter of a million or more.[75] A year later, Gilbert Kirby urged evangelicals to give up 'internal strife over matters of secondary importance' and declare the 'faith once for all delivered to the saints'.[76] This was the conviction he would take to LBC as principal.

Pentecostalism – Old and New

In the early 1960s LBC was faced with decisions about whether 'matters of secondary importance' included Pentecostalism's

---

[73] Colin Chapman to the author, 11 Dec. 1998.
[74] *Chr* (29 June 1962), 1.
[75] *Chr* (9 Oct. 1964), 1.
[76] *Chr* (29 Jan. 1965), 12.

belief in a baptism in the Spirit accompanied by gifts of the Spirit
such as speaking in tongues. The 1920s and 1930s had been
decades in which the three main British Pentecostal groups – the
Assemblies of God, the Elim Pentecostal Church and the
Apostolic Church – had grown significantly.[77] J. Nelson Parr,
Assemblies of God (AOG) general secretary, complained, however, that despite their belief in such doctrines as the verbal
inspiration of the Bible, millions of Pentecostals worldwide had
been ejected from their churches.[78] By the 1960s the previous
hostility of evangelicals towards Pentecostals was waning and the
EA, under Kirby, appointed a Pentecostal minister to its staff. But
in 1961 David Petts, who had been a student at Brasenose
College, Oxford, expressed Pentecostal convictions at his LBC
intake interview and was not accepted. A year previously Petts
had described in the AOG's *Redemption Tidings* how, as a
Baptist, he had been 'baptised in the Spirit' following contact with
Pentecostals.[79] The LBC faculty felt that Petts would be more at
home in an environment where he would not be 'under the
restraint of adapting himself to the outlook of the majority of
students at L.B.C.'[80] Petts was later to become principal of
Mattersey Hall, the Assemblies of God college near Doncaster.

A few Pentecostally minded students were accepted by LBC,
but there were concerns that they should not press their views.
The issue of whether speaking in tongues was the evidence of the
fullness of the Spirit was particularly sensitive. George Jeffreys,
the founder of Elim, had suggested that tongues were normal but
not essential evidence.[81] One student from an Elim background,

[77] For AOG history see D. Allen, 'Signs and Wonders: The Origins,
Growth, Development and Significance of Assemblies of God in Great
Britain and Ireland, 1900–1980', University of London PhD thesis
(1990).

[78] *R T* (Dec. 1928), 6.

[79] *R T* (27 May 1960), 12–13.

[80] Notes of interviewing subcommittee, 1 Nov. 1961.

[81] See I.M. Randall, 'Old Time Power: Relationships between
Pentecostalism and Evangelical Spirituality in England', *Pneuma* 19.1
(1997), 53–80.

LBC Principals

Ernest Kevan
1946–65

Gilbert Kirby
1966–80

Michael Griffiths
1980–89

LBC Principals

Peter Cotterell, 1990–95

Derek Tidball, 1995–

Founders and Presidents

W.H. Aldis

Montague Goodman

P.S. Henman

Founders and Presidents

Sir John and
Lady Beatrice Laing

Martyn Lloyd-Jones

Sir Eric Richardson

Founders and Presidents

Sir Maurice Laing

Baroness Cox, President

Faculty with over 20 years service

H.D. McDonald
1948–75

Donald Guthrie
1949–83

Tim Buckley
1950–90

Faculty with over 20 years service

Owen J. Thomas
1951–76

Harold H. Rowdon
1954–91

J.C. Connell
1953–78

Faculty with over 20 years service

Tony Lane
1973–

Max Turner
1974–1986; 1991–

Mary Evans
1978–

Marylebone Road Site

St Andrews' Church Hall where the first evening classes were held in 1943

The original building, 19 Marylebone Road

Marylebone Road Site

Left & Middle
LBC in Marylebone Road

Bottom
Student accommodation in
Nottingham Place

Northwood Site

Through the decades – chapel

19 Marylebone Road

Refurbished chapel at Northwood

Through the decades – study

Through the decades – lectures

Original building in Marylebone

Graham McFarlane lecturing at Northwood campus

Third year students in 1995

Famous visitors to LBC

F.F. Bruce
giving the first
Laing Lecture

Billy Graham's
visit in 1970

Luis Palau preaching
in College Chapel

Famous visitors to LBC

John Stott

Clive Calver

The Archbishop of Canterbury, George Carey

Tony Sargent, was admitted to LBC in 1961. Sargent was a student contemporary of Richard Massey, who belonged to an unusual Congregational church in Stanton-under-Barden, Leicestershire, in which the elders had been baptized in the Spirit in the Pentecostal sense.[82] Both Sargent and Massey were to become Bible college principals – at the International Christian College, Glasgow, and the Birmingham Bible Institute, respectively. When interviewed at LBC, Massey was asked by Kevan if he believed speaking in tongues was the *sine qua non* of the filling of the Spirit. Since Massey was unsure at that time about the meaning of *sine qua non*, his reply was sufficiently undogmatic to satisfy Kevan.[83] Two other known Pentecostals at LBC in the early 1960s were Sonia Hill and Keith Southworth. Southworth edited *The Pentecostal* in 1964–65, a (short-lived) magazine which was the mouthpiece of the Students' Pentecostal Fellowship. This fellowship was active in some universities and was led by a friend of Southworth's, Richard Bolt.[84]

From the perspective of Keith Southworth, there was no serious engagement with Pentecostal theology in LBC lectures.[85] There were, however, points of contact. In 1962, when George Jeffreys died, Ralph Martin spoke of Jeffreys' significance as an evangelist. At one Quiet Day a student stood up and referred in prayer to a specific text which the speaker would be expounding. There was understandable interest in whether this 'prophecy' would be fulfilled: had the speaker chosen this text? She had. Leslie Allen was one of those present on whom this incident made a considerable impression.[86] During the early 1960s there were debates within LBC not only about prophecy but also about healing. An evangelical 'Divine Healing' movement had informal

---

[82] P. Hocken, *Streams of Renewal*, 231.

[83] Conversation with Richard Massey, 16 Dec. 1998. Richard Massey's PhD thesis was 'A Sound and Scriptural Union: An Examination of the Origins of the Assemblies of God of Great Britain and Ireland During the Years 1920–1925', University of Birmingham (1987), 286.

[84] Peter Hocken to the author, 24 Dec. 1998.

[85] Keith Southworth to the author, 26 Jan. 1999.

[86] L. Allen to the author, 7 July 1999.

connections with the Congregational Revival Fellowship, then newly formed and supported by Gilbert Kirby.[87] Richard Massey, through his early links, had been inspired by Donald Gee, Pentecostalism's leading writer and principal of the AOG's Bible school at Kenley, south of Croydon – a college Massey attended prior to studying at LBC.[88] Gee was known to some at LBC since he was a member of a theological study group chaired by John Stott and attended by Kirby.[89] In 1963 Massey wrote for the LBC student magazine, *Areopagus*, on spiritual gifts. The article, which Donald Guthrie found 'interesting', suggested that 'the baptism in the Holy Spirit' was a key to the Spirit's work in giving spiritual gifts.[90]

Even more significant for LBC and for British evangelicalism was what was initially called the 'new Pentecostalism', or the charismatic movement. The growth of this movement was intimately bound up from 1962 with Anglican figures such as Michael Harper, a curate at All Souls, Langham Place. In 1960 Dennis Bennett, an Episcopalian clergyman, announced to his parish in Van Nuys, California, that he had received the baptism of the Spirit and had spoken in tongues. Two years later Philip Hughes, a well-known Anglican scholar and editor of *The Churchman*, visited California and wrote in the September 1962 issue of *The Churchman* about 'indications of a new movement of the Holy Spirit within the Church'.[91] Hughes gave a (somewhat critical) report at a meeting at LBC attended by over thirty people, while Jean Stone, from Bennett's congregation, delivered a powerful address to an EA group which included Ernest Kevan and Ralph Martin. In May 1963, Harper, who by then had entered into a charismatic experience, invited Frank Macguire, another Episcopalian from California, to speak to about fifty leaders including Stott and Lloyd-Jones. Members of two groups

---

[87] Hocken, *Streams*, 23, 223.
[88] R. Massey, *Another Springtime* (Guildford: Eagle, 1992).
[89] W.K. Kay, *Inside Story*, 310.
[90] *Areopagus* (Summer 1963), 7–8.
[91] 'Editorial', *Churchman* (Sept. 1962), 131.

praying for revival, one the Anglican Prayer Fellowship for Revival (of which Colin Kerr was president), reprinted Hughes' assessment. Demand was such that thirty-nine thousand copies were printed.[92]

One of those who read Hughes' report was Douglas McBain, by then minister of Wishaw Baptist church in Scotland. In 1963 McBain began to speak in tongues. He drew together other former LBC students and also became a central figure within charismatic renewal in Scotland.[93] A few months after McBain's renewal experience, Cynthia Peppiatt, who had been a student at LBC, and her husband Martin, one of John Stott's curates, were drawn into 'deeper awe and wonder in the whole spiritual life' through the ministry of Larry Christenson, an American Lutheran charismatic.[94] Such developments bore similarities to Pentecostal developments in Britain in the first decade of the twentieth century, in which some Anglican had embraced Pentecostal thinking.[95] Martyn Lloyd-Jones, who had met with Michael Harper and with other Anglican charismatics, spoke about the subject in an address to the annual meeting of the Evangelical Library in December 1963. He viewed the interest in Pentecostal spirituality as evidence of a 'longing for something deeper'.[96] Tony Sargent has noted George Jeffreys' support for Lloyd-Jones' advocacy of the baptism of the Spirit.[97] In early 1964 Donald Gee, from his increasingly ecumenical perspective, exhorted his wary fellow-Pentecostals to accept the new

---

[92] Hocken, *Streams*, ch. 17.

[93] D. McBain, *Fire over the Waters: Renewal among Baptists and Others from the 1960s to the 1990s*, 37–8.

[94] Martin Peppiatt to the author, 13 Feb. 1999; Hocken, *Streams*, 78, 100, 113.

[95] M. Harper, *As at the Beginning: The Twentieth-Century Pentecostal Movement*, ch. 4; cf. M. Robinson, 'The Charismatic Anglican – Historical and Contemporary: A Comparison of the Life and Work of Alexander Boddy (1854–1930) and Michael C. Harper', University of Birmingham MLitt thesis (1976).

[96] Murray, *Fight of Faith*, 480–2.

[97] Sargent, *Sacred Anointing*, 29.

movement.[98] But John Stott, addressing a record number of Anglicans at the 1964 Islington Conference, rejected the idea of a post-conversion experience of baptism with the Spirit.[99]

Gilbert Kirby spoke in February 1964 about what he saw as two dangers posed by these developments within evangelicalism. One was the claim that speaking in tongues was essential evidence of Spirit-baptism. The other was the danger of dismissing tongues, since 'whenever and wherever God pours out His Spirit in abundance there are unusual manifestations'.[100] Michael Harper resigned from his curacy at All Souls, and in September 1964 the Fountain Trust was formed, with Harper as general secretary. From 1964 until it closed in 1980, the Fountain Trust would draw together charismatics within Anglicanism, the Free Churches and, more controversially, Roman Catholicism. *Renewal* magazine, as the trust's mouthpiece, was launched in 1965. By the middle of 1965 it was reckoned that over one hundred ministers in the mainline denominations were known to speak in tongues.[101] A number of those who were to be active within charismatic renewal were trained at LBC. They included Edmund Heddle, McBain and Tony Higton. Other LBC students, as will be seen later, were to leave existing denominations and take leadership positions within 'house churches', as they were initially termed. Higton and Kirby addressed this phenomenon in *The Challenge of the Housechurches*.[102] Charismatic developments would draw new boundary lines within evangelicalism.

Conclusion

The 1960s introduced British evangelicals to opportunities for constructive theological work as well as new ecclesiological

---

[98] D. Gee, 'The "Old" and "New" Pentecostal Movements', *Min* (Jan.–March 1964), 14–16.

[99] *Ch E News* (10 Jan. 1964), 1.

[100] *Crusade* (Feb. 1964), 33.

[101] Michael Bennett, to the editor, *Chr* (2 July 1965), 4.

[102] T. Higton and G.W. Kirby, *The Challenge of the Housechurches*.

complexities. LBC's evangelical stance made it attractive to people not only from Britain but also from many other countries. Its London location had many advantages. Students came from such places as Brazil, Rhodesia, Nigeria, Japan, India, Argentina, Switzerland and Hong Kong. The student body in this period reached almost two hundred and forty. A community of the size LBC had become inevitably incorporated differing outlooks, a situation Ernest Kevan believed to be healthy. However, during the latter part of Kevan's principalship, until his death in 1965, it was becoming increasingly evident that a more confident evangelical scholarship was opening up fresh questions and that the lines between conservative and liberal thinking were not always easy to draw. Evangelicals were also looking far more seriously than had sometimes been the case at the doctrine of the church. Kevan, and later Gilbert Kirby, were aware that calls for evangelical unity could be seen as implying that evangelicals should not be denominationally committed. Such calls could also be pursued in a way that was narrowly separatist and divisive. Pentecostalism and charismatic renewal, which began to affect LBC in the 1960s, were part of a search for a deeper spirituality – but would also exacerbate evangelical divisions. This tendency to division, as the next chapter shows, was to become painfully evident in the area of ecclesiological issues in the later 1960s.

7

'A Somewhat Dismal Picture'? 1965–70

Commenting in 1968 on British church life, Gilbert Kirby, who had taken up the LBC principalship in autumn 1966, suggested that it would be easy 'to paint a somewhat dismal picture'. He pointed to the decline in numbers of those offering for ordination in the major denominations, the active opposition of humanists to the teaching of Scripture in schools and the fact that many countries overseas were refusing entry to missionaries. Each of these developments had serious implications for LBC, since the college was training ministers, teachers and missionary personnel. Kirby, however, observed that despite these 'depressing facts' evangelicals wanted an adequately trained ministry, schools were appointing students trained at LBC and churches overseas were calling for those who could enter the field of theological education.[1] Kirby's tendency was almost always to emphasize signs of hope, although in private settings he could be less optimistic. At an LBC board meeting in May 1969 Kirby anticipated a reduction in the number of college students and attributed this to 'the general spiritual climate of the country and to tensions within evangelical circles'. The chairman of the meeting on that occasion, John Laird, an experienced secretary of SU, added that he had never known such disturbance within the evangelical world.[2] This chapter engages with some of the issues which marked the period 1965–70.

---

[1] G.W. Kirby, 'What of the Future?' 138–40.
[2] Minutes of a meeting of governors, 16 May 1969.

New Leadership

The search for a new principal for LBC following Ernest Kevan's death was not a straightforward one. In the early 1960s, when Kevan's health was a cause for concern, Philip Henman, as board chairman, had encouraged him to think about who might be a suitable successor. Kevan mentioned those he felt were *not* suitable, but he had been reluctant to name anyone whom he favoured. In the event, Henman believed that this gave greater freedom to those involved in the search for a new leader. On 21 January 1966 Henman furnished the governors and tutors with a lengthy account of the thinking leading to the proposal to appoint Gilbert Kirby. Clearly he felt that total transparency was vital, since Kirby, who did not see himself as an academic 'high flyer', was not viewed by everyone as an obvious candidate. Henman recalled the circumstances that had obtained 21 years before, when the college had appointed Ernest Kevan, 'a comparatively young man of forty who had never been to College, had little or no experience in training students, who apart from Strict Baptist circles was not widely known to the Christian public, and whose academic attainments at this stage were modest'.[3] It was Henman's hope that those at the heart of LBC's life would recognize that once again a discerning choice had been made. Through his work as general secretary of the EA, Kirby had undoubtedly become an outstanding evangelical figure.

Kirby had not, however, been the first choice of the governors. At an early stage in the search the board members had been unanimous about approaching John Stott. Henman, in a meeting with Stott, had explained LBC's principles and also details concerning the college. At that stage, in early November 1965, Stott was willing to consider the matter of the principalship.[4] But by the end of November Stott had responded that he did not feel it right to leave All Souls Church.[5] His comment was that 'if he had two lives

---

[3] Minutes of a meeting of governors, 21 Jan. 1966.
[4] Minutes of a meeting of governors, 4 Nov. 1965.
[5] Minutes of a meeting of governors, 26 Nov. 1965.

he would gladly give one to the college'. Accordingly, the governors conducted internal interviews and also asked that the opinions of the faculty members should be conveyed in writing. As a result of this process, which threw up differing views, those responsible for interviewing were left with eight names from outside the college to consider. Of these names, the one that stood out was Gilbert Kirby, who was already an LBC governor. It was at a prayer meeting of the board that a fellow-governor, Tony Dannatt, who acted as LBC's architect, had suggested Kirby.[6] In January 1966, when Henman brought Kirby's name to the board and the faculty, he asked everyone to register a vote. Seventeen out of the nineteen present voted for Kirby.[7] In due course Kirby, using his considerable skills as a team leader, was to win total support.

From an early stage in his Christian life, Gilbert Kirby displayed an unusual ability to foster good relationships with evangelicals of varied hues. He had sharpened this skill over three decades. Before going to Cambridge in 1933 Kirby was involved in the Crusader class in Bromley, Kent, and attended a Congregational church in the mornings and a flourishing evangelical Anglican church in the evenings. At Cambridge – Cheshunt College and Fitzwilliam College – Kirby was committed to the Cambridge Inter-Collegiate Christian Union (CICCU) and although he was training for Congregational ministry he normally worshipped at St Paul's, an Anglican church frequented by a CICCU father figure, Basil Atkinson. From 1938 to 1945 Kirby was minister of Halstead Congregational Church, Essex, where he continued his pan-evangelical approach by inviting Anglicans and Baptists to speak. Kirby's first wife, Joan, whom he had met at the Keswick Convention in 1937, died in 1943 of meningitis and a cerebral abscess. Two years later Kirby moved to the pastorate of Ashford Congregational Church, Middlesex, by which time he had married Connie, the sister of Edmund Heddle. From this point, Kirby's enormous capacity for wider evangelical activity flourished. Soon

---

[6] Brady, 'Gilbert Kirby', 10.
[7] Minutes of a meeting of governors, 21 Jan. 1966.

he was involved in the teaching programme at LBC, the growth of the EA, Tom Rees' work at Hildenborough Hall, Kent, and Lloyd-Jones' ministers' fellowship.

Gilbert Kirby's LBC and EA interests often overlapped. In 1950, at the Ashford church's diamond jubilee, guests and speakers who came to Ashford at Kirby's invitation included Lieutenant-General Sir Arthur Smith, chairman of the EA, as well as John Laing and Eric Richardson, later an LBC board chairman. Kirby was also in close touch with Lloyd-Jones, who preached at his induction as honorary pastor of Turners Hill Free Church, Sussex, in 1957. As general secretary of the EA, Kirby's range of evangelical contacts became even broader. His taking up the LBC principalship ensured that the college was even more firmly identified with pan-evangelicalism. Through Kirby, well-known figures who came to LBC included Billy Graham, Luis Palau (the Argentinian evangelist), a number of bishops and MPs, Cliff Richard, Malcolm Muggeridge and Sir David McNee, commissioner of the Metropolitan police. Many visitors were introduced as Kirby's 'old friends'. Kirby also brought to LBC the remarkable knowledge he had gained of international evangelicalism. He made many links through his secretaryship of the EMA and the World Evangelical Fellowship and had visited most of the countries of western Europe as well as the USA and India. This broad perspective was of great value to LBC.

Breadth of vision was in somewhat short supply in some sections of British evangelicalism in the later 1960s. At the time of the 1965 NAE, held in Church House, Westminster, a number of Baptists, Methodists and Congregationalists were questioning whether their position in their denominations was tenable. For his part Kirby, to some extent echoing Kevan, stated: 'The Evangelical is the loyalist in his denomination – our denominations owe their origins to the very things that we hold dear ... There is good historic evidence for staying in until we are thrown out.'[8] Kirby's outlook was to prove unpalatable to those who were strongly separatist as well as to those whose thinking was rigidly denominational.

---

[8] *Chr* (8 Oct. 1965), 1.

Herbert Carson, who left Anglican ministry on grounds of conscience, criticized what he saw as Kirby's inconsistency. 'Mr Kirby and many of his friends', said Carson, 'come from the ranks of the Inter Varsity Fellowship. For years the central plank of the policy of the I.V.F. has been non-co-operation with the doctrinally liberal Student Christian Movement.' For Carson, the only consistent choice was to 'come out'.[9] Yet Kirby's inclusiveness enabled him to work with Howard Belben of the Methodist Cliff College in initiating the Association of Bible College Principals and also to foster closer relationships between LBC and other colleges in the London area – All Nations, Spurgeon's and Oak Hill. Kirby personified broad evangelical statesmanship.

Inherited Positions

The years 1965 and 1966, however, saw Gilbert Kirby's inclusivist approach being put under enormous strain. Of the 1,155 delegates who attended the NAE in September 1965, most Anglicans (the largest group) gave qualified support to ecumenical involvement, while many Baptists, together with FIEC representatives (these were the next largest groups), were unhappy about such involvement. The assembly decided to set up a study group to examine evangelical attitudes to ecumenism, denominationalism and a possible future united evangelical church.[10] A nine-member commission was convened and several leaders, including Lloyd-Jones, were invited to present their views. Lloyd-Jones himself never advocated – indeed he repudiated – the idea of a new evangelical denomination, but there were those close to Lloyd-Jones who spoke in terms which seemed to suggest such a concept.[11] Thus the EA report prepared for the October 1966 assembly referred to the option of 'a united evangelical Church on denominational lines'.[12]

---

[9] *Ev T* (March 1968), 11.

[10] *Crusade* (Dec. 1965), 18–21.

[11] Murray, *Fight of Faith*, 508–11.

[12] *Report of the Commission on Church Unity to the National Assembly of Evangelicals* (London, 1966), 10.

Kirby himself wanted to present a balanced picture that included both inclusive and exclusive options. He suggested to the EA executive in July 1966 that deference should not be given to either the right or left wings of evangelicalism.[13] Within a few months, however, these wings had publicly gone their separate ways.

In planning for the 1966 NAE, Gilbert Kirby took a calculated risk by asking Martyn Lloyd-Jones and John Stott to play a prominent part in the opening session. What Lloyd-Jones said on that occasion did not surprise Kirby. Others such as Tim Buckley and Owen Thomas, who were present as LBC representatives, also knew the views Lloyd-Jones espoused. Indeed, he was asked to state publicly what he had said in private. He issued a passionate call for a fellowship or association of evangelical churches, which would be free from what he saw as the compromises entailed in ecumenical or wider denominational involvement, and which instead would express 'evangelical ecumenicity'. It was inconsistent, in Lloyd-Jones' view, for evangelicals to unite with those with whom they agreed only on secondary matters. 'Why is it', he asked, 'that we are so anxious to hold on to our inherited positions?' John Stott, the chairman, brought the evening to a sensational end by adding his own comments. Both history and Scripture, asserted Stott, were against what Lloyd-Jones had said.[14] Positions had publicly polarized. Looking back later, Kirby felt that encouraging Lloyd-Jones to put his case had been 'probably one of my biggest mistakes'.[15] Evangelicals committed to separation from theologically 'mixed' denominations would associate increasingly with the British Evangelical Council (BEC). Morgan Derham, who followed Kirby as EA general secretary, commented gloomily that evangelicals were being pushed to make a choice between denominations and individualistic anarchy.[16]

---

[13] Executive committee minutes, EA, 27 July 1966; cf. I.M. Randall, 'Schism and Unity', 173.

[14] Murray, *Fight of Faith*, 523–5.

[15] *Crusade* (Oct. 1979), 56.

[16] *Crusade* (Oct. 1966), 13.

According to several commentators at the time and subsequently, Martyn Lloyd-Jones was advocating at the 1966 assembly that evangelicals should leave their denominations. Secession had not, in fact, been the thrust of Lloyd-Jones' call. Attitudes, however, were palpably hardening. *The Church of England Newspaper* dismissed what Lloyd-Jones had said as 'nothing short of hare-brained'.[17] The reporter for *Crusade*, influenced no doubt by Kirby's restraint, was content to call the opening session 'adult stuff'.[18] Hopes of conciliation were largely dashed at a packed meeting of the Westminster Fellowship of ministers in November 1966, when Lloyd-Jones made the issues clear. There was, he said, an unmistakeable cleavage between those who believed in staying in their denominations and those who saw no purpose in so doing. From now on, he added, he would offer his help only to ministers already out of their denominations or thinking of leaving.[19] The position of Lloyd-Jones gave a huge boost to the FIEC and the BEC. In 1967 Westminster Chapel, which had previously been in the Congregational Union, joined the FIEC, and the numbers at the BEC's 1967 conference mushroomed to 2,700 when Lloyd-Jones spoke. The same year saw the launch of *Evangelical Times*, a monthly 'separatist' newspaper edited by Peter Masters, previously a member of Westminster Chapel. Two former LBC students, Michael Buss and David Potter, later joined the editorial team.

Soon the *Evangelical Times* was publicizing statements that had a direct bearing on the position of LBC. At the Baptist Revival Fellowship conference at Swanwick in 1967, attended by about two hundred and fifty people (mainly ministers), David Kingdon, principal of the Irish Baptist College, called for the formation of an Evangelical Baptist Union.[20] This call put LBC's aim of co-operating with the major denominations under the spotlight. Some former LBC students changed their allegiance from the BU

---

[17] *Ch E News* (28 Oct. 1966), 5.
[18] *Crusade* (Dec. 1966), 33.
[19] Murray, *Fight of Faith*, 528–31.
[20] *Ev T* (Dec. 1967), 1.

to the FIEC. One example was Ken Patterson, who was committed to the Baptist denomination during his time at college but by the late 1960s was prominent in FIEC affairs. At the FIEC's 1968 assembly Patterson, who since 1965 had been pastor of Trinity Road Chapel (Kevan's congregation), drew a distinction between separation from false doctrine and 'secondary separation' from fellow-evangelicals in mixed denominations. He said that the FIEC stood for the first approach. Other pastors present stressed 'guilt by association', although no one publicly advocated secondary separation.[21] Also in 1968, *The Evangelical Times* applauded the small Kensit Memorial College in London, which was preparing people for ministry and was 'undenominational, evangelical and has a refreshingly sound approach to modern BD courses and the like – it doesn't touch them!'[22] Although not mentioned, LBC was clearly in the firing line.

It was not only LBC that was feeling the pressure. The EA's position, as a force for evangelical unity, was under threat. Morgan Derham considered that it was essential for the EA to find ways of restoring belief in pan-evangelical co-operation. The EA attempted to do this by encouraging, for example, the setting up of regional and local evangelical fellowships. Morgan Derham's vision was of the Alliance providing opportunities for united service and helping to shape evangelical opinion. His secretaryship, however, lasted for just two years, and in 1968 he left to undertake Bible Society work. The NAE in that year mustered only six hundred delegates, far less than the number the BEC could attract when Lloyd-Jones was speaking. Evangelicals who had known and enjoyed the less complex days of the 1950s, when Keswick and the Billy Graham crusades were providing foci of unity, were caught off guard by the force of the new movement for separation. The EA was able in 1968 to launch TEAR Fund as its relief agency, but even this was subjected to scathing comment in the *Evangelical Times*. The EA was 'high and dry' and was left 'with nothing to do except to shed a TEAR – a useful form of

---

[21] *Ev T* (May 1968), 3; (May 1969), 15.
[22] *Ev T* (July 1968), 3.

penance'.[23] The prospects for evangelical unity appeared some-what dismal.

Fresh Initiatives

Many evangelicals in the later 1960s, however, were far from gloomy. Fresh initiatives were taking place. Of these initiatives, by far the most important was the National Evangelical Anglican Congress (NEAC) at the University of Keele in April 1967. It was perceived at the time that Keele would loom large in the annals of Anglican evangelicalism.[24] One thousand evangelical Anglicans (519 clergy and 481 lay people) gathered at Keele in 1967 to review their agenda. NEAC was a turning point in evangelical self-identity. David Bebbington has described it as the 'chief land-mark' in the post-war evangelical renaissance,[25] and Alister McGrath has spoken of it as 'a watershed, not merely in the history of English evangelicalism, but also in the history of the Church of England'.[26] Baptists such as Michael Eastman were inspired by the call to involvement in the world issued at Keele by Norman Anderson, a professor of law at London University.[27] Keele also affirmed that evangelical Anglicans intended to work within the Anglican structures much more than before. A study guide to the Keele resolutions, to be used by local churches, was soon published.[28] Keele was not a reaction to separatism: it came

---

[23] *Ev T* (April 1969), 13 (Paul Cook).

[24] Editorial, *Chr* (14 April 1967), 2.

[25] Bebbington, *Evangelicalism*, 249.

[26] A.E. McGrath, 'Evangelical Anglicanism: A Contradiction in Terms?' 17.

[27] Interview with Michael Eastman, 28 Jan. 1999. See J.N.D. Anderson, *Into the World: The Needs and Limits of Christian Involvement* (London: Church Pastoral Aid Society, 1968), for Anderson's thinking.

[28] P. Crowe (ed.), *Keele '67: The National Evangelical Anglican Congress Statement, with Study Material* (London: Church Pastoral Aid Society, 1967).

out of evangelical Anglican conferences held in the north of England in the 1960s and its planning group, chaired by John Stott, met initially in 1964.

As the congress considered the future it was Stott, then aged forty-six, who set the tone. He acknowledged that evangelicals within the Church of England had previously had a reputation for narrow partisanship. By contrast, leaders at NEAC expressed their openness to other Christian traditions. Michael Green, later principal of the London College of Divinity (LCD) and then, at thirty-six, the youngest conference speaker, placed emphasis on the centrality of the Eucharist.[29] The stress on learning from and co-operating with the wider church had appeared in a book in 1965 edited by J.I. Packer, *All in Each Place: Towards Reunion in England*. This focus on reunion did not, however, appear to affirm the historic pan-evangelicalism which figures such as Kirby were seeking to promote. Certainly Stott, A.T. Houghton, Philip Hughes and other speakers at Keele supported transdenominational evangelical organizations, but, as Oliver Barclay notes, the 'short paragraph in the Keele statement about relationships with evangelicals in other churches did not seem to require any action'.[30] At the BEC conference in November 1967 the 'compromises' of Keele were, predictably, denounced,[31] and Michael Buss added that too many evangelicals were 'sitting on the fence' over ecumenism.[32] Given the fragmentation of this period it is not surprising that LBC experienced some decline in student numbers.

Nonetheless, the college continued to make its mark on the evangelical scene. There were those in the mid-1960s who did not wish either to 'come out from among them' or to take the route of full involvement in wider ecclesiastical affairs if this was at the expense of evangelical relationships. Peter Johnston, vicar of St

---

[29] M. Green, 'Christ's Sacrifice and Ours: Relating Holy Communion to the Cross'.
[30] Barclay, *Evangelicalism*, 84.
[31] *Chr* (10 Nov. 1967), 3.
[32] *Chr* (8 Dec. 1967), 10.

Mary's, Islington (the venue for the Islington Clerical Conferences), argued in 1965 that resurgent evangelical scholarship owed much to two evangelical bodies that straddled the denominations: the IVF and LBC. Looking back over two decades since the commencement of LBC, Johnston highlighted its growth to over two hundred students, its academic standards – 'second to none' – and the fact that five of its staff had obtained doctorates.[33] In 1967, as if in confirmation of Johnston's optimism, Dermot McDonald was awarded the degree of Doctor of Divinity by London University as a recognition of his contribution to historical theology and the philosophy of religion. His book *Jesus Human and Divine* was published in 1968. In the same year, at the EA assembly, Arthur Cundall from LBC gave the Bible readings; Anne Long, a former LBC student, was involved in the theological debate on evangelism; and another former student, Bruce Nicholls, chaired the assembly's session on global evangelicalism.[34]

The global context was one in which LBC had consciously invested to a considerable degree. There was concern at LBC, however, that mission leaders did not understand the nature of the college courses. So LBC invited representatives from the main societies to LBC to explain the training the college offered.[35] In 1968, a questionnaire which was distributed to one thousand former LBC students showed that one-third had gone overseas.[36] Almost two hundred of these were working as missionaries and were linked with at least fifty mission bodies. The survey also showed that over one hundred of LBC's students up to that date had come to college from the medical profession. Many were to serve in other countries in a medical missionary capacity. Eighteen former students, for instance, had joined the Bible and Medical Missionary Fellowship (later Interserve). Two doctors

---

[33] *Chr* (1 Oct. 1965), 8.

[34] *Chr* (25 Oct. 1968), 1, 4.

[35] Minutes of faculty meeting, 30 June 1965.

[36] Much of the information in this section is derived from Rowdon, *London Bible College*, ch. 5.

who had studied at LBC in the 1950s, Peter and Carol Hover, had helped to set up a hospital in the Sindh desert area of West Pakistan, a huge logistical exercise involving six hospital caravans. Bill Gould was a doctor in Nepal and was experimenting with making limbs for amputees – a very necessary initiative. Denis and Ann Roche were also in Nepal, in charge of a small hospital in Bhadgaon.

Many students came to LBC from overseas and returned to their home regions or moved on elsewhere. Nationals from Germany, Belgium, Greece, Ghana, Rhodesia, India, Nepal and Singapore became ministers in their own countries. Apostolos Bliates was giving theological and pastoral leadership to Greek evangelicals. Robert Karthak, who returned to Nepal, achieved a doctorate in theology and as a pastor in Kathmandu became something of a father figure to the growing number of Nepali pastors. Another student from the 1960s, Subodh Sahu, who had been converted through SU in India, returned to India after his LBC studies to give training in evangelism and discipleship. Perhaps the non-western leader who became best known was Byang Kato, who left LBC in 1966. Kato was born in 1936 and was converted to Christianity in Nigeria through churches related to the Sudan Interior Mission. He gained a BD through LBC and in 1974 added to that a ThD from Dallas Theological Seminary, USA. In the interim period Kato was active in encouraging theological work among African evangelicals. He became the first African general secretary of the Association of Evangelicals of Africa and Madagascar and was also secretary of the Association's theological commission. His strategic contribution was cut short, however, through his death in a drowning accident off the coast of Kenya in 1975.

Overseas service continued to offer many opportunities for women trained at LBC to exercise leadership – opportunities often denied them in Britain. Sometimes wives lectured at Bible colleges in partnership with their husbands. At the Bible Institute of South Africa, which looked to LBC for its staff, David Carnegie was vice-principal and Dorothy Carnegie was a lecturer. Bruce and Kathleen Nicholls were at that stage at the Union Biblical

Seminary, Yeotmal, India, which had about one hundred students. Michael and Una Herbage were theological teachers in Barcelona. In other cases women who had studied at LBC were taking sole leadership positions within a variety of institutions. Vivienne Stacey, for example, was leading the United Bible Training Centre, Gujranwala, Pakistan, and training teachers, youth leaders and nurses. Betty Shelton was principal of the Queen Mary High School, Bombay, with 1,200 children as her responsibility, many from influential Indian families. Nor was this kind of leadership role restricted to western women. In the 1960s, Florence Yeboah came from Ghana under the auspices of SU to study at LBC. She then returned to Ghana, becoming director of an organization promoting women's ministries. Global initiatives, involving women as well as men, were being taken.

Ministry in the World

The trend towards globalization was linked with another trend – towards more holistic ministry. The launch of TEAR Fund in 1968 took place in part because Mary Jean Duffield, a twenty-one year old who was concerned about the famine in the Bihar region of India, joined the EA and was given the task of examining the potential for a relief fund. Evangelicals were reawakening to a world of material need.[37] George Hoffman, who became TEAR Fund's first director, had been profoundly affected by the 1967 Keele congress. The section on social responsibility in the Keele report was later described by one commentator, Michael Saward, as 'full of well-meaning platitudes', but nonetheless Saward argued that because Keele acknowledged the past failures of evangelicals it marked a turning point in British evangelical thinking about social responsibility.[38] In this period, as David Smith notes

---

[37] T. Chester, *Awakening to a World of Need*, 41–2.
[38] M. Saward, *The Anglican Church Today: Evangelicals on the Move*, 63.

in his study of the social impact of British evangelicalism, younger evangelicals in particular 'began to turn from a preoccupation with the salvation of individuals towards a more comprehensive view of its [evangelicalism's] mission'.[39] It was a position that appealed to an increasing number of those within LBC's orbit.

In 1967, when Michael Eastman transferred from the ISCF to become the development officer of the newly formed Frontier Youth Trust (FYT), he soon found common cause with other 'radical evangelicals' in Britain and beyond who were rediscovering and emphasizing the social and political dimensions of the gospel. LBC's training, by facilitating student work among unchurched young people and among the hundreds of needy older people housed at Luxborough Lodge (near the college), brought into focus the reality of social deprivation. The issue of justice, however, was to become more central. FYT, which entered into partnership with SU in 1966, was pioneering long-term youth work which combined evangelism and social action among the disadvantaged young in deprived communities. One result was an evangelical presence within the state youth service.[40] Another key figure was David Blair, who left LBC in 1961 to work for SU and became head of SU's schools department in 1974. He and Eastman were among those behind the formation of the Association of Christian Teachers in 1971. Evangelical engagement with society was – as we shall see – to become even more evident in Britain in the 1970s.

Evangelicals were also beginning to express concern for issues of social justice at an international level. In 1966, at the Billy Graham-sponsored World Congress on Evangelism in Berlin, which drew together over one thousand selected leaders from one hundred countries, the closing statement condemned racism. LBC was represented at Berlin and some of the congress delegates visited the college. Billy Graham returned to Britain for crusades

---

[39] Smith, *Transforming*, 88. Remarkably, Smith does not mention TEAR Fund.

[40] I am indebted to notes from Michael Eastman; Chester, *Awakening*, 80–2.

in 1966–67. The numbers coming to Earl's Court in London to listen to Graham reached twenty-five thousand, and through 23 relay centres Graham was heard by one hundred and six thousand people elsewhere in Britain. Unsurprisingly, the Calvinist wing of evangelicalism was not impressed, as evidenced by the critique of Graham's methods produced in 1966 by Erroll Hulse, then minister of Cuckfield Baptist Church, Sussex, a church which would establish international Reformed links through its magazine, *Reformation Today*.[41] But criticisms of American mass evangelism were also coming from elsewhere. David Winter, editor of *Crusade*, commented in 1966 that the preliminaries in the crusade of that year seemed rather dated.[42] Even more seriously, an important EA report entitled *On the Other Side*, published in 1968, concluded (on a deliberately controversial note) that the crusade model of evangelism had made minimal impact on modern culture. It called for fresh thinking.[43]

New thinking was spreading in IVF circles. In the 1960s, books by Francis Schaeffer published by Inter-Varsity Press were being widely read. Schaeffer, an American Presbyterian who had founded the L'Abri community in Switzerland in 1954, emphasized Christian apologetics. His talks in 1965 to the IVF's Graduates' Fellowship conference in England were the basis for his most popular book, *Escape from Reason*. About a dozen LBC students attended a TSF conference at which Schaeffer was the main speaker. In typical fashion, he gave a historical sketch of philosophy from Thomas Aquinas through the Reformation and Renaissance to the present time. His argument was that there had been an ever-growing rift between faith and reason until, in the contemporary world, people were 'locked and barred inside a system of their own reasoning with no means of escape from it'. For the LBC students who were present Schaeffer made the state of those without God, as expressed in literature, art, radio and

---

[41] E. Hulse, *Billy Graham: The Pastor's Dilemma*.

[42] D. Winter, *Decision* (Sept. 1966), 11.

[43] *On the Other Side: The Report of the Evangelical Alliance's Commission on Evangelism* (London: SU, 1968), 168.

television 'horrifyingly clear'.[44] A serious challenge for LBC was to apply Christian thinking to the surrounding culture.

Others were also responding to this challenge. The 1960s saw John Stott speaking a number of times at Regent College, Vancouver, Canada, where he was impressed by the issues being tackled. An increasing number of students and graduates worldwide, often encouraged by the International Fellowship of Evangelical Students (IFES), wanted to relate Christianity to their context. IFES leaders included Jo Gardner, Jim Johnson in South Africa, Ronald Fung in Hong Kong, and Chua Wee Hian (Freddie Chua), who was later well known as IFES general secretary. All of these had studied at LBC in the 1960s. Within the British student scene, Stott made his priorities more explicit in an address to the IVF in 1972, published as *Your Mind Matters*, and in his initiation of lectures in Contemporary Christianity. Those working with Stott in the lecture project included Os Guinness and Roy Clements, both of whom had been at LBC. Guinness wrote in *Areopagus* about the way in which apologetics should involve pressing home the logical implications of doubt. Os Guinness's ideas were to be spread through such books as *The Dust of Death* (1973). Roy Clements worked for IVF and had influential Baptist pastorates in Nairobi and at Eden Chapel, Cambridge.[45]

Evangelicals working with students and other young people were acutely aware of the way in which ministry in the world outside the church was changing. By the later 1960s many former LBC students were in the field of education, some taking key positions as school RE specialists and college lecturers. A few were working with the Schools Council and with syllabus revision committees. In 1968 Michael Eastman and Peter Cousins published *The Open Approach to Religious Education*. In this approach the starting point was not the Bible but the experience of young people. Elmira Hill (later Masters) was editing the

---

[44] Report on TSF Conference in *Areopagus* (Spring 1967).

[45] J.R.W. Stott, *Your Mind Matters: The Place of the Mind in the Christian Life*; Chester, *Awakening*, 89–90; Os Guinness, 'Dismantling his Lightning Conductor', *Areopagus* (Christmas 1964), 6–7.

Primary Teachers' Magazine, which was recommended by the London County Council education authority for use in infant schools. Many children in Britain in the 1960s had little religious knowledge, but three former LBC students – Howard Sainsbury, Esther Edwards and Michael Cartwright, all of whom taught RE at Pollards Hill, in the south London area – were able to generate enthusiasm for SU activities. Each of these three progressed further in the field of education. There was a concern to inform evangelicals about the fact that traditional methods of communicating to young people were becoming less relevant, and Eastman, Sainsbury and others contributed material to *Crusade*.

A letter from Michael Eastman to Harold Rowdon in 1968, which gave information about several SU staff who had studied at LBC,[46] illustrated the degree to which LBC's pan-denominational evangelicalism was in tune with the ethos of groups such as SU. Some former students were with SU overseas. David Cunningham was in Zimbabwe and would become secretary of SU in southern Africa. He pioneered SU's Aid for AIDS programme. Elizabeth de Benoit was leading SU work in Ivory Coast and Cameroon and was later a tutor at the Emmaus Bible Institute in Switzerland. Alethe Clezy went to the Philippines with SU and then to Australia to undertake editorial work. Shoko Hirata was translating Bible reading materials into Japanese. Within Britain, SU leaders who had been at LBC included Paul Marsh, who (after missionary service in Pakistan) was appointed SU's Bible reading editor, succeeding Morgan Derham. Pat Eastman was the first female representative for SU's eastern counties region. She later married Stephen Travis and joined him in lecturing at St John's College, Nottingham. Henry Warde was responsible for directing eighteen SU evangelists, and his wife, Margaret, was editor of *Homes and Parents*. Ian Cory, previously with Tom Rees and later on LBC's staff, was then establishing SU's northern region.

Other outreach was being carried on in local settings. In 1966, for instance, Martin Gouldthorpe, who had left LBC and become a schoolteacher, took over 'The Dive' in west London, a club

---

[46] Rowdon, *London Bible College*, 119–25.

often raided by the police because of drugs, and turned it into a Christian coffee bar. Gouldthorpe and his wife worked with two other former LBC students, Denis Paterson and Eric Westwood, in the 'Come Back to God Campaign'. An example of local church growth under the leadership of ministers trained at LBC was St James's Road Baptist Church, Watford. Roy Bell became minister in 1952, followed by Norman Archer in 1957 and Norman Trussler in 1964. The church grew significantly up to 1970, in a period of general decline in churchgoing, with new buildings being erected. J. Clement Connell acted as moderator for the church and no doubt suggested LBC students to the deacons. There had also been LBC evangelistic teams assisting the congregation. Roy Bell moved to Canada, becoming a lecturer and then a pastor in Vancouver. The St James's Road church secretary, reviewing the LBC contribution, recalled how Bell 'inspired us with his simple, crystal-clear exposition of the Gospel' and spoke of Archer's 'vivid preaching'. He saw Trussler's aim in the 1960s as being 'closer fellowship with the Lord in worship'.[47]

Charismatic Perplexities

Emphasis on the renewal of worship was typical of a further trend among evangelicals in the later 1960s. Questions about spiritual renewal were, in the minds of some, as pressing as the call to mission. St Mark's, Gillingham, Kent, became the first Anglican parish to be substantially affected by charismatic experience and worship. From the mid-1960s people who wished to discover more about what Michael Harper was calling the 'third force in the body of Christ' (Protestantism and Catholicism were the other two) were being directed to St Mark's. John Collins was the vicar and for a time David MacInnes and David Watson, both of whom would become prominent in Anglican charismatic renewal, were curates. By the end of 1965 the Fountain Trust, with Harper as secretary, had published five booklets. Harper suggested that 'the

---

[47] Rowdon, *London Bible College*, 112–14.

most important truth which the new movement of the Holy Spirit is revealing concerns a dynamic conception of the Body of Christ equipped with all the ministries and gifts of the Spirit'.[48] At a time of evangelical disunity, a Fountain Trust conference at High Leigh in 1967 could draw Anglicans (both evangelical and Anglo-Catholic), Baptists, Brethren, Presbyterians, Pentecostals and members of the Salvation Army. Douglas McBain, a participant at High Leigh, saw there 'the beginning stages of a movement of massive significance'.[49]

Some students at LBC in the 1960s shared this belief in the significance of the new movement. One was Terry Virgo, who met his wife, Wendy, while they were at LBC. As a young member of Holland Road Baptist Church, Hove, Virgo had been challenged about the baptism of the Spirit through a friend and had entered into this experience in 1962. The widely respected Holland Road minister, George Rudman, encouraged Virgo to speak about what he had experienced. Virgo started as a student at LBC in 1965 and on Sunday mornings attended Richard Bolt's charismatic church in Buckingham Street, off the Strand.[50] Two other LBC students, Arnold Bell and John Houghton, would later work with Virgo in a 'house church' (a term increasingly used in the 1970s) network which he set up, initially operating in the south-east of England. Gilbert Kirby, whose instincts were to encourage, was sympathetic to this growing charismatic circle within LBC. Although Kirby deplored the tendency of some charismatics to be divisive, he believed that 'something of God' was in the movement.[51] In 1967 he commented on the poor spiritual state of many churches and on difficulties some LBC students were experiencing in finding pastorates.[52] In due course

---

[48] M.C. Harper, *The Third Force in the Body of Christ* (London, 1965), 15. Harper acknowledged his debt to Lesslie Newbigin for the idea of the third force.

[49] McBain, *Fire*, 47.

[50] Hocken, *Streams*, 263.

[51] Interview with Gilbert Kirby, 30 Jan. 1998.

[52] Minutes of the AGM, 17 Nov. 1967.

new groups, such as that led by Virgo, would offer fresh opportunities.

Most of the charismatic movement's leaders in the 1960s, however, were not interested in setting up separatist congregations. Their vision was of renewal affecting the historic denominations. As if to affirm this vision, the bishop of Southwark, Mervyn Stockwood, who was not an evangelical, invited Dennis Bennett of Van Nuys, California, to speak to a group of about two hundred clergy at the chapter house of Southwark Cathedral in November 1965.[53] Bennett was also invited by the EA to address a meeting of leaders which Gilbert Kirby attended. Morgan Derham commented that the chief subject being aired in theological colleges, churches and groups where ministers were meeting was speaking in tongues. The EA's theological study group, which contained two Pentecostal members, considered the implications of the new movement. J.I. Packer, too, addressed the subject of 'the New Pentecostalism' at the TSF's 1965 conference at Swanwick. Renewal, in Morgan Derham's view, was being welcomed because of the prevailing 'formality and dullness'.[54] Kirby was well aware of the desire for new life, and (as Luis Palau later commented) he acted as a bridge between older and younger evangelical leaders.[55]

This desire for renewal presented evangelical theology with new challenges. In 1965 Michael Harper addressed the criticism that the charismatic movement had no theology. He said: 'Theology itself does not provide strength. There is good and bad theology. Bad theology can be more harmful than no theology at all.' For Harper, the neglect of the Holy Spirit was one aspect of theological weakness.[56] Lloyd-Jones, a sympathetic but critical observer of charismatic phenomena, was worried about those who were playing down doctrine and claiming that the important question was whether 'a man has got the Spirit'. Lloyd-Jones was

---

[53] *Chr* (19 Nov. 1965), 20.

[54] *Chr* (10 Dec. 1965), 2.

[55] L. Palau to S. Brady, cited in Brady, 'Gilbert Kirby', 12.

[56] Harper, *Beginning*, 94.

aware, in 1966, of reports that 'bishops and even cardinals in the Roman Catholic Church have been baptized with the Spirit'. In 1967, a group of Roman Catholics in Pittsburgh who had read *The Cross and the Switchblade* (by a Pentecostal pastor, David Wilkerson), spoke in tongues. Lloyd-Jones found it quite unacceptable that Catholic teachings that were 'contrary to Scripture' should be condoned by charismatics.[57] On the subject of prophecy, Lloyd-Jones spoke approvingly of the position adopted by the Pentecostal statesman, Donald Gee, that spiritual gifts were not to be 'directive'.[58] Pentecostals who came to LBC in the later 1960s, such as Julian Ward (later on the staff of the Elim Bible College, which became Regents Park Theological College), were to grapple with such issues.

The charismatic movement was in fact part of a wider change taking place in styles of church life. What was being created through charismatic renewal, Bebbington argues, was 'a Christian version of the counter-culture', mirroring major social trends – rejection of the institutional and bureaucratic in favour of self-expression.[59] New music was entering evangelical worship, with *Youth Praise* being produced in 1966 and renewal songs subsequently proliferating. The annual five thousand-strong Filey Convention, held at Butlin's holiday camp in Filey, Yorkshire, under the auspices of the Movement for World Evangelisation (MWE), was more innovative than Keswick. It was called 'Swinging Filey' because of its new musical sounds. Kirby was a popular Filey figure and was to become chairman of MWE. Christian-run coffee bars proliferated in the 1960s, often featuring bands that had adopted the musical ethos of the Beatles or leading folk groups. Frank Colquhoun, who had been on the first LBC faculty, observed in the mid-1960s that it was becoming almost impossible to persuade unchurched people to attend church services. Indications were that churchgoing in cities such as Birmingham was under ten per cent. Colquhoun was in favour

---

[57] Murray, *Fight of Faith*, 661.

[58] Murray, *Fight of Faith*, 663; cf. Massey, *Springtime*, chs. 6 and 8.

[59] Bebbington, *Evangelicalism*, 233.

of inviting non-Christians to informal house meetings rather than to services where they would be expected to sing hymns and recite creeds.[60] LBC would have to engage with changing spiritual and societal trends.

Theological Challenges

Although the charismatic dimension promoted lively discussion at LBC, it would not become a subject for theological study by anyone on the faculty until Max Turner, who joined the college staff in 1974, gave it his attention. A more serious theological challenge in the 1960s was coming from the WCC. At the fourth assembly of the WCC in Uppsala, Sweden, in 1968, the concern seemed to be with enabling people to be truly human rather than with evangelism. WCC thinking had been developing at a conference in Geneva in 1966 on church and society and in reports on *The Church for Others* and *The Church for the World*. A 'Programme to Combat Racism' was set up following Uppsala. John Stott, who was at Uppsala, protested that the assembly stressed physical need but did not seem to take note of spiritual hunger.[61] For many western evangelicals, the themes of humanization and liberation signalled abandonment of the gospel. But what was also evident was that voices from the Third World were beginning to affect evangelical theological thinking. An important influence within evangelical circles was Samuel Escobar of Peru. In the period 1967–70, at conferences in Britain (organized by the IVF), South America and the USA, Escobar, who was then working for IFES, argued that the gospel was 'for the whole man and cannot be sliced up into social and spiritual pieces'.[62] It was a theological perspective that would powerfully affect evangelicalism.

---

[60] *Chr* (26 Nov. 1965), 2.

[61] O. Costas, *The Church and its Mission: A Shattering Critique from the Third World*, 182–6.

[62] Chester, *Awakening*, 57.

Some non-western theologians, however, were wary about the new emphases. Byang Kato was opposed to the WCC and to its African arm, the All Africa Conference of Churches, and used the phrase 'unity in the dark' to describe ecumenism. No doubt he had read the Banner of Truth book with that title while at LBC. British divisions affected Africa. Yet Kato, an outstandingly able evangelical African, wanted, as Paul Bowers put it, a Christianity that was 'truly African and truly biblical'.[63] Kato was critical of John Mbiti of Kenya, who was regarded as Africa's leading theologian, and Kato also rejected the conclusions of the 1965 consultation of African theologians which spoke of God's revelation in Christ as 'not totally discontinuous with our people's previous traditional knowledge of Him'.[64] At the same time, Kato acknowledged that among his own Jaba in Nigeria there was a prophetess who predicted that white people would tell them about the Supreme Being. This was fulfilled when white missionaries arrived.[65] One critic of Kato, Timothy Njoya, wrote: 'Byang Kato's fear of African religion and philosophy is genuinely grounded in his evangelical tradition. Evangelicalism in Africa claims itself to be cultureless, timeless and unhistorical in order to cover up the fact that it is American and conservative.'[66] Kwame Bediako, a student at LBC in the 1970s, noted how far removed Kato was from the dominant emphasis in African Christian scholarship.[67]

There were a few figures like Kato who kept abreast of theological issues in both the western and non-western worlds. Much evangelical theological traffic, however, was transatlantic,

---

[63] P. Bowers, 'Evangelical Theology in Africa: Byang Kato's Legacy', 35–9.

[64] B. Kato, *Theological Pitfalls in Africa*, 154–5.

[65] Kato, *Pitfalls*, 36.

[66] T. Njoya, 'Dynamics of Change in African Christianity', Princeton Seminary PhD thesis (1976), 60, cited by K. Bediako, *Theology and Identity*, 387.

[67] Bediako, *Theology*, 417. See further discussion of Bediako's evaluation of Kato in ch. 8.

especially between Britain and America. In 1966 Dermot McDonald and Donald Guthrie were invited to attend an international conference at Gordon Divinity School, Wenham, Massachusetts, USA, on biblical authority. Fifty-one biblical scholars from ten countries attended the conference, from 20 to 29 June. The subject of 'biblical inerrancy' was at that point a highly sensitive one in the USA. Harold Lindsell was gathering evidence about Fuller Seminary, where he had been on the staff, to seek to show that the seminary had moved away from an insistence on inerrancy as the proper way to describe the truthfulness of the Bible. In his combative *The Battle for the Bible*, Lindsell regards the Wenham conference of 1966 as one that showed the 'deep cleavage' among evangelical scholars over inerrancy.[68] Donald Guthrie's personal papers from that conference make clear that discussions were not to be taped or reported, although the presentations – which included a substantial paper by J.I. Packer on hermeneutics – were available.[69] The conference report stated that the concept of inerrancy required further study, but participants were united in believing that the Scriptures were 'completely truthful' and 'authoritative as the only infallible rule of faith and practice'.

Members of the LBC faculty did not normally allow themselves to be drawn into such theological battles. Through scholars such as Donald Guthrie, LBC has probably been better known for its contribution to the field of biblical study than to aspects of systematic theology. Yet David Wells, who studied at LBC from 1963 to 1966 and later completed a PhD at Manchester, saw systematic theology as at the apex of all he received from LBC.

---

[68] H. Lindsell, *The Battle for the Bible*, 131–2.

[69] Personal papers of Donald Guthrie held at LBC. Other presenters at the Wenham conference included Kenneth Kantzer, Earle Ellis, Donald Wiseman, Gleason Archer, Leon Morris, Bruce Metzger, John Walvoord, Roger Nicole, E.J. Young, David Hubbard, Oswald Hoffman, John Warwick Montgomery and Herbert Ridderbos. In his paper on hermeneutics Packer said that he had not found a single article or book covering his subject by an evangelical.

Ernest Kevan's teaching within the college was, for him, reinforced by the influence of Stott, Lloyd-Jones and Packer.[70] Wells was later to become concerned about theological disintegration within evangelicalism and would write extensively on the subject. Following Ernest Kevan's death, the teaching of theology at LBC was largely in the hands of Geoffrey Grogan, who had come from the BTI in Glasgow in 1965 and returned there in 1969 as principal. LBC added David Carnegie to the faculty to specialize in dogmatics, and David Jackson and Peggy Knight to teach primarily in the biblical field. Jackson taught Greek. Peggy Knight, who established herself over the next two decades as a teacher of the highest quality, replaced Margaret Manton, who became vice-principal of Ridgelands College. LBC's scholarly output in this era included the following: in 1968 Leslie Allen completed his doctoral thesis on 1 and 2 Chronicles, McDonald's study of New Testament Christology appeared, and Tyndale Press published Arthur Cundall's commentary on Judges.

There were concerns, however, over the extent to which the expertise of LBC's teaching staff was being translated into successful London University degree results. A number of student failures in the BD degree provoked the faculty to conduct investigations. By 1968, more written work, extra exams and personal interviews with advisers had been introduced.[71] It was also decided in the same year to pursue the possibility of LBC's moving from London University to the Council for National Academic Awards (CNAA), established in 1964. Donald Guthrie had been gathering information on CNAA.[72] Sir Eric Richardson, who had a distinguished educational career, latterly as director of education at the Polytechnic of Central London, joined the LBC board in 1968 (becoming chairman in 1970) and gave enormous assistance. He encouraged LBC to apply to the CNAA, of which he was a member, for recognition for a degree in theology – the great advantage being that LBC would be able to draw up its own

---

[70] David Wells to the author, 17 Feb. 1998.

[71] Minutes of a meeting of governors, 19 Jan. 1968.

[72] Minutes of faculty meeting, 14 June 1967.

syllabus.[73] The CNAA's background was technological, and it was initially thrown into confusion by the LBC application.[74] In due course, however, CNAA brought into being a board and committee for theological studies. Subsequently other independent theological colleges were to pursue the CNAA option. The move to the CNAA was of enormous significance since it allowed LBC to construct its own courses and design its own examinations.

Not only was LBC investigating a new academic framework for its theological study, it was also looking for a new geographical setting. An obvious option was to move out of central London to a less expensive area. Such a decision could not, however, be taken lightly since there was a feeling in some quarters that LBC needed to be central to fulfil its function. It was also argued that a central London location made it easier for students to find lodgings and to radiate out to take preaching engagements. On the other hand, the accommodation at Marylebone Road was hopelessly inadequate. Apart from the lack of space, the ventilation system militated against concentration in lectures. Students near an air duct had unacceptably cold air, while those near a heating duct were scorched. In addition, only the principal, J. Clement Connell as director of studies, and Owen Thomas as chaplain had their own study rooms. It was recognized that extra space would probably be essential in order to gain CNAA's approval. Through his struggles to work in the Marylebone Road environment Donald Guthrie became convinced that a move must be made. He heard that the London College of Divinity was moving from Northwood to Nottingham, and he immediately concluded that for LBC to buy the LCD site was 'God's answer to our problem'.[75]

The LBC board agreed to explore this idea and a building committee, which included Guthrie, was then set up. Philip

---

[73] Minutes of faculty meeting, 15 May 1968.
[74] Sir Eric Richardson to the author, 4 Nov. 1997.
[75] Guthrie, *I Stand for Truth*, 50–1; G. Grogan to the author, 7 May 1998.

Henman, the board chairman, was deeply involved in the project. The LCD asking price was in the region of £350,000, and the LBC board agreed to offer this amount since it was anticipated that at least that sum would be realized from the sale of LBC's central London site. Dermot McDonald was concerned that, in any move, existing library and study space should at least be doubled. Plans were drawn up to turn the LCD's extensive chapel into a two-storey library and to build a new chapel for LBC's use. New lecture rooms were to be built. In May 1968 Kirby reported to the LBC governors that the announcement of the intended move to Northwood had been commented upon favourably in various quarters. The news had apparently been well received by the Anglican community in Northwood. Kirby was also delighted to report that after a fall in student numbers, which had contributed to an excess of expenditure over income, LBC was virtually full for the next academic year. In February 1969, contracts were exchanged with the LCD. LBC was able to purchase and adapt the Northwood site without incurring debt. A new decade would see LBC moving to a new location.

Conclusion

At its twenty-fifth anniversary in 1968, LBC could look back with some satisfaction. Its beginnings had been on a small scale, but by 1968 over five hundred students had spent three or more years studying full-time at LBC for theological degrees. Many more had obtained diplomas and certificates. Thirteen students had gained higher degrees after leaving LBC. The denominational affiliation of LBC students was varied. Up to 1968, 340 of the full-time students were Baptists, 192 were Anglicans, 107 were Free Evangelicals, 84 were Brethren and 56 were Methodists. Former students from outside Britain were spreading evangelical influence – for example through pan-European EA links.[76] Gilbert Kirby, moving from the EA and international evangelical

---

[76] A.D. Bliates to the author, 17 May 1999.

work to take up the principalship in 1966, wanted to build on these successes. He was aware that the college had to move into a new era. A number of its early backers, such as A.J. Vereker and Clarence Foster, died in this period. Kirby was also fully conversant with the difficulties facing evangelicals. The new impetus towards separation on the one hand, and the Keele agenda within Anglicanism on the other, tended to divide evangelicals from one another. The result in both cases was that interdenominational causes such as LBC were regarded with less favour. Hugh Gough, for example, who had been heavily involved in the EA and also in LBC, said in 1965 how important it was to be a committed Anglican.[77] Kirby, while sensitive to these trends, was also convinced that LBC, as an interdenominational theological college, had a crucial role in equipping leaders to contribute to pan-evangelical renewal and to tackle the challenge of emerging theological issues. Adrian Hastings says of the evangelicals that they came through the sixties in far better shape than other groups.[78] To that extent, the picture was not as dismal as some, in their gloomier moments, may have thought.

---

[77] *Chr* (31 Dec. 1965), 5.
[78] Hastings, *History of English Christianity*, 552.

8

'A Measure of Comprehensiveness' 1970–80

The decade of the 1970s began with LBC's move to Northwood and ended with the retirement of Gilbert Kirby as principal. Three long-standing staff – Dermot McDonald, Owen Thomas and J. Clement Connell – left or retired, and new, younger staff members were appointed. In 1978 Donald Guthrie became vice-principal. New directions were also evident in worldwide evangelicalism. The single most important event was the International Congress on World Evangelization, held in July 1974 at Lausanne, Switzerland. There were nearly two thousand seven hundred participants and over a thousand observers. From Lausanne came a more comprehensive understanding of the evangelical movement as global, rather than western, and a more holistic view of the gospel. Gilbert Kirby was chairman of the congress when the final statement – the Lausanne Covenant – was presented. It included an affirmation of evangelical socio-political involvement. René Padilla, a younger South American theologian, set the congress alight, speaking scathingly about an evangelical sub-culture playing down radical discipleship.[1] Evangelicalism was also being broadened through charismatic influences. At the 1977 Nottingham Evangelical Anglican Conference (a follow-up to Keele), David Watson, by then an outstanding Anglican charismatic leader, lamented the way the Christian church had been 'torn limb from limb into hundreds of separate pieces' and attempted to bring Protestants and Catholics

---

[1] *Crusade* (Sept. 1974), 26.

together.[2] As we will see, LBC added its own contribution to the diverse streams of the decade.

At the end of the decade, in 1979, the college had to grapple with a challenge to the inclusive evangelicalism which Gilbert Kirby espoused. The college president, Sir Eric Richardson, received a letter signed by 18 former students of LBC. This letter, dated 13 December 1979, complained that there had been a 'steady erosion' over the previous 15 years of LBC's early purpose to 'train men in the Word of God'.[3] Since that was the period in which Gilbert Kirby had been principal, there was an obvious reference to his leadership. The academic staff, meeting on 9 January 1980, 'unanimously felt that they should inform the Board that they subscribed to the conservative evangelical position of the College, and that they had complete confidence in the leadership given by the present Principal'. Later in the month the board of governors replied to the complainants saying that differences of interpretation 'need to be recognised and debated, but should not be a cause for division or the occasion of questioning one another's integrity'. As will be seen later in this chapter, the issue was one of differing approaches to biblical interpretation. The governors were adamant that the college was required by its constitution to operate in fellowship with all evangelical movements and that given the schools of thought in the evangelical world this implied 'a measure of comprehensiveness'.[4]

Broadening Leadership

As in previous decades, students who left LBC in the 1970s took up a wide variety of posts, with several subsequently moving into positions of evangelical leadership and influence. Many of them

---

[2] T. Saunders and H. Sansom, *David Watson*, 186–91.

[3] Letter to Sir Eric Richardson, 13 Dec. 1979, signed by Michael Buss and James Wood on behalf of the 18 named at the end of the letter.

[4] Minutes of academic board, 9 Jan. 1980; letter dated 25 Jan. 1980 from Derek Warren, chairman of the board of governors.

owed a great deal to the personal encouragement of Gilbert Kirby, who was unusually gifted in this area. One of these young leaders was Clive Calver, who was at LBC from 1968 to 1971. He went on to work for BYFC, becoming its director in 1975, and then, in 1983, general secretary of the EA. Calver's initial Christian commitment owed much to Roger Forster, whose background was Brethren and who, with his wife Faith, pioneered the Ichthus group of churches in London.[5] Another important aspect of Calver's experience was his membership of the Young Liberals in their politically radical phase. In 1980 Kirby could describe BYFC under Calver's leadership as one of the most dynamic youth movements in the country.[6] During the 1970s Calver drew together a varied team – one member of which was the songwriter Graham Kendrick – that was to have a considerable impact on evangelical life in Britain. Calver's achievement in developing BYFC as an evangelistic force was remarkable. The full-time staff, for example, increased from 12 in 1975 to 45 members four years later. At that stage Calver's assessment of his own style was that he had a tendency to be 'stroppy and bolshie', but he praised the way LBC had given him positions of trust and so had contributed to his training for leadership.[7] While at LBC Calver married Gilbert Kirby's daughter Ruth, a fellow student.

Another of the young evangelical leaders of this period was Derek Tidball, who completed his BD at LBC in 1972. He became pastor of the Baptist church in Northchurch, Berkhamsted, and also part-time lecturer in sociology and director of student evangelism at LBC. In 1977, with the impending retirement of Clement Connell, Tidball became a full-time member of the college staff and a year later director of studies. In the 1970s Tidball was chairman of BYFC, served on the executive of the EA, and was on the council of the socially orientated Shaftesbury Project. These networks were to be crucial in the continuing development of LBC

[5] Chester, *Awakening*, 50.
[6] G.W. Kirby in C. Calver, *Sold Out: Taking the Lid off Evangelism* (London: Lakeland, Marshall, Morgan & Stott, 1980), vii.
[7] *Crusade* (April 1979), 51–3.

as a resource for evangelicals. Tidball was interviewed in 1977 about his vision for the future, especially in the field of theological education. He indicated that his priorities included academic work which connected with contemporary issues and the training of students in a way that would enable them to grow in maturity and use their gifts.[8] In 1978 Tidball, with Peter Cotterell, who joined the LBC staff in 1976, was a driving force behind the first UK Church Growth Consultation, jointly sponsored by the EA and LBC. The main speaker at the conference, which drew together 50 British church leaders, was Peter Wagner from the School of World Mission, Fuller Theological Seminary.[9] LBC was facilitating initiatives in leadership training.

New evangelical leadership had to take account of the way in which Britain was becoming a more diverse country. Patrick and Rosemary Sookhdeo, who completed their studies at LBC in 1969, were engaged in ministry within immigrant communities in London. Patrick Sookhdeo was appointed to the EA staff and also inspired 'In Contact', an organization which developed a number of centres in East London. In 1974 Patrick Sookhdeo edited a book on racial issues, *All One in Christ?* to which Dermot McDonald and Geoffrey Grogan (amongst others) contributed. In the following year, multifaith and multiracial questions were taken up at an EA conference. In 1978 Sookhdeo edited *Jesus Christ the Only Way*, which included a chapter by Gilbert Kirby and also chapters written by representatives of non-Christian faiths explaining their beliefs. By this stage there were at least a dozen former LBC students working in the East End of London. At a conference in 1978 on 'evangelism in a plural society' it was suggested that Patrick Sookhdeo had done more than any other evangelical leader to explore the outworking of this theme.[10] Sookhdeo had himself experienced racist attitudes within evangelicalism, and his call was for the church to make plain 'God's anger at all forms of racism and injustice'.[11]

---

[8] *C Rev* (Spring 1977), 8–9.

[9] *C Rev* (Autumn 1978), 18–19.

[10] *Journal of the Evangelical Race Relations Group* (Sept. 1978), 8.

[11] P. Sookhdeo, 'Race in Britain – A Challenge to the Church', 5.

Joel Edwards, a Black Pentecostal (New Testament Church of God) who came to LBC in 1972, felt that the college, with its White Anglo-evangelical culture, did not understand him. Nonetheless, Edwards was one of a group of LBC students who made links with each other in the mid-1970s and who would later work together in transdenominational evangelical leadership. This group included Alistair Begg, Steve Brady and Ian Coffey. It was Begg, later well known for his preaching at large evangelical events such as Keswick and for his ministry in America, who helped to broaden Edwards' experience of British evangelicalism by taking him to Gold Hill Baptist Church. There Edwards saw in Jim Graham, the pastor, what Black Pentecostals normally called 'a man of God'. Edwards was appointed the first general secretary of the West Indian (later African and Caribbean) EA in 1988, and nine years later he succeeded Clive Calver as EA's general director. In his autobiography Edwards writes of his period at LBC: 'What I could never realize at that time was the degree to which God had sovereignly instigated friendships and networks that would last many years and which would later blossom into working relationships.'[12]

By 1970 another batch of former LBC students had moved into teaching positions in the world of theological education. Newer appointments included Claire Spivey at the Anglican St Michael's House, Cambridge, and Mally Shaw at St John's, Durham. Norman Shields was lecturing at the Irish Baptist College, and at the Belfast Bible College Ron Evans was principal and Vic Reid a tutor. Reid would succeed to the principalship at Belfast and would later become principal of Redcliffe College. Among the LBC-trained staff at All Nations were Ron Davies and then Margaret Jones. Anne Long would make a significant contribution at St John's, Nottingham, in the areas of pastoralia and spirituality. George Mitchell, who had been part of the small but vocal Scottish contingent at LBC in the 1960s, had taken up a teaching post at the BTI in Glasgow. Another Scot, Ian Macnair, was at LBC from 1971 and three years later became a pastor in

---

[12] Edwards, *Lord, Make us One*, ch. 3.

Kirkwall, in the Orkney Islands. Macnair moved from there to the Birmingham Bible Institute and returned to LBC in 1983 as lecturer in Greek. Steve Brady left LBC in 1975 and his pastoral ministries included the East London Tabernacle and Lansdowne Baptist Church, Bournemouth. He completed a PhD as an LBC Laing scholar and using his mixture of experience was to become a lecturer and then principal at Moorlands College.

The LBC networks were also international. Ron Piper came to LBC in 1972 from an American Presbyterian background. He later became professor of New Testament at the University of St Andrew's in Scotland. Haward Beckett in Zimbabwe, Amos Udonsak in Nigeria, and John Barnett in Brazil, all former LBC students, took up principalship responsibilities. Students at LBC from the non-western world in the 1970s included Kwame Bediako, a Presbyterian from Ghana, and Ken Gnanakan, a Methodist from India. Both would become leading evangelical theologians and founders of theological centres. Bediako's seminal doctoral thesis, published as *Theology and Identity*, examined culture and Christian thought in the second century and in modern Africa. One chapter evaluated Byang Kato, who had been an LBC student. Bediako praised Kato for insisting on the centrality of the Bible, but criticized his conception of theology as a-cultural. For Bediako, this approach 'defeated the very purpose of theology as the struggle with culturally-rooted questions'.[13] Bediako's theological leadership was unusually cross-cultural. He established a centre for mission research and applied theology in Ghana, founded and became secretary of the Africa Theological Fraternity and became a director of the Oxford Centre for Mission Studies. He was also a research fellow of (Edinburgh's) Centre for the Study of Christianity in the Non-Western World.

LBC also wished to train women for leadership. As has been noted, this usually meant leadership in an overseas setting, and women students often ran missionary activities. Donald Guthrie, who believed that the contribution of women had been vital to the success of LBC, felt some incongruity between the responsible

---

[13] Bediako, *Theology*, xviii.

positions given to women missionaries and the restrictions often placed upon them in Britain.[14] During the first half of the 1970s Peggy Knight was the only female on the LBC staff. Her perception was that the place of women within the college was affirmed by faculty and students.[15] From its inception the college had trained women who became missionaries and teachers, but in the 1970s the college began to receive increasing numbers of applications from women who would take up ordained ministry. The best known of these was Elizabeth Canham, who was at LBC from 1970 to 1972. Canham became a lecturer at the Church Army's training college in London in 1974, and in 1981 she became associate rector at an Episcopal church in New Jersey, USA. Her ordination meant that she was the first Englishwoman to become an Anglican priest. She later provoked controversy by conducting an 'unauthorised' communion service at St Paul's Deanery in London.[16] Judith Rose, an LBC student from 1971 to 1973, had been a parish worker and was later to be involved in directing Anglican ordinands. In 1996 Rose became the Church of England's first female archdeacon – of Tonbridge, Kent.

An article by Gillian Cooke in *Areopagus* in 1972 queried whether LBC, as a college with 45 per cent women, was at that point taking the training of its female students seriously enough. Cooke argued that women were given relatively few responsibilities in the college, whether as student representatives or as leaders of evangelistic and other teams.[17] Judith Rose's experience was that LBC did not actively encourage pastoral leadership and associated teaching gifts in women. What the college did offer Rose, however, was a knowledge of theology and of evangelical life which enabled her to take up later ministerial opportunities.[18] In 1974 women students at LBC made it clear that they felt they

---

[14] Guthrie, *I Stand for Truth*, 48.

[15] Interview with Peggy Knight, 16 Jan. 1999.

[16] J. Field-Bibb, *Women towards Priesthood: Ministerial Politics and Feminist Praxis*, 296.

[17] G. Cooke, 'Why Women at London Bible College?' 3–4. Gillian was later ordained.

[18] J. Rose to the author, 18 Feb. 1999.

were being overlooked. Gilbert Kirby responded by announcing that he was intending to give a talk on women and ministry. His aim, as ever, was to encourage. As if to highlight the issue, at one of the intake interviews in 1975 seven of the 12 students accepted were women. Mary Evans, who had a background in education, graduated from LBC in 1975 and became first a tutorial assistant and then a lecturer. With Donald Guthrie's encouragement, Evans undertook research on the biblical approach to women's roles. Guthrie believed that the traditional belief in the subjugation of women needed re-examination. In the conclusion to her book *Woman in the Bible*, based on her MPhil thesis, Mary Evans argued for a 'drastic reappraisal of our whole outlook' on men and women working together in the church.[19]

Missionary Responsibility

This 'working together' was taking place in the area of evangelism and in other aspects of mission. When Billy Graham gave an address to LBC students in 1970 he entitled it 'The man God can use', but he made it clear that his message applied equally to men and women. For Graham, the person whom God could use in the presentation of the gospel was one who had an experience of Christ, a clear call, a regular devotional life, a relevant theology, an authoritative message and social concern. Towards the end of his address he issued a challenge to the student body. 'What would it be like', he asked, 'if 200 Spirit-filled people were unleashed on London. I mean men and women really filled with the Holy Spirit.'[20] Graham was appreciative of the work of LBC and in particular of the contribution of Gilbert Kirby. In 1994 Graham recalled an occasion when he had been about to speak but had been feeling tense about his lack of preparation. Kirby, who was also on the platform, realized this and offered Graham encouragement.[21]

---

[19] M. Evans, *Woman in the Bible*, 132.

[20] *C Rev* (Spring 1971), 14–19.

[21] Billy Graham to Steve Brady, 17 Oct. 1994, cited in Brady, 'Gilbert Kirby', 1.

Kirby was to commit himself to a number of international con-
gresses and other events related to evangelism both in Britain and in
other countries – especially other parts of Europe.

LBC itself continued to be a strongly international community.
In intake interviews held in mid-1975, for example, of 40 new
students accepted 16 were from outside Britain. They came from
Switzerland, Hong Kong, Denmark, South Africa, Rhodesia,
Norway, Malaysia, Switzerland, Kenya, Pakistan, Sri Lanka,
Indonesia, USA and Finland. LBC was undertaking training for
global mission, since most of these would return to their own
countries after their time at LBC. Yet the college was often
perceived as much more interested in preparing people for
ministry in the western world. Uncertainty about the precise role
of LBC as a centre for training missionaries and overseas leaders
grew somewhat around 1971 with the launch of All Nations
Christian College (ANCC), at Ware, which combined the
previous All Nations college with Mount Hermon and
Ridgelands colleges. All Nations, with 130 male and female
students taking its basic courses, soon established itself as a
significant centre for missionary training, and some missionary
thinkers saw the possibility of it offering postgraduate study.

Against this background, the LBC faculty discussed the
college's missionary responsibility at a meeting in December
1971. Harold Rowdon wanted closer connections with
missionary societies and also advocated stronger links between
LBC and theological colleges overseas, including exchange visits
of students and staff. Dermot McDonald saw LBC as offering
important research opportunities for those who had done their
undergraduate work in other countries.[22] Ernest Oliver of the
EMA, who had replaced John Savage as part-time missions
lecturer, found the student body responsive to mission
possibilities.[23] But there was an increasing feeling that a full-time
staff member to teach missiology was needed. Faculty members
stated that LBC was not being mentioned by missionary society

---

[22] Minutes of faculty meeting, 14 Dec. 1971.
[23] E. Oliver to the author, 19 Jan. 1999.

personnel officers as a college training missionaries, despite the fact that it was teaching the same subjects as those being offered in most missionary training colleges. Bruce Nicholls, who had studied at LBC and who was a theologian with a profound appreciation of the global scene, was approached about becoming a lecturer at the college, but he was committed to India. Peter Cotterell, who had enormous experience in Ethiopia, was appointed.

As part of a process of reappraisal, Harold Rowdon and John Balchin attended the 1973 EMA conference. It was hoped that as a result of such links there would be closer working relationships with some of the societies represented. There was a concern that the profile of overseas missionary societies needed to be raised among the student body. David Robinson, who would later become an Overseas Missionary Fellowship (OMF) field superintendent, wrote in LBC's *College Review* in 1971 about crises facing world mission. There existed, he argued, a crisis of finance, a crisis of dwindling church concern for world mission and a crisis of falling numbers of missionary personnel. The sights were then turned on LBC, with Robinson alleging that 'a certain number of the student body, though evangelical in faith and doctrine, appear to have almost no interest in world mission'. Although over a dozen leaving students in the previous year had gone overseas, that was out of 80 leavers.[24] A number of students in the later 1970s were to be challenged by world needs. John Chapman, for example, who entered LBC in 1977, went to Papua New Guinea. In the 1990s he was to become international director of Latin Link.

Those who went overseas as missionaries after having trained at LBC did not always move into positions of major mission leadership. Many served for decades without coming to the attention of the wider evangelical community. Each edition of the LBC Old Students' Association list contains names and addresses of large numbers of people working in a variety of roles throughout the

---

[24] *C Rev* (Summer 1971), 12–13.

non-western world. Some have had their ministry cut short, on occasions in tragic circumstances. Mary Fisher, who was an LBC student from 1971 to 1973, went to teach at a Pentecostal Mission School in Umtali, Rhodesia. She was a quiet person from an Elim background in Wales. Mary Fisher's missionary service lasted for five years. In June 1978 a group of terrorists attacked the missionary compound in Umtali and quite a number of people died or were injured. Among those seriously injured was Mary Fisher, who survived one week and died on 30 June 1978. It was, poignantly, the LBC graduation day. The sadness was deeply felt and a bursary fund was set up at LBC bearing Mary's name.[25]

Newer missionary agencies were growing in the 1970s, the best-known within LBC circles being Operation Mobilisation (OM), founded by a dynamic American, George Verwer. In the 1960s there had been some concern expressed by established missionary societies about the activities of OM's youthful teams, and John Savage had kept LBC informed of EMA deliberations on this topic.[26] By the early 1970s, however, evangelical leaders in general had come to appreciate OM's fast-growing international work. One student who entered LBC in 1971, Bill Musk, had previously spent eighty days in a Turkish gaol for undertaking evangelistic work in connection with OM. Musk later undertook scholarly missiological research and wrote on Islam. Richard Sharp, an OM leader, was at LBC in the mid-1970s, and several LBC students were joining OM teams. Another OM member, Peter Hill, was behind what Gilbert Kirby described as one of the largest demonstrations against moral decline ever undertaken by Christians in Britain – the Festival of Light. Hill was appalled at the low moral standards in Britain and began to plan a campaign culminating in a rally on 25 September 1972 in Trafalgar Square, followed by a march and concert in Hyde Park. At least sixty thousand people converged on London. In line with evangelical thinking, the

---

[25] D. Tidball to the author, 12 June 1999.
[26] Minutes of faculty meeting, 9 Dec. 1964.

concert turned into a massive evangelistic event, with cheering when Jesus was mentioned.[27]

In a personal review of the 1970s, Kirby drew attention to the influence of gospel concerts and gospel musicals, particularly those sponsored by Youth for Christ. He was impressed, too, by Jimmy and Carol Owens, with their musicals 'Come Together', 'If My People' and 'The Witness'. Kirby welcomed any initiatives which had the potential to bring evangelicalism into the public arena. Well-known figures such as Lord Longford and Malcolm Muggeridge, for example, supported the Festival of Light. But Kirby was less enthusiastic about some evangelistic ventures which drew evangelicals and non-evangelicals together. There was, for example, the 'Call to the North', first mooted in 1970 when Donald Coggan was Archbishop of York. The support for 'Call to the North' came from the whole spectrum of Christian faith – from Roman Catholics to Open Brethren. Many evangelicals, however, held aloof because there was no adequate doctrinal basis for evangelism, and in Kirby's view it was doubtful whether any significant impact was made on non-churchgoers. Nonetheless, Kirby was encouraged that in 1975 England had two archbishops – Donald Coggan and Stuart Blanch – who were known to be broadly evangelical in their sympathies.[28]

Conferences to consider evangelism across Europe and in Britain were held at Amsterdam in 1971 and at Morecambe in the following year. Kirby was actively involved on both occasions. The Amsterdam congress, Kirby considered, drew together diverse European evangelicals in larger numbers than ever before. There were thirteen hundred participants and observers from 35 countries, of whom half were lay people. Although Billy Graham delivered the keynote address, the other speakers were Europeans. Kirby himself gave the closing message, arguing the case for contemporary mission to take account of social changes.[29] A few months later Kirby reported at LBC on his

---

[27] *Crusade* (Sept. 1971), 24–5; (Nov. 1971), 1.

[28] G.W. Kirby, 'An Age of Ferment'.

[29] *Chr T* (24 Sept. 1971), 40–1.

attendance at the 'Strategy for Evangelism' congress at
Morecambe. He highlighted Tim Buckley's contribution to the
congress and noted the numbers of former LBC students
present.[30] This was a period when analysis of church growth was
becoming much more common. Kirby's view was that the 'church
growth movement', which had originated in America, needed to
be adapted to the British context. In the 1970s there was considerable interest in the possibility of LBC having a department of
applied theology that would specialize in such areas.[31] This
thinking was to develop further.

Mission and Socio-Political Action

The understanding of the nature of mission was also developing.
This was reflected in part by the way that the word 'mission' was
replacing 'evangelism'. The latter concept was still an extremely
important one for evangelicals, and in the 1970s their ideas
about evangelism influenced other sections of the church in
Britain. In 1976 a group of denominational leaders met with EA
leaders, and as a result a 'Nationwide Initiative in Evangelism'
was agreed. But developing evangelical thinking about the
kingdom of God saw the confining of the idea of mission to
'churchy' activities as unsatisfactory. An LBC survey showed
that 30 per cent of former students were in 'secular' occupations
such as social work. Reg Piesse, for example, worked as a
probation officer and a prison welfare officer, later becoming a
lecturer in sociology, and John Pearce became an inspector with
the probation service. Were they also in mission? Certainly
Kirby thought so. Others, such as Anne Carruthers, Bert Hearn
and Raymond Johnston (lecturing at the University of
Newcastle), were employed in higher education. Barbara Parfitt,
who left LBC in 1970, would become a professor of nursing in
Glasgow. Michael Eastman and Patrick Sookhdeo were among

---

[30] Minutes of a meeting of governors, 19 May 1972.
[31] Memorandum from the principal, 23 Feb. 1978.

those who highlighted issues of racial injustice through the Evangelical Race Relations Group. A more holistic concept of mission, embracing the socio-political dimensions of the gospel, was affecting British evangelical priorities.

This process of reappraisal was given considerable impetus by the Lausanne Congress in 1974. Donald Hoke, director of the congress, said before it took place that its goals were imparting vision and motivation for world evangelism; informing churches of strategies and methods; encouraging unity in evangelization; and identifying unreached people. Hoke stated that in his opinion Lausanne might be a 'bomb', and he pointed to the significance of the unprecedented Third World presence at the congress. One hundred and fifty nations were represented at Lausanne, and 1,200 of the 2,700 delegates were from the Third World.[32] But whereas Hoke was looking for an evangelistic explosion, what the congress experienced was a different kind of eruption, led by Samuel Escobar and René Padilla. These South Americans were seen as the most vocal advocates of evangelical social responsibility. A report on Lausanne by two LBC students highlighted precisely this issue. The Lausanne Covenant, as they saw it, would 'strongly influence a more balanced approach to world mission, for example, in its reaffirmation of the Christian's social responsibility, the recognition of culture, and a re-evaluation of our missionary responsibility in a growing partnership of Churches'.[33]

Gilbert Kirby attempted to ensure that the thinking of Lausanne was conveyed to LBC. His own role as a planner and a co-chair of the congress meant that he was at the heart of Lausanne. Derek Tidball, as LBC's director of evangelism, also attended. Twelve LBC students were present, including some who helped with the practical organization of the congress. A former LBC student, Chua Wee Hian, led the congress members in considering mission in some of the difficult places in the

---

[32] *Chr T* (15 March 1974), 12–16.

[33] *C Rev* (Autumn 1974), 10–11. Report by John Howell and Laurence Moscrop.

world. *Crusade* described 1974 as the year of the evangelicals – referring to Lausanne, the charismatic movement, the growth of SU and the Universities and Colleges Christian Fellowship (UCCF, formerly IVF), evangelical publishing, the role of evangelical theological colleges and the success of TEAR Fund.[34] The summer after Lausanne saw LBC acting as host to the executive of the Lausanne Continuation Committee, chaired by Bishop Jack Dain. LBC also welcomed the theological commission of the World Evangelical Fellowship. Kirby was keen to stress the role of former LBC students such as Bruce Nicholls, Byang Kato, Ken Gnanakan, John Langlois and Peter Savage in WEF. From 1992 Langlois, a leading lawyer and public figure in Guernsey, chaired WEF's religious liberty commission.[35]

One direct result of Lausanne was the 1977 launch of *Third Way* – a journal aiming to bring a biblical approach to current societal issues and working explicitly from the starting point of the Lausanne Covenant. The assistant editor of *Third Way*, Mary Endersbee, had been an LBC student in the 1960s, and a number of students from this period were now vigorously pursuing the radical discipleship agenda. At Lausanne a Radical Discipleship Group had suggested that the congress' position on social responsibility did not go far enough, and this perspective was to gain more adherents. In Britain the Shaftesbury Project, which had associations with IVF, came into existence in 1969 to encourage evangelical thinking and action directed towards society. Gilbert Kirby and Fred Catherwood (who was to set out his views on the social order in *A Better Way*) were two of the four project trustees. But Derek Tidball believed that evangelical leaders needed to address more seriously questions about women in society, political devolution, housing and unemployment.[36] One contribution to this discussion which was extremely influential was *Rich Christians in an Age of Hunger* (1977), by an American Mennonite, Ron Sider. The writings of another

---

[34] *Crusade* (Nov. 1974), 7.

[35] *C Rev* (Autumn 1975), 5.

[36] *C Rev* (Autumn 1976). Review of *A Better Way*.

Mennonite, J.H. Yoder, were also important. Indeed, by 1977 the literature on social issues was such that Tidball was able to produce a wide-ranging survey of 'Contemporary Evangelical Social Thinking'.[37]

In a comment on increased social action, Gilbert Kirby reflected on the fact that some were fearful that evangelicals would fall into the same trap as the 'liberals' of the 1920s and 1930s and embrace a 'social gospel'. But Kirby believed that what was happening represented a welcome turning of the tide, with evangelicals showing proper social concern.[38] His own position on matters such as race and world poverty was clear. Given the way fears about other races were being stirred up – Enoch Powell was speaking about 'the new enemy in our midst' – it was vital for evangelicals to make a vigorous response.[39] Kirby supported the EA's work in creating a study group to discuss race relations. On the question of world poverty he applauded TEAR Fund for its investment in development projects. By the later 1970s TEAR Fund's income was approaching £2 million. In addition, the work of the Festival of Light (then under the direction of Raymond Johnston) was seen by Kirby as contributing to evangelical social awareness. Kirby considered that papers at the Nottingham Anglican Conference in 1977 on 'Obeying Christ in a Changing World' included both conservative thinking and social radicalism.[40] At the radical end was a fringe meeting at Nottingham on urban mission which was organized by Michael Eastman and which was to produce the Evangelical Coalition for Urban Mission (ECUM).[41]

---

[37] D.J. Tidball, *Contemporary Evangelical Social Thinking – A Review*. This was the Shaftesbury Project's first published monograph.

[38] *LF* (17 April 1971), 3.

[39] *Crusade* (Aug. 1970), 6.

[40] Kirby, 'Ferment'. In 1978 there was an evangelical consultation on social ethics at High Leigh.

[41] I am indebted to Michael Eastman for the unpublished paper, 'The ECUM Story' (1991).

Integrating Charismatic Developments

New directions were also evident within the charismatic movement. The first Roman Catholic renewal groups in Britain met in 1970, with Cardinal Suenens, primate of Belgium, supporting the movement. After an international charismatic conference in Guildford in July 1971, which brought together Protestants and Catholics, *Crusade* ventured the opinion that 'neo-Pentecostalism' had become 'the most important single development in British church life since the War; possibly this century'.[42] As Gilbert Kirby analysed the development of this movement up to the end of the 1970s, he recognized its 'profound effect on church life in Britain'. He identified three crucial characteristics: the rediscovery and use of spiritual gifts; the enjoyment of fellowship at a deeper level in the local church; and greater liberty in worship. There had, he suggested, been unfortunate excesses and schisms, but many churches and leaders had experienced genuine renewal.[43] The main impact was felt within Anglican and Baptist life, but in 1977 one-third of the speakers at a Fountain Trust conference were Catholic. Tom Smail, a Presbyterian minister who became a leading Anglican theologian, took over the general secretaryship of the trust from Michael Harper. The trust disbanded in 1980, the idea being that renewal would move into the denominations. Harper himself subsequently became an Orthodox priest.[44]

The charismatic influence at LBC became more pronounced in the early 1970s. In 1971 it was noted in faculty discussions that there were sizeable numbers of 'Pentecostalists' in the college, particularly among the younger women.[45] Three years later, Kirby proposed that Donald Bridge from Frinton-on-Sea, Essex, should be approached to come and speak on the subject of spiritual gifts and offer 'a balanced presentation of this aspect of

---

[42] *Crusade* (Sept. 1971), 1.
[43] Kirby, 'Ferment'.
[44] M.C. Harper, *The True Light*.
[45] Minutes of faculty meeting, 24 Feb. 1971.

truth'.[46] The charismata were now being acknowledged as biblical, which was something of a contrast with a decade before when a book defending the Pentecostal view of tongues was initially placed in the 'Christian Deviations' section of the library.[47] When Max Turner was appointed in 1974 to the LBC staff – as librarian, but with teaching responsibilities in the area of New Testament – he began to attend a charismatic prayer group organized by the students. Turner's formative Christian experience had included a year spent at a college led by Richard Bolt, the pioneer of the Students' Pentecostal Fellowship.[48] From 1974 Kirby's own church, an independent evangelical church in Roxeth Green where he was honorary pastor, felt the impact of renewal. Frank Gamble, who had entered LBC in 1971 as a Baptist, joined Kirby at Roxeth and introduced a 'charismatic style of worship, replete with tongues and prophecies'.[49]

Charismatics were, however, far from being the dominant group at LBC in the mid-1970s. There were 220 students enrolled in 1974–75 and only a small minority were to become leaders within the charismatic movement. Nonetheless, LBC became a place where charismatics, denominational Pentecostals and non-charismatics were able to exchange opinions. The contribution of older Pentecostalism was important: in January–February 1974, six students who were accepted as a result of the interview process were from Pentecostal denominations. Pentecostal students in the 1970s included Lyndon Bowring, who was on the leadership team at Elim's Kensington Temple, became involved in the Festival of Light and was to become chief executive of its successor, Christian Action, Research and Education (CARE). At the same time, the impact of the 'house church' movement, or Restorationism (restoring the New Testament church), was beginning to be felt. In *Restoring the Kingdom*, Andrew Walker

---

[46] Minutes of faculty meeting, 13 Feb. 1974.
[47] The book was moved to the Holy Spirit section after protests were made. I am indebted to Tony Sargent for this information.
[48] Interview with Max Turner, 16 Jan. 1999.
[49] Brady, 'Gilbert Kirby', 13.

has traced the story of Restorationism and the divisions which marked its development.[50] The leadership of this stream in the early 1970s had its focus in the 'London Brothers', which included Gerald Coates (in Cobham) and Terry Virgo, both of whom would attract students from LBC into their enterprises. An important shop window was the Capel Bible Week, held at the Elim Bible College, which was run by a committee that included George Tarleton, who had been at LBC in the mid-1960s.[51]

Gilbert Kirby made efforts to keep in touch with the thinking of Gerald Coates and of Bryn Jones, a Welshman based in Bradford. He considered they were having a crucial influence in the 1970s on charismatic groups outside the main-line denominations. Michael Harper, in 1976, saw what was happening as the emergence of a new denomination, and spoke of 'the baneful history of schism repeating itself'.[52] Tim Brawn, an LBC student from 1973 to 1976, invited Coates to speak at LBC, and for a time Brawn worked with Coates.[53] Another student, Steve Clifford (originally FIEC), also joined Coates, while David Holden (originally Baptist), who left LBC in 1977, aligned himself with Terry Virgo. *Restoration* magazine, dedicated to the spread of the Restorationist vision, began in 1975. It was edited by Bryn Jones, who had been influenced by Pentecostalism, and by Arthur Wallis, whose background was Open Brethren. By that stage the new movement was itself diversifying. In 1976 Jones launched the Dales Bible Week, which within two years was attracting nine thousand people to the Great Yorkshire Showground in Harrogate. In 1977 Virgo started monthly Bible Days in Hove, Sussex, and these developed into the Downs Bible Week. Virgo became an editorial associate of *Restoration*. The impact of this charismatic upsurge in the later 1970s was, inevitably, felt in LBC.

[50] A. Walker, *Restoring the Kingdom*, esp. chs. 2–5.
[51] George Tarleton was to sever his connections with the movement. See Walker, *Kingdom*, 286–8.
[52] *Crusade* (March 1976), 29.
[53] G. Coates, *An Intelligent Fire*, 97.

In November 1976 the LBC faculty discussed the style of worship in college chapel. There was at the time, as the staff saw it, a 'strong charismatic element' in the student body and student leaders of the services were seeking to handle the situation. It was agreed that staff would consider the nature of worship at a college gathering in the spring.[54] Kirby, a natural bridge-builder, appreciated the fact that the 'house church movement' was to some extent a legitimate protest against unduly institutionalized church structures, but he was disappointed at the proliferation of 'splinter groups'. He was also concerned about those within the new movement who were emphasizing authority and oversight – what became known as the shepherding movement – and who were, in his view, tending to rob individuals of their right of private judgement.[55] The activities of a few over-zealous charismatic students in the college – for example, pressure was put on some students to receive prayer for charismatic experiences – led the faculty, in November 1977, to stress the need for 'balance in worship and in all aspects of College activity'. The strong charismatic stance that characterized 'certain quarters' of the student body was, it was observed, affecting chapel services to a considerable extent and it was decided that in the autumn term members of the faculty would alternate with visiting speakers in leading main devotional occasions.[56]

Yet Kirby was not seeking to dampen down genuine spiritual experience. Kirby invited David Pawson, a charismatic leader within Baptist circles, to speak at LBC on the current work of the Holy Spirit. Kirby was encouraged at the way renewal was being accepted within the major denominations. In July 1977, following the Nottingham Anglican conference, John Stott suggested (somewhat optimistically) that controversy over the charismatic movement was now past.[57] A few months later Douglas McBain met with Raymond Brown, principal of Spurgeon's College, and

---

[54] Minutes of faculty meeting, 3 Nov. 1976.
[55] Kirby, 'Ferment'.
[56] Minutes of faculty meeting, 23 Nov. 1977.
[57] *Chr T* (8 July 1977), 31.

Paul Beasley-Murray, who would succeed Brown as principal, to discuss forming a group within the BU committed to reformation and renewal. Seven hundred people attended the launch of this group, Mainstream, a year later, and the editorial in *Crusade* suggested that the inaugural meeting indicated how charismatic renewal was bringing dynamism to the whole church.[58] At the same time, however, Bryn Jones was arguing not for denominational renewal but for a 'move of God that will restore the apostles, the prophets, the evangelists, pastors and teachers'.[59] In similar vein, Terry Virgo stated that churches 'not open to the manifestation of the Holy Spirit' had to be prepared to lose members to fellowships providing 'proper scriptural oversight'.[60] Sharply contrasting charismatic directions were evident.

Church Relations

Although new Restorationist groups emerged in the 1970s, the denominational mix at LBC did not alter to any significant degree. With two exceptions – Gilbert Kirby and Owen Thomas – the LBC staff who were ordained ministers were Baptists, although staff who were not ordained contributed to a more varied denominational mix. As before, Baptists remained the largest group within the student body, followed by Anglicans. There were more students from independent groups, reflecting the growth in independency within evangelicalism in the 1960s. Some students identified themselves as belonging to two denominations (e.g. Open Brethren/Baptist), which indicated the greater ease of movement across denominational boundaries. Although there was a continuing Brethren presence in LBC – Clive Calver, for example, was listed as Brethren when he entered college – this was declining. Reservations expressed in 1971 about a suggestion from Owen Thomas to place a 'Christian symbol' (a cross) in the

---

[58] McBain, *Fire*, 82–5; *Crusade* (June 1979), 5.
[59] *Restoration* (July/Aug. 1978), 11.
[60] *Restoration* (Nov./Dec. 1978), 13.

LBC chapel highlighted a persistent conservatism, probably due in part to Brethren influence. It was decided to display a biblical text instead. By the end of the 1970s, Brethren numbers were reckoned to be falling quite rapidly and the death of John Laing in 1978 marked the passing of a unique Brethren figure. At a Brethren conference at Swanwick in autumn 1978 Michael Griffiths, then general director of OMF and soon to be principal-designate of LBC, warned Brethren against leadership by 'geriatric generals'.[61]

A different kind of crisis was facing the Baptist denomination in the early 1970s. In 1971 Michael Taylor, principal of the Northern Baptist College, gave an address at the BU assembly on the theme 'How much of a man was Jesus Christ?' The content of this address, with its apparent questioning of orthodox Christology, provoked a huge reaction from conservative evangelicals. The BRF, at its annual conference in Swanwick, made this forthright statement: 'We cannot in conscience remain associated with the life of a Union which has decided to tolerate the denial of the deity of our Lord Jesus Christ.'[62] In January 1972 there was a meeting of over one hundred Baptists, 82 of whom were ministers, to discuss the possibility of a new fellow-ship of evangelical Baptist churches. Many of the ministers had been affected by calls in the 1960s to leave mixed denominations. At the 1972 BU assembly a resolution was passed – by 1,800 votes to 46, with 72 abstentions – which insisted that Christ was 'truly God and truly man'. But by the end of 1972 a new Association of Evangelical Baptist Churches had been formed, with Keith Mawdsley (a student at LBC in the 1950s) acting as its secretary. At least forty churches left the BU, including West Street, Crewe, where James Wood was minister. Wood was a contemporary of Mawdsley's at LBC in the 1950s and had become a BRF leader.[63]

---

[61] 'Brethren in Crisis', *Crusade* (Nov. 1978).

[62] McBain, *Fire*, 62.

[63] *Ev T* (Feb. 1972), 1; (Nov. 1972), 1.

Many Baptist ministers who trained at LBC were, however, committed to staying within the Baptist Union. Among these ministers was Bill Hancock, later the BU's head of ministry, who went to Mount Pleasant, Northampton, in 1969. At a meeting with the Mount Pleasant deacons, Hancock told them what he felt he could offer the church and one deacon said it was 'time they got back to the Bible'. Before the call was formally issued, Ernest Payne, the former BU general secretary, met with Hancock – ostensibly to talk about the church but also to assess Hancock's denominational loyalty. Payne was satisfied, and at Hancock's induction service Payne led worship and Gilbert Kirby preached.[64] Other figures from the LBC network who were to be influential within the BU included Douglas McBain, Derek Tidball and Paul Mortimore. From 1968 to 1982 McBain was minister of Lewin Road, Streatham. This was followed by itinerant ministry before he became London superintendent and then, in 1998, BU president. Tidball, after eight years on the full-time LBC staff, returned to Baptist pastoral ministry, at Mutley Baptist Church, Plymouth. He was BU president in 1990–91, then took the post of secretary for evangelism and mission, and became LBC principal four years later.

The other major denomination with significant representation at LBC was the Church of England. Methodists and members of the United Reformed Church (created in 1972 by the union of Congregational and Presbyterian churches) formed a relatively small section of the LBC student body. In 1977 Kirby was pleased to mention two former students (from the 1950s) who had made their mark in the Anglican world. He congratulated David Wheaton, principal of Oak Hill College, on becoming a canon of St Albans Cathedral, and Michael Baughen and his colleagues at All Souls, Langham Place, on their magnificent new premises. Kirby was delighted that LBC embraced 'Anglicans and Baptists, Charismatics and non-Charismatics, Methodists and Brethren, those who can happily subscribe to the five points of Calvinism and those who feel unable to do so'.[65] Indeed, surveys of evangelical

---

[64] W.C.R. Hancock to the author, 9 April 1998.
[65] *C Rev* (Autumn 1976), 5; (Spring 1977), 6–7.

diversity became a feature of Kirby's writings. In 1978 he published *Too Hot to Handle*, a book seeking to promote mutual tolerance among evangelicals. A review in the *Christian Graduate* welcomed the way Kirby put 'charity before polemics', but regretted 'a certain prosaic reductionism' in his handling of theological debates, suggesting that Kirby was 'so afraid of tramping on people's toes that he scarcely leaves a footprint of his own'.[66]

One denomination with which LBC had minimal contact was the Roman Catholic Church. Kirby was aware of the increasing interest in Bible reading among lay Catholics and of the appeal to Scripture by theologians such as Hans Küng. The issue of whether Roman Catholics could be admitted to LBC was problematic in the early 1970s. Faculty members received an application in 1970 from Sister Alphonsus to complete a BD. Although she was willing to set out her experience of Christ and was able to agree in general with LBC's basis of faith, she said that she would be bound to add the authority of the Church to that of Scripture. The faculty members were divided, some thinking she could be accepted and others worried about how this would be perceived. 'Somewhat reluctantly', the minutes recorded, 'it was decided not to accept the candidate'.[67] Two years later, when a young Roman Catholic was interviewed, Donald Guthrie argued in favour of accepting her. He suggested that some students might be able to come to LBC without being full-time college members.[68] Others were unconvinced, and the faculty found that several of the student committee opposed accepting a Roman Catholic. Again, apparently with some reluctance, the applicant was rejected 'in her own interests'.[69]

Attitudes were, however, changing. A few members of LBC's TSF group visited a London Catholic centre serving the White Fathers (missionaries to Africa), and there was a request from the

---

[66] *Chr Grad* (Dec. 1978), 38. The reviewer of *Too Hot to Handle* was David Hempton.

[67] Minutes of faculty meeting, 18 March 1970.

[68] Minutes of faculty meeting, 31 May 1972.

[69] Minutes of faculty meeting, 23 June 1972.

White Fathers for preachers from LBC. Some of the faculty indicated a willingness to speak there in an individual capacity.[70] In 1974 Don Ford, who had left LBC in 1970, reported from South America on the changing face of Catholicism. He argued that it was 'incumbent upon evangelical Christians to think positively about Catholicism', and he spoke about 'evangelical Catholics' who had 'come into a genuine, personal knowledge of the Lord Jesus Christ'.[71] Kirby, despite his broad sympathies, did not hesitate to highlight traditional Roman Catholic practices, such as the mass and the veneration of the Virgin Mary, which were unacceptable to those in the Reformed tradition. But Kirby saw strengths in more eucharistic forms of worship, welcoming the way the liturgical movement had emphasized the need for the Lord's Supper to be given a more central place. When Timothy Tierney, a Carmelite friar, applied to LBC in 1977, he was accepted as a full-time (though technically 'visiting') student. Tierney had been introduced to LBC by an Ulster Protestant whom he knew through a local charismatic prayer group.[72]

Spiritual Formation

The issues raised by charismatic renewal and by broader traditions of Christian spirituality had implications for LBC as a place of spiritual formation. A number of discussions took place in 1973 and 1974 about questions of spirituality. There was a general feeling that students needed to be reminded that LBC was not a university but a Christian training college. The college was becoming more informal – for example, in 1972 it was decided that the wearing of gowns was becoming anachronistic and this rule was discontinued – but there was a concern to ensure that standards of behaviour and levels of commitment were maintained. Character training was discussed at faculty meetings.

---

[70] Minutes of faculty meeting, 7 June 1971.

[71] *Chr Grad* (March 1974), 9; (June 1974), 41.

[72] I am indebted to Tony Lane for this information.

Students were encouraged to be committed to the small fellow-ship groups to which each student was allocated. Within each group was a member of staff. The faculty also agreed that, com-pared to two decades before, many students had much less grounding in basic biblical knowledge. *Areopagus* attempted to fill this gap with a guide to the *lingua franca* of Zion – explaining, for example, that 'in this corner of thy vineyard' meant 'here'.[73] In a more substantial response, the faculty decided that in the 1974 autumn term tutors taking chapel should offer instruction in basic Christian living. In addition, it was emphasized that the limited number of college rules should be properly observed.[74]

Consideration of these issues continued. As a result of reflection by faculty members in 1976 on the relationship of theological training to spiritual life, Frank Lake, who was well known for his pioneering work in 'Clinical Theology', was invited to speak to the faculty. He talked about his experience in counselling ministers and theological students (including those suffering from depression), describing his approach as biblical and experiential. Lake stressed the need for people to come to know and to come to terms with themselves.[75] Although some evangelicals regarded Lake with suspicion, this talk generated interest in the area of counselling and a wish on the part of some to take the matter further. Accordingly, five faculty members and two faculty wives attended a short weekend course led by Lake. It was felt that certain students would benefit from such a course, and Anne Long, a former LBC student who had worked with Lake, was booked to come to LBC and lead a group which would focus on clinical theology. In addition, Ruth Fowke, whose field was psychiatry and who would later write on personality and prayer, came to the college to speak on coping

---

[73] *Areopagus* (Dec. 1972). This issue carried English translations of 'Zionese'.

[74] Minutes of faculty meeting, 24 April 1974.

[75] Minutes of faculty meeting, 21 April 1976; for Lake see J. Peters, *Frank Lake: The Man and His Work* (London: Darton, Longman & Todd, 1989).

with crisis. There were hopes for an LBC course in pastoral care and counselling.

As always, Gilbert Kirby emphasized spiritual balance. He repudiated, in an article in 1977, the views of those who said that evangelicals needed 'not doctrine but experience', and argued strongly for the rigours of intellectual theological training. But Kirby also insisted he was 'acutely aware of the dangers of a coldly intellectual approach to the Christian faith'. Quoting from a Keswick speaker of an earlier generation, Guy King, he pleaded for the partnership of head and heart. 'A visitor to our Theological Study week in the summer vacation', Kirby reported, 'remarked to me that what most impressed him was that men of undoubtedly high intellectual calibre nevertheless were men of true faith.'[76] The college was not yet, however, giving a central place to spirituality. The Keswick influence at LBC was less marked by the 1970s, although Alex Ross, an Anglican, Alistair Begg, Steve Brady and Ian Coffey were among former students who became Keswick speakers. Ross spoke of how LBC had shown him 'the power of God's word to transform and equip us for ministry'.[77] David Wells, then at Trinity Evangelical Divinity School, Deerfield, Illinois, was arguing for reflective spirituality – what he called 'Musing on God's Ways'.[78] Approaches to spirituality and personal formation were introduced in lectures given at LBC by a psychotherapist, Myra Chave-Jones.

An important aspect of the changing attitude to spirituality on the part of evangelicals was a new outlook on 'the world'. The field of the arts, for example, which had long been a no-go area for many evangelicals, was now increasingly seen as a vocation. The Arts Centre Group was launched in 1971 and later expanded, with Cliff Richard, Roy Castle and Thora Hird among its best-known supporters. The Greenbelt Festival, which began in 1974 and owed a great deal to John Peck, also encouraged a more holistic perspective on spirituality. In 1975, John Stott retired

---

[76] *C Rev* (Autumn 1977), 6–7.
[77] Alex Ross to the author, 1 Dec. 1998.
[78] *Chr T* (29 Sept. 1972), 16–18.

from All Souls and gave more time to the London Institute for Contemporary Christianity – another indication of renewed evangelical commitment to engagement with the world. Early in 1979 Stott was asked to talk to the LBC faculty. He suggested three areas requiring particular attention from evangelical educators: theology, the knowledge of which was often too superficial; pastoralia, in particular the standard of preaching; and spirituality, since the aim of any Bible college should primarily be to produce men and women of God. As a result of these discussions a planning committee was set up to look at directions for the 1980s.[79] In addition, Kirby produced a paper, 'The question of spirituality', which examined discipleship and church life.[80]

Educational and Theological Developments

In 1977, in an appraisal of LBC, Gilbert Kirby noted that the college was in a period of transition. He highlighted the longer-term potential of newer members of staff, particularly Max Turner, Tony Lane, who lectured in historical theology, and Peter Cotterell, director of overseas studies. These staff were to be significant for the college's standing. Two other newer staff members, Douglas de Lacey, lecturer in New Testament and Greek, and Richard Sturch, in philosophy, were to move on.[81] Donald Guthrie was, said Kirby, 'a scholar of international repute and far better known than anyone else'. Reflecting on charges that LBC was too academic, Kirby suggested that such accusations were inevitable. He wished the college to offer quality practical training while also continuing to be 'unashamedly academic'. In a follow-up paper, he predicted that in the 1980s fewer LBC students would come from very conservative evangelical churches, whether Anglican or Free Church, and that most would come from churches 'which to a greater or lesser

---

[79] Minutes of academic board, 14 March 1979.
[80] Minutes of academic board, 25 April 1979.
[81] Two decades later Richard Sturch won the UK Mastermind contest.

extent have been caught up in the renewal movement'. As Kirby looked forward to the appointment of a new principal he believed that the college would need someone who commanded the respect of evangelicals generally and who could lead LBC into a new phase.[82]

A highly important aspect of this new phase was LBC's move in the early 1970s from the London University BD to the CNAA's BA degree. LBC was the first evangelical college to make the move to CNAA accreditation, which gave LBC freedom in planning its own syllabus. External exams were phased out. In 1972, 39 LBC students enrolled for the new BA, as against 24 for the BD in the previous year. There was CNAA pressure for LBC to increase staffing, and this led to Tony Lane's appointment. Gilbert Kirby wanted each student to take homiletics, mission studies, pastoral theology, Christian education and psychology. Derek Tidball suggested that in the vocational area LBC compared unfavourably with other colleges, and in the mid-1970s students expressed worries about the academic approach. The possibility of more vocational training was considered. The college was by then using the Cambridge Diploma/Certificate and there were suggestions that eventually it might design its own LBC Diploma Course.[83] It was only in the 1990s that this direction was to be successfully pursued. CNAA validation was renewed for another five years in 1977, by which time CNAA observed that LBC could properly be 'regarded as a pacemaker for other institutions developing similar courses'.[84] The CNAA visitors, Kirby reported, were impressed by the imaginative way Cotterell and Tidball had presented vocational training.[85]

Within the world of academic theology there was talk in the mid-1970s of evangelical scholarship coming of age. A number of LBC staff, such as Tony Lane, John Balchin and Max Turner,

---

[82] G.W. Kirby, 'An Appraisal of LBC'; G.W. Kirby, 'Social Trends in the 1980s' (both unpublished papers, 1980).

[83] Minutes of academic board, 9 Jan. 1979.

[84] Minutes of faculty meeting, 28 Sept. 1977.

[85] *C Rev* (Autumn 1977), 7.

were completing research degrees in the 1970s, and the fruits of new theological enquiry were to be found in articles in *Vox Evangelica*. The CNAA view was that staff should be given adequate time for research. On the wider academic front, it was estimated that there were now around thirty evangelicals holding academic theological posts in British universities, a huge change from the immediate post-war years. The best-known British evangelical academic, F.F. Bruce, an external examiner for LBC and the first Laing lecturer in 1971, mused that in the 1940s he had been seen as somewhat radical in IVF circles but was now considered fairly conservative.[86] Evangelical theology was treated rather dismissively in *Fundamentalism* (1977), by James Barr, who claimed to have undertaken a review of evangelical literature. 'This', said John Stott, was 'a false claim', since reputable scholars such as Bruce had been virtually ignored.[87] One student who left LBC in 1970, Paul Avis, was exhilarated to discover while at LBC larger dimensions of theology and in particular how the Reformers emphasized the catholicity of the church. Avis was to become a prolific writer on a range of theological issues and also general secretary of the Council for Christian Unity of the Church of England, a position in which he could use his broad sympathies to work for ecumenical understanding.[88]

Despite LBC's progress, there was no room for complacency. The educational world was continuing to change and there was a danger that evangelical colleges might be left behind. Sir Eric Richardson encouraged the use of video equipment for communications training at LBC. In 1972 students criticized some lecturers for giving material in their lectures that could easily be obtained from textbooks. In some cases lecturing was at dictation speed, and there was a suggestion that if the college purchased a

---

[86] *Crusade* (April 1976), 40. The Laing lecture has since become an annual event in the LBC calendar.

[87] *Chr T* (8 Sept. 1978), 44.

[88] I am grateful to Paul Avis for his comments. *Areopagus*, in autumn 1968, carried an article by Avis which drew attention to the importance of the creeds and the works of Augustine and Calvin.

photocopier then summary notes could be copied and distributed. There was also a request for more seminar discussion. Faculty members were asked to seek to remedy the situation where applicable, but in 1978 there were continued comments about the inadequacy of the method of dictating notes in lectures and suggestions that synopses could be provided. Justin Dennison, who was the student academic affairs representative (and who would go on to Baptist ministries in England and Canada), conveyed the feelings of students that the faculty could make more imaginative use of modern teaching aids such as overhead projectors. The faculty accepted the points made.

The need to be contemporary and technologically up to date became more pressing as the college's involvement in delivering theological education took new forms. Moira Anderson, the registrar of the extension department, reported in 1978 on the scale of LBC's correspondence, evening class, weekend and summer courses. In a single year, 840 new correspondence course students – including blind students using Braille – had been enrolled.[89] Weekend workshops in practical theology could attract up to one hundred participants and summer schools drew even larger numbers. Some of these events were aimed at ministers. LBC was also keen to develop further its links with the world of education. The Association of Christian Teachers, created by the ISCF and two other organizations, was launched in 1971. Conferences were arranged at LBC for Scripture specialists in schools, for university students and for sixth formers. Theological education was moving to a point where skills as well as knowledge were taught. Experience, and reflection upon it, was now being seen in the broader theological world as an integral part of applied theology.

Many theological developments were creative, but issues were also raised that caused tensions for LBC. On 9 January 1980 Gilbert Kirby shared with the faculty the letter of 13 December 1979 that had been received from 18 former students – mostly pastors of independent churches within the Reformed

---

[89] *C Rev* (Autumn 1978), 21.

constituency – alleging that the college had left its original theo-logical position. In what he felt was a scriptural approach, Kirby first attempted to deal with this privately, writing on 20 December 1979 to Michael Buss, the first signatory to the letter. Kirby expressed to Buss his sense of personal hurt at the insinua-tion 'that the College has gone to pieces theologically during the period of my Principalship' and he insisted that 'my own position in relation to Scripture and the truths contained therein is every bit as conservative as that of my predecessor'. The accusation was also made in the 13 December letter that the college had ceased to be a handmaid of the churches and had become an innovator. In Kirby's view LBC had been innovative from the beginning, as an institution that was evangelical and academic, and he could not see that this was a matter for condemnation.[90] The faculty agreed with Kirby that the letter was badly constructed, contained broad generalizations and offered no concrete evidence.[91]

The accusations were not entirely new. Concerns about LBC's theological stance had been raised by John Waite, a former LBC staff member, writing a review in the *Evangelical Times* of Leslie Allen's 1976 commentary on Jonah. In his introduction to the book of Jonah, Allen suggested that there might well be 'a histori-cal nucleus behind the story', but argued that its form was that of a parable.[92] Waite said in his review that he was profoundly disturbed and saddened by this interpretation. He saw scholar-ship being pursued at the expense of confidence in Scripture as 'the inerrant Word of God'.[93] Kirby was well aware of the views of the Reformed constituency. With the backing of Martyn Lloyd-Jones, the London Theological Seminary, a college which embodied Lloyd-Jones' opposition to sitting examinations, was launched in 1977. At its opening Lloyd-Jones spoke of the 'fatal mistake' that Bible colleges (LBC was not mentioned but was surely in mind) had made in allowing curricula to be determined

---

[90] G.W. Kirby to M. Buss, 20 Dec. 1979.
[91] Minutes of academic board, 9 Jan. 1980.
[92] L.C. Allen, *The Books of Joel, Obadiah, Jonah and Micah*, 179.
[93] *Ev T* (April 1979), 10–11.

by 'the liberal outlook' and he described examinations in biblical knowledge as 'almost blasphemous'.[94] In fact, LBC was by this time shaping its own courses and methods of assessment. Nor was the teaching at LBC out of line with wider evangelical scholarship. Leslie Allen's commentaries on Joel, Obadiah, Jonah and Micah were in an evangelical commentary series and the editor, R.K. Harrison, did not query what Allen wrote.

Gilbert Kirby, although he felt keenly attacks on himself and Leslie Allen – the slogan 'Allen must go' was used – was determined, as he said to Allen, not to yield to the pressure of an unrepresentative minority. On the other hand, Kirby was insistent that the college should not be stranded on the liberal wing of evangelical thought. In typical Kirby style, it was agreed that Allen be asked to take care to present 'a balanced view' in his lectures and writings.[95] In the aftermath of this controversy, Gilbert Kirby suggested to Leslie Allen that he might be better suited to university work. This disappointed Allen. Although he did follow up some possibilities of this nature, he was in fact committed to continuing to teach Bible college students. Later Gilbert Kirby moved Leslie Allen to teaching Hebrew, Aramaic and Judaism. The move was made in part to ease tensions still being felt over the Jonah affair. If Allen no longer had the responsibility for Old Testament lecturing at LBC it was possible that the criticisms being made about the approach to the Bible being promulgated at the college would lose their force.[96] The evangelical diversity that had been such a feature of Kirby's policy had been strained to the limit.

Conclusion

LBC both grew and changed in the 1970s. Numbers in one year reached 232 students and there was discussion about the likely

---

[94] D.M. Lloyd-Jones, *Training for the Ministry Today*, 5, 9.

[95] Minutes of a meeting of governors, 25 Jan. 1980.

[96] L. Allen to the author, 7 July 1999.

growth of the college to 250. LBC was recognized as a theological facility that was producing increasing numbers of evangelical leaders at a time when evangelicalism was grappling with new challenges to its thinking – socio-political, charismatic and ecumenical. Kirby argued in 1977 that LBC stood where it had always done in regard to Scripture, but he also showed a willingness to respond to the need for change, especially in areas such as the practical aspects of education. Kirby was determined to ensure that the college was up to date. Under his leadership its style became more informal, with the faculty ethos being affected by younger staff. Students were seen increasingly as adults with their own insights to offer. As a small indicator of change, 1975 saw the abandonment of high table for the faculty. After discussions, Kirby simply decided that he would not sit at high table himself, and the system collapsed. Dermot McDonald spoke of Kirby as a 'thoughtful, congenial and informed leader' who did not expect from others what he would not share.[97]

A number of those with whom Kirby shared leadership left or retired during the 1970s. Dermot McDonald, having been LBC's vice-principal since 1958, retired in 1975 at a time when he was still at the height of his writing powers. Owen Thomas and his wife Peggy, who had given much pastoral care to LBC students, moved in 1976, returning to pastoral ministry. J. Clement Connell retired two years later. New staff members brought fresh approaches – something Kirby relished. When Leslie Allen's views were criticized, however, Kirby as well as Allen found it deeply painful. It was important to LBC, as the governors put it in their discussions, that the impression should not be given that more liberal views were to be preferred to more conservative views. At the same time, the letter replying to those who were critical of Allen, an important letter which was approved and signed by Derek Warren as board chairman, said that LBC 'respects the integrity of its Faculty'. Despite the pressure, Allen remained a member of the faculty, by contrast with the crises in

---

[97] H.D. McDonald to Steve Brady, 18 Aug. 1994, cited in Brady, 'Gilbert Kirby', 15.

the 1950s and 1960s when H.L. Ellison and Ralph Martin had not been able to continue at LBC because of their views. By the 1970s LBC had greater theological confidence, and the letter from Warren insisted that within the parameters of the conservative evangelical view of Scripture, LBC allowed 'freedom of expression'.[98]

---

[98] Minutes of a meeting of governors, 25 Jan. 1980; letter from Derek Warren dated 25 Jan. 1980.

9

'A More Goal-Orientated Model' 1980–90

During the 1980s LBC was to move on from the issue of freedom of academic expression and was to concentrate more on the way in which theology was to be applied. In 1980, following the retirement of Gilbert Kirby, Michael Griffiths became LBC's third principal. In his book *Shaking the Sleeping Beauty* (1980), which was designed to help in arousing the church to mission, Griffiths spoke about the way in which Christ's commission was a call to teaching that would yield disciples. He issued a challenge: 'We are thus to get rid of the mental image of merely imparting information to people long enough to enable them to pass examinations.' Teaching, for him, was designed to produce transformation.[1] His thinking about discipleship, expressed in a number of books (for example *Take my Life*, *Give up your Small Ambitions* and *Cinderella with Amnesia*) and in his preaching and lecturing, had made a profound impact on many students and others in the 1960s and 1970s. *Shaking the Sleeping Beauty* contained the substance of lectures given in 1978 at Wycliffe Hall, Oxford.

It was against this background that the LBC board, as they looked for new leadership for the college, considered that Michael Griffiths, with his challenging style of speaking and writing, would have much to offer as LBC's principal. His principalship, from 1980 to 1989, highlighted certain distinctives. For Griffiths, the future of theological education at

---

[1] M. Griffiths, *Shaking the Sleeping Beauty: Arousing the Church to its Mission*, 167.

institutions such as LBC lay in a shift from the approach in which students were simply fed information 'like animated memory banks'. He argued for goal-orientated ideas about 'being' and 'doing' as well as 'knowing'.[2] These issues were already the subject of much discussion at LBC and were to be explored further in the 1980s as the college launched new courses in 'applied theology', a theology rooted in Christian discipleship and the practice of ministry. One particularly creative venture was the CLAM (Christian Life and Ministry) course, to which Mary Evans made an immense contribution. On a wider front, the decade saw the impact of fresh evangelical leadership in Britain – a development in which LBC played a significant part. At the close of the decade, however, issues of leadership were to cause tensions within LBC.

A New Principal

Until he became the college's principal, Michael Griffiths had not had much contact with LBC. In the 1950s he studied theology at Ridley Hall, Cambridge, and then worked as an IVF travelling secretary. It seemed to him from his involvement with university witness that evangelicals should seek to establish a presence in university theological faculties. This was the strategy espoused by F.F. Bruce and also by W.J. Martin, another IVF figure of the period, and Tyndale House, Cambridge, had encouraged the approach from the 1940s. From this perspective, the potential danger with institutions such as LBC was that they could become evangelical ghettos, largely cut off from mainstream academic life. After twenty years in the Far East, which included ten years in Japan with the OMF and a second decade, from 1969, as general director of OMF, Griffiths could see more clearly the value of a two-pronged approach to theological education: independent as well as mainstream. Independent colleges such as the Singapore and Bangkok Bible Colleges, the Malaysian Bible Seminary, the China Graduate School of Theology, the China Evangelical

---

[2] *C Rev* (Summer 1983), 1–2.

Seminary, Taiwan, and the Asian Theological Seminary in Manila had provided him with examples of good practice.[3] It had not, however, been his intention to move into Bible college training himself.

In the later 1970s, various people asked Griffiths to consider positions in Britain. He was approached by SU, but this was at a time when it would have been difficult for him to move from OMF. When Oliver Barclay later spoke to Griffiths about the possibility of his taking over (from Barclay himself) the general secretaryship of the UCCF, a move from Singapore seemed possible. Michael and Valerie Griffiths came to England to talk about this post, but it became clear that there was no role for Valerie with UCCF. By contrast, Valerie, who had studied theology at Oxford, had a clear part to play within OMF. Griffiths reluctantly said 'no' to UCCF. Derek Warren, on behalf of the LBC board, then contacted him about the college principalship. The college had been interested in George Carey, who had been on the staff of St John's College, Nottingham, and was then in parish ministry in Durham. When discussions with Carey did not go beyond the preliminary stage, the board turned to Griffiths, now unexpectedly available and widely known as a best-selling author, a conference speaker and a university missioner. With his UCCF commitment, his conservative evangelical credentials were not in doubt.[4]

When he met the LBC board representatives, Griffiths emphasized that he was not experienced in the academic field and that he did not regard himself as an administrator. Although he had been responsible within OMF for nine hundred missionaries, who were working in ten countries, he had to a large extent been able to delegate the administrative tasks. If he were to come to LBC he wanted to give leadership in the college and also function as a speaker and motivator in the wider world.[5] In 1979 he was

---

[3] M. Griffiths to the author, 16 June 1998.

[4] D. Warren to the author, 2 June 1998.

[5] M. Griffiths to the author, 16 June 1998; interview with Michael Griffiths, 5 Jan. 1999.

conducting university missions in Oxford and Durham and, ideally, he wished to have opportunity to continue with this kind of ministry. He was aware, however, of the expectation at LBC that the principal would be at the helm. As a result of the discussions about the principalship, the LBC leadership agreed to offer the position to Griffiths – and he accepted. It was hoped that Valerie would be able to be involved in some lecturing. In the summer of 1979 Griffiths was interviewed for the *College Review* and outlined something of his vision. He was looking forward to working with the faculty to seek to combine the finest academic standards with preparation for practical ministry and with spiritual development.[6]

On 9 October 1980 Griffiths presented a personal policy statement to the board. He wanted, through his leadership, to ensure clear commitment to the biblical position of LBC; to raise the spiritual level in the college; to maintain high academic standards; to upgrade the college's distance learning materials; and to bring about a better staff/student ratio. The biblical teaching should, in his view, be designed to give students the tools to teach others. 'It is this determination to stop studying academic recipes and to produce master-bakers who will really teach others to bake cakes', he stated in 1981, 'which represents the most needed and important shift in theological education.'[7] On the question of spiritual formation he spoke two years later about well-deserved criticism of 'content-orientated theological education'. This had given way increasingly, he claimed, to a more goal-orientated model which involved training geared to encouraging the formation of Christian disciples and the honing of skills for ministry. But, despite this welcome change, there was still the danger of a theological production line 'churning out graduates like rows of identical spiritual sausages'. He emphasized that LBC should recognize individuality.[8]

---

[6] *C Rev* (Summer 1979), 9–11.
[7] *C Rev* (Summer 1981), 5.
[8] *C Rev* (Summer 1983), 1–2.

These bold statements by Griffiths meant that he was soon in demand as a representative of thinking taking place in colleges. He wrote an introductory article, for example, for a survey in *Today* magazine of Bible college training in the 1980s. The study showed that LBC was the largest such college, with 230 students. All Nations was next in size with 155 students. Most of the colleges featured were interdenominational, but some denominational colleges – Spurgeon's, Oak Hill, the Pentecostal colleges and the Nazarene college – were included. Griffiths became chairman of the Association of Bible College Principals and president of the European Evangelical Accreditation Association. He also became involved in some EA affairs, although the college's EA links would not be as strong as they had been under Gilbert Kirby. Nonetheless, Griffiths gave the first message at an EA-sponsored meeting of invited evangelical leaders in 1981.[9] The background to this meeting was continuing strains within evangelicalism over such issues as the charismatic movement and ecumenism. Through his involvement when in Guildford in the (charismatic Baptist) Millmead Centre, Griffiths knew charismatic leaders. He also knew key Reformed and separatist figures such as Alan Gibson, who in 1982 took over the general secretaryship of the British Evangelical Council.

Like Ernest Kevan and Gilbert Kirby, Michael Griffiths was keen that the LBC faculty should represent the range of evangelical life. In 1981 he was delighted that LBC was able to appoint R.T. France, an Anglican scholar who was at Tyndale House, Cambridge. France was a highly effective writer and lecturer. Griffiths was also eager to foster LBC's missionary interests. The role of Peter Cotterell, with his long experience in Ethiopia, was crucial. Co-operative arrangements were made with All Nations and with Wycliffe Bible Translators through their Summer Institute of Linguistics.[10] Relationships with denominational bodies, too, were important. Peter Hicks came from a Baptist pastorate to the college staff in 1981 to lecture in philosophy. He

---

[9] Report on the Evangelical Leaders Consultation, 9–11 Sept. 1981.
[10] *C Rev* (Summer 1984), 1.

returned to pastoral ministry but would rejoin the college faculty
in 1991. Derek Tidball and John Balchin had many Baptist
connections. Griffiths attended Northwood Hills Evangelical
Church, the Brethren fellowship where Harold Rowdon
worshipped. Rowdon, a widely known Brethren figure, was
central to the Partnership network with its progressive vision for
Brethren churches. For a short time LBC had the services of a
United Reformed Church minister, Bob Gordon, who was known
within charismatic renewal circles. There were also wider
European contacts. Tony Lane had been visiting lecturer at the
Freie Theologische Akademie at Seeheim, and subsequently at
Giessen, West Germany.

Applied Theology

What the LBC staff wanted to avoid, however, was the merely
academic approach to theology. As Griffiths reiterated in 1985, in
an article in *Today* magazine, theological education was about
combining scholarship with practical usefulness and involved
much more than students being 'stuffed with theological
information'.[11] The conviction that a new style of 'applied
theology' was necessary was by that time one that was widely
shared within LBC. In 1980 Derek Tidball had prepared and
submitted to the staff a discussion paper which argued that while
biblical studies was a primary discipline and should continue to
remain central at LBC, the context in which theological work was
being undertaken had to be taken much more seriously. The
issues highlighted in the paper included growing secularization, a
world dominated by change, modern communication methods,
changing patterns of education, and the rise of Islam. In response
to the paper, staff members suggested that LBC should consider
how best to offer training for pastoral ministry, fuller integration
of extension studies into mainstream courses, new diploma

---

[11] *Today* (Aug. 1985), 22.

courses, increased short-term training, a centre for applied theology and, finally, more postgraduate options.[12]

At a faculty quiet day for prayer and discussion in May 1980 to consider these proposals, clearer aims for the college were agreed. It is evident that there was considerable enthusiasm and momentum. The agreed aims were to teach people who came to LBC to think biblically, to help them discover and use their gifts, and to train them in communication skills. The key outcomes were defined as biblical knowledge, ability to handle theological textbooks, discovery of personal aptitudes, disciplined living 'in the power of the Spirit', and ability to communicate. Those accepted for training at LBC should have motivation and potential to proceed to pastoral or other ministries. Peter Cotterell believed that LBC's emphasis should be on offering training to people from the UK, although there were differences among the staff over this standpoint. It was, Cotterell argued, more difficult for LBC to prepare people from overseas or for overseas contexts adequately. Changes for the future were to be examined in the light of the analysis that had been undertaken. In order to integrate distance learning, Moira Anderson, who was in charge of extension studies, was to attend faculty meetings in future. As part of the applied theology vision, the college would look at sandwich courses, at shorter study periods, a centre for Islamic studies, an MA course and greater use of audio-visuals.[13]

The momentum was not lost. In October 1980 Max Turner presented to the staff a paper on 'The Primary Aims and Goals of LBC'. This paper incorporated work by a group comprising Turner, Balchin, Cotterell and Arthur Cundall – who after almost two decades at LBC was returning to Australia. The paper suggested three primary goals. LBC should serve the UK Christian community; develop theologically trained leadership for the world church; and train missionaries. At first sight this agenda appeared to be at odds with the view expressed by Cotterell that the UK should be LBC's focus. In fact, there was a strong

---

[12] D.J. Tidball, 'A Discussion Paper', 8 May 1980.
[13] Notes on faculty quiet day, 15 May 1980.

emphasis on the 'products' that LBC could offer to the UK scene: ministers, primarily for Free Churches, RE teachers and evangelists. This had implications in terms of applied theology. Ministers required pastoral theology, teachers needed contextual studies and evangelists had to have training in apologetics. In addition, it was felt that LBC could offer education to the Third World at a higher level, especially through second degrees. Given these primary aims, secondary goals followed. It was considered that in revising courses attention should be given to spiritual formation, biblical foundations, exegetical skills, study of cultural influences (e.g. through looking at church history) and communication.[14]

Further discussions about a sharpened vision for LBC took place at academic board meetings in October and November. Proper ministerial formation was seen to be a vital area. What LBC could offer that was relevant to those from a non-western context was a further matter for debate.[15] Conversations were taking place with John Bendor-Samuel of Wycliffe Bible Translators about an MA that would concentrate on approaches to biblical interpretation. In 1981 the college submitted proposals to CNAA for a Master's degree in theology. Considerable thought was also devoted to the college's role in relation to spirituality. At the June academic board meeting it had been proposed that, in light of the difficulties many students were having with basic spirituality, a book by the late Methodist W.E. Sangster, *Spiritual Check-Up*, might be available to all students entering LBC.[16] There was discussion about offering spirituality as an optional course in the BA degree, as part of what became a firm intention – although CNAA representatives were somewhat wary about it – to incorporate more practical training into the BA.[17]

---

[14] Max Turner, 'A Paper on the Primary Aims and Goals of LBC', 9 Oct. 1980.
[15] Minutes of academic board, 29 Oct. 1980.
[16] Minutes of academic board, 4 June 1980.
[17] Minutes of academic board, 12 Nov. 1980.

The area of applied theology was strengthened in 1984 with the appointment to the staff of Sheena Gillies as associate director of training and evangelism. In part this was in response to a motion the board received from the student body. It read: 'We, the student body of the London Bible College, would like to bring to the attention of the faculty and board our concern regarding the imbalance of the academic work to the practical training which we receive. We gratefully acknowledge the fact that the academic standard of the college is high but feel that it is appropriate the quality of the practical training be of a similar standard.'[18] Ian Cory was head of training, while Derek Tidball had responsibilities as director of studies, together with involvement in applied theology and college pastoral work. The governors wanted an additional staff member with expertise to train others,[19] and Gillies fulfilled the criteria. She had been a teacher and a UCCF travelling secretary in Scotland and had taught at Capernwray Hall, Carnforth, a centre for biblical training. Most of LBC's applied theology was delivered by Griffiths, Cotterell, Tidball and Gillies. Derek Tidball, who was writing on issues of social context and pastoral/evangelistic ministry, left the college in 1985 to return to the pastorate. In 1986 two further appointments were made. Nick Mercer and Jack Ramsbottom, both Baptist ministers, were appointed as (respectively) director of vocational training and pastoral studies lecturer.

The later 1980s saw even closer attention being given to pastoral care in the college. It was accepted that, to have integrity, applied theology must have practical implications outside the classroom. There were proposals in 1986 for restructuring pastoral care. The college had employed Gwen Hicks, the wife of Peter Hicks, as a pastoral assistant. She was a trained teacher and social worker. Visiting teaching staff such as Myra Chave-Jones, on care and counsel, and David Atkinson from Oxford, on ethics, also made important contributions. There was, however, no

---

[18] Minutes of board of governors, 17 Feb. 1984.
[19] Minutes of board of governors, 30 March 1984.

college chaplain. A small college think-tank looked at LBC's pastoral needs. This group included the college warden, Harold Rowdon, and Arthur Cundall, known for his penetrating observations. It was proposed that, to foster spiritual growth and encourage proper moral standards (there had been some cases of stealing and of unacceptable sexual relationships), it should be the responsibility of the lecturer in pastoral theology to take an overall role in spiritual formation.[20] Within a large community there were inevitably occasional failures, and the faculty suffered a blow when the college's lecturer in ethics had to resign. He became involved in an inappropriate relationship with one of the students and left his wife. Such disappointments brought the issues into sharper focus, and when Clive Calver visited LBC in the late 1980s he applauded the increased stress on spiritual formation training.

Mission and Ministry

Michael Griffiths, although delighted about the stress on applied theology, was concerned that the students' experience could be too narrow. He wanted them to have more understanding of inner city and multiracial situations. Several former LBC students, such as Michael Eastman and Patrick Sookhdeo, were working in this field, and in 1981 the Evangelical Coalition for Urban Mission was launched. The day of the launch, in April 1981, was the day on which riots erupted in Brixton and Toxteth, and widespread concern about these riots led to the setting up of the Archbishops' Commission on Urban Priority Areas.[21] In 1982 John Stott suggested that, given national developments, probably the most important evangelical initiative in the past few years had been the formation of ECUM.[22] Eastman, who was its secretary, was also an adviser to the Archbishops' Commission and thus had

---

[20] 'Proposals for Restructuring Pastoral Care', Feb. 1986.

[21] Chester, *Awakening*, 162.

[22] *Third Way* (Feb. 1982), 9.

an influence on the major report, *Faith in the City*, which was produced in 1985. Indeed Robert Runcie, Archbishop of Canterbury, commented when he spoke at the third NEAC, held in Caister, Norfolk, in 1988, on how momentum for *Faith in the City* had come from evangelicals linking theology and worship, witness and social action. He challenged evangelicals to go on to take ecclesiology more seriously.[23]

It was precisely at this point that LBC, as a trans-denominational body, was vulnerable. The 1980s saw a continuation of the trend that had become evident in the later 1960s and throughout the 1970s for many evangelical Anglicans, and also Baptists, to give energy to denominational renewal. R.T. France found LBC academically very satisfying, and the standards easily as high as those in university faculties, but ultimately he felt that the college's non-denominationalism (rather than interdenominationalism) was cutting him off from the mainstream of Anglicanism.[24] Of the new staff appointed in the 1980s, most continued to be drawn from Free Church life. In 1983, for example, two Baptists (French and Scottish respectively) were appointed – Jean-Marc Heimerdinger to teach Hebrew and Ian Macnair to teach Greek. Several members of LBC's teaching staff in the later 1980s, however, were attending Anglican churches. Griffiths spoke about the way in which a number of factors had to be taken into account when making a teaching appointment – spirituality, interdenominational sympathies, teaching competence, academic background, lay or ordained, gender and ability to be a team player. It was crucial that those on the staff should be involved in the practice of ministry.

There were worries in the later 1980s, however, about the fact that (despite the emphasis on practical training) student numbers were falling. A report to the board in October 1988 noted there were two hundred students at LBC, compared with a budget figure of 220. In the previous year there had been 213 (although

---

[23] R. Steer, *Church on Fire: The Story of Anglican Evangelicals*, 330.
[24] R.T. France to the author, 4 Jan. 1999.

the early 1980s had seen figures around the two hundred mark), and questions were raised about the reason for the recent reduction. Griffiths pointed out that the number of overseas students had fallen in one year from 57 to 36. There was also, as will be seen later, increasing uncertainty about the future location of the college. In 1985 three members of staff – John Balchin, Derek Tidball and Peter Hicks – returned to pastoral ministry. Ian Cory also moved, becoming editor of *Today* magazine. Others, such as Deryck Sheriffs (from South Africa), Heimerdinger, Macnair and Robert Willoughby, had joined in the period 1982–84 and would make their mark in biblical studies, but those leaving were better known figures than most of the new staff. Finally, at a time when greater attention was being given to Baptist identity, LBC's traditional interdenominationalism made it a less attractive option for some Baptist students. In 1986 Paul Beasley-Murray became principal of Spurgeon's College, which was to see significant advance. Baptist Mainstream figures, such as David Coffey, later general secretary of the BU, and Derek Tidball, were helping to shape BU thinking.[25]

Coupled with some queries about LBC and ministerial training, there were continued questions about LBC's relationship with overseas mission. There were strong bonds, as there had been from the beginning, between LBC and interdenominational missions. Michael Griffiths continued to take a keen interest in OMF's affairs and in the Far East generally. In 1981–82 David Pickard, who at that stage was responsible for nearly three hundred OMF missionaries, completed his LBC studies. He went on to become general director of OMF. In 1986 Griffiths toured the Far East, visiting former LBC students working with organizations such as OMF and SU or teaching in theological seminaries. Among these former students were well-known Asian theologians such as Ronald Fung, teaching at the China Graduate School of Theology, who was an LBC student in the 1960s. Lish Eves, who had been with OMF in Indonesia and whom Griffiths knew as a

---

[25] McBain, *Fire*, 123–4.

superb teacher, joined the LBC staff in 1988 to teach applied theology. Arthur Pont, a member of the LBC board, was general secretary of the Bible and Medical Missionary Fellowship. Links with outreach to young people were also important. Griffiths admired George Verwer and OM's many younger leaders.[26] Before studying at LBC together, Robert Willoughby had worked for OM and his wife, Ro, had been on the staff of UCCF.

LBC's strategy of training national leaders from overseas appeared to have been successful. For example Chun Chaeok, who had been at LBC in the 1960s, had gone on to take a doctorate at Fuller Seminary's School of World Mission and then became head of Christian studies at a Women's University in Seoul, South Korea, which had nine thousand undergraduates. In the view of Nigel Sylvester, who had been at Ridley Hall with Griffiths and who had gone on to international leadership with SU, LBC had a continuing role in training African students. Kwame Bediako, in Ghana, and Phineas Dube, in Harare, were examples adduced. Griffiths himself noted that 20 per cent of LBC's students came from overseas and instanced strategic leaders in the 1980s such as Joe Kapolyo, from Zambia, and several SU general secretaries overseas. Such people could still usefully be trained at LBC, it was suggested, but on the whole it was advisable for students to do theological training in their own environment.[27] Yet LBC continued to seek to make itself known overseas. Students in the 1980s who took up non-western leadership posts included Ken Tan, who became OMF's Singapore director, the brothers Norman and Gordon Wong, both scholars and Methodist ministers in Singapore, and Rennie Tsang, who went on to teach at the Alliance Bible Seminary in Hong Kong.

The overseas scene was traditionally one in which women trained at LBC found scope to use their gifts. This continued to be the case, but Michael and Valerie Griffiths both argued for wider acceptance of the ministry of women. In 1984 Griffiths devoted a

---

[26] *LBC Rev* (Summer 1982), 5.
[27] Report for the governors, Michael Griffiths, 9 July 1981.

section of the *College Review* to the subject. He noted how LBC had trained women for RE teaching and missionary or pastoral work. Peggy Knight, Mary Evans and Sheena Gillies were now on the LBC staff, and the *Review* article recommended Evans' book on the role of women, *Woman in the Bible*. The article also expressed pleasure that even some Brethren assemblies, traditionally very conservative over women in leadership, were setting women aside for pastoral work. The views of Michael and Valerie Griffiths were set out in their contribution to an IVP book on the subject, *Where Christians Disagree*.[28] Readers of the *College Review* were probably surprised to discover in a book review that Max Turner had seemingly written a book, *Men in the Bible*, which pointed out that the Pauline corpus was 'essentially male'. The spoof review was by Elizabeth Bush.[29] Ro Willoughby, who left LBC in 1983, became a writer, working with IVP and SU. When at LBC, Ro was the first woman to be elected LBC student president.

The view that women should not take leadership roles was, on the whole, dismissed at LBC in this period. It was Donald Guthrie's perception that the presence of increasing numbers of women on the teaching staff was of the greatest value to the college.[30] Yet, ironically, in this period the contribution to LBC of faculty wives, which had always been a feature of college life, seemed not to be explicitly encouraged.[31] To some extent this was an inevitable change, given the wider social context in which more and more wives were pursuing their own careers. By contrast with this trend, there were some in the student body – not all of them men – who defended restrictions in the public roles of women. More conservative thinking in this area was a feature of some strands of the Restorationist movement which, as we will

---

[28] *C Rev* (Autumn 1984), 1; Shirley Lees, *Where Christians Disagree: The Role of Women* (Leicester: IVP, 1984), see pp. 64–112 for the contributions of the Griffiths.
[29] *C Rev* (Autumn 1985), 8.
[30] Guthrie, *I Stand for Truth*, 47.
[31] I am indebted to Ian Macnair for this observation.

see below, had been growing in the later 1970s. For example, Jean Brand, who left LBC in 1972 and who was in a Restorationist church in Southampton led by Tony Morton, argued that in church decision-making women could offer their spiritual insights and should then 'withdraw to give men the final say'.[32] Given that LBC had been training women from its inception, restrictive approaches to their work were never likely to command much support.

A more pressing issue was the extent to which non-western perspectives should be shaping LBC's theological studies. From his years in Ethiopia – written about so passionately in *Cry Ethiopia* – Peter Cotterell was implacably opposed to what he saw as the paternalism of many western missionary societies. His view was that missiology should start with indigenous peoples and churches. This approach was queried by some mission figures, but through former LBC students such as David Pickard of OMF, and Michael Crowley of the South American Missionary Society, fresh emphases spread. In 1984, Cotterell pointed out, there was only one professor of missions in Britain, and LBC, through its undergraduate course and especially through its MA, contributed to making missiology better known. The vision went beyond traditional ideas of western churches giving leadership to the rest. At a conference convened in 1987 in Stuttgart by the Commission on World Mission and Evangelism of the World Council of Churches, most of the contributors were evangelical theologians from the non-western world. David Bosch, from South Africa, who spoke at meetings jointly sponsored by LBC and the London Institute, saw a new evangelical/ecumenical convergence over mission, and Cotterell was able to explain his views in WCC circles.[33] LBC was becoming known for creative thinking in the field of mission and culture.

---

[32] *Restoration* (Jan./Feb. 1980), 19.
[33] Chester, *Awakening*, 118–19; interview with Peter Cotterell, 10 Aug. 1998.

The Academic World

As well as giving energy to advances in applied theology, LBC staff continued to contribute to wider academic affairs. In May 1981 Donald Guthrie's magisterial 1,000-page *New Testament Theology* was published. R.T. France, when he joined LBC in the same year, had already written in the area of New Testament studies. He and David Wenham were editing three volumes of studies of history and tradition in the gospels. Dick France was LBC's vice-principal from 1983 to 1988, before moving on to become principal of Wycliffe Hall, Oxford. In 1981 Joyce Baldwin, then principal at Trinity College, Bristol, was the first female to give the annual Laing lecture. Max Turner, who had obtained his PhD on 'Luke and the Spirit' in 1980, became secretary of the Tyndale Fellowship New Testament Study Group in 1981 and also became a full-time lecturer in New Testament at LBC. Three other research degrees were soon to be awarded to LBC staff: Derek Tidball obtained his PhD for his research on Nonconformist Home Missions, Tony Lane an Oxford BD for his work on Calvin and Bernard, and John Balchin a PhD for a study of Colossians chapter 1.

The network of former LBC students taking up teaching posts was also continuing to grow in the 1980s. David Runcorn, who left LBC in the late 1970s, was to teach at Trinity College, Bristol, after a period of Anglican pastoral ministry. Mark Cartledge was to become a tutor at St John's College, Nottingham. Within the Baptist world, Ken Roxburgh combined pastoral ministry with further study and was to be appointed principal of the Scottish Baptist College, while Brian Howden, who left LBC in 1985, would become a tutor at the Northern Baptist College. Robert Cook and Richard Johnson were two former students who took posts at Redcliffe College. John Horder was to become director of pastoral training at Moorlands. The long association continued between LBC and the BTI, which became the Glasgow Bible College and then (through amalgamation with the Northumbria Bible College) the International Christian College (ICC). Ian Shaw, who left LBC in 1985, went first to Manchester, where he studied for his PhD, and then became (the future) ICC's church history lecturer. In the university world Brian Capper, New Testament lecturer at the University of Kent, was amongst those making an important contribution to scholarship.

Several LBC staff were playing a part in the evangelical theological network which had Tyndale House as its focus. LBC staff members on the Tyndale Fellowship (TF) committee included Guthrie, France and Lane. For a time, before coming to LBC, Lane had been employed by the TF on a part-time basis. He was involved in the fellowship's theology project, which in due course led to the setting up of the TF doctrine and ethics groups, which brought together the increasing numbers of evangelicals working in the various areas of academic theology. Gilbert Kirby had indicated to Lane that he was keen to see the links between LBC and TF strengthened.[34] The serious scholarship represented by the members of the TF was something with which LBC wished to be aligned. LBC staff members were also involved in professional/academic bodies that were not confined to evangelicals. Guthrie wrote a paper in 1980 on what he saw as the theological trends that would characterize the 1980s. In it, he indicated that he was keen that LBC should continue to ensure that evangelical scholarship retained a central position within its life and also that LBC was itself in the mainstream of such scholarship.[35]

A volume of essays was produced in 1982 to mark the retirement of Guthrie, who had been on the staff since 1949. Leslie Allen, Harold Rowdon and Tim Buckley were colleagues who dated back to Ernest Kevan's era. Guthrie's contribution to the reputation of the college had been massive. His three-volume *New Testament Introduction* went to a fourth edition in 1990. From 1983 until his death in 1992 he was president of the college, and a few months before he died he was awarded the CNAA honorary degree of Doctor of Letters. 1983 saw Leslie Allen, whose scholarship had also done much to enhance the standing of LBC in Old Testament

---

[34] I am indebted to Tony Lane for this information.

[35] D. Guthrie, 'Current Theological Trends' (unpublished paper, 1980).

circles, take up the Old Testament chair at Fuller Theological Seminary. Griffiths, aware of the problems over the Jonah commentary, had read Allen's writings and, although he did not agree with all the conclusions, he found them 'very attractive and readable'. 'Apart from Donald Guthrie', Griffiths wrote to Derek Warren (as board chairman), with reference to Allen, 'he would be the most appreciated of our faculty in academic circles.'[36] Griffiths had assured Allen that he did not need to look for a post elsewhere. When Allen received an approach from Fuller, however, after 23 years at LBC, and given the painful experiences he had gone through, he decided to move. Allen's personal contribution to LBC was greatly valued by staff and students.

The college was well aware of the fact that, having lost its two most prominent academics, it would need to give priority to maintaining its hard-won reputation for credible academic scholarship. Guthrie observed in 1980 that there were now many evangelicals teaching in university theological faculties. While this was encouraging there was, Guthrie noted, concern amongst some evangelical leaders that a looser approach to the biblical text was being adopted. At the conservative extreme, Guthrie commented, there was a tendency to criticize all other evangelicals and to call them liberal. He anticipated that attacks on LBC would come mainly from the right wing.[37] In fact LBC was not particularly troubled by theological conflicts in the 1980s, but Guthrie's prophecy was partly right in that within the evangelical theological scene as a whole the early 1980s saw public divisions. In 1982 James Dunn, who was soon to be professor of divinity at Durham, wrote two articles on Scripture for *The Churchman* that were deemed unacceptable by the more conservative. This dispute brought a new journal, *Anvil*, into being. LBC did not take sides in this period of tension, but Tony Thiselton, a former LBC student, became a member of the new Anvil Trust.[38]

---

[36] M. Griffiths to D. Warren, 30 March 1981.
[37] Guthrie, 'Current Trends'.
[38] Bebbington, *Evangelicalism*, 269.

Throughout the later 1980s, LBC signalled its continued determination to espouse mainstream evangelical scholarship. In 1985 David Payne, who had been an assistant to F.F. Bruce at the University of Sheffield and then moved to Queen's University, Belfast, joined the LBC faculty. At Queen's Payne had become dean of the faculty of theology, and at LBC, as academic registrar, he took on an augmented director of studies role. Bruce, who had not forgotten the Ellison affair (in 1978 he and Ellison wrote about the arbitrary way evangelical institutions sometimes handled staff),[39] was concerned about whether LBC would give Payne academic freedom.[40] Payne encountered no difficulties and enhanced the prestige of the college. LBC did not have the services of Max Turner from 1986 to 1991. He was seconded to King's College, Aberdeen – and was engaged in climbing Scottish mountains in his spare time. But the field of biblical studies at LBC was strengthened in 1987 by the addition of Steve Motyer, who had taught at Oak Hill and had also been in Anglican ministry. The staff/student ratio, which in 1980 had been 1:14, was 1:12.5 by the end of the 1980s. Conrad Gempf, who had completed his PhD in Aberdeen, joined the LBC staff as a New Testament lecturer in 1989 – Dick France having moved to Oxford.

In order to clarify, especially for the American market, the fact that LBC was a thoroughly academic institution, it was decided (after considerable discussion in the early 1980s) that the college should retain its name but add a sub-title, 'Centre for Undergraduate and Postgraduate Theological Studies'. At the same time, the college wanted to ensure that its courses remained practical. In its submissions to CNAA about a new one-year MA course, LBC stressed its academic resources – for example the extensive college library.[41] When CNAA visited the college and produced a report in early 1983 it welcomed the college's own recognition of the

---

[39] *Harvester* (Aug. 1978), 236. I am indebted to John Andrews for this reference.
[40] Interview with David Payne, 16 Jan. 1999.
[41] 'Institutional Review Document', Nov. 1982.

danger of becoming a 'theological ghetto'.[42] LBC's MA, in Aspects of Biblical Interpretation, was approved in 1983, and the first intake of students began with the core module in hermeneutics. Other modules covered Old Testament, New Testament and Christology. An option on the theology of the poor was to follow. Peter Cotterell, with his wealth of experience and his postgraduate work in linguistics and missiology, became MA course leader. In its early period the MA was a joint enterprise between LBC and the Summer Institute of Linguistics. Numbers grew, and in 1988 there were 19 students. As the first independent college offering such an MA, LBC charted a path others were to follow.

Evangelical Confidence

Growing evangelical confidence was discernible in the 1980s. An EA leaders' consultation in 1981 brought together 52 people, representing independent as well as denominational churches. Gilbert Kirby, who sensed that more promising days for evangelical unity were dawning, was chairman. At a further gathering held in the following year, Roy Clements spoke on biblical authority; Michael Griffiths, who had also been a speaker at the first consultation, took up the subject of handling differences between evangelicals; and David Watson, by then the best-known Anglican renewal leader, described his approach to missions.[43] With the appointment of Clive Calver as general secretary of the EA, confidence grew still faster. Soon the national press was giving coverage to EA activities and opinions. In 1984 Calver took part in debates over statements by David Jenkins, then bishop of Durham. Calver aligned himself with Tony Higton, whose robust defence of the historic Christian faith were being widely quoted. The *Daily Mail* said that in the 1980s these

---

[42] CNAA report, Jan. 1983.
[43] Report in the EA archives, Whitefield House, London, 22–24 Sept. 1982.

new voices sounded more modern than the words of modernist vicars. Using examples from history, such as the Methodist Holy Club and the Anglican Clapham Sect, Calver spoke of the power of small but committed groups of Christians to effect change.[44]

Leadership '84, a conference which brought together about a thousand evangelical leaders, was an attempt by Clive Calver to focus evangelical attention on changes taking place in society and to engender vision for mission, social involvement and international affairs. It produced a statement, 'Converted to Wholeness', which called for local churches to be involved in issues of justice. Against the background of the ethos of Margaret Thatcher's government, with its scepticism about the churches becoming engaged in politics, the theme of justice was highlighted by Calver and others. Lyndon Bowring, another former LBC student, the executive chairman of CARE, was alerting evangelicals to their responsibility in relation to ethical questions.

One crucial platform by the late 1980s was Spring Harvest, which began in 1979 with an attendance of two thousand and grew to fifty thousand people, becoming the major gathering of evangelicals in Britain. Seminars on a wide variety of topics supplemented Bible teaching. Clive Calver was a co-initiator of Spring Harvest. Such new initiatives meant the UCCF and its associated bodies, which constituted Michael Griffiths' natural milieu, were becoming less central within British evangelicalism.

Former LBC students were influential in other areas. Several were working in the media. Nigel Gibbons was a researcher with Central TV, Anne Tyler was editor of the *Church of England Newspaper* and Colin Blakely was a writer for several magazines and newspapers. Steve Goddard, who left LBC in 1976, became editor of the popular *Buzz* magazine. *Buzz* had a circulation of thirty thousand in 1981, although it was to decline later. Another former student, Dave Roberts, became editor of *Today*, *21CC* and *Alpha*, and then executive editor of *Renewal*. Martin Wroe, who was at LBC in the early 1980s, became chair of the Greenbelt festival – attended by over twenty thousand people – and also a

---

[44] *Today* (Sept. 1984), 13–15.

writer for *The Observer*. In the same period another former LBC student, Simon Jenkins, was working for the BBC (while at LBC he had founded and he continued to edit *Ship of Fools*, a Christian version of *Private Eye*). Iwan Russell-Jones, a contemporary of Goddard's, worked as a BBC producer, moved to the USA, and subsequently returned to BBC Wales. Within LBC, John Webb gave media and communications training. In 1985 Clive Lawless of the Open University ran workshops at LBC on teaching skills.[45] LBC students indicated that the style of communication within the college had become more varied.[46]

These developments were in line with wider social trends and were part of a process of engagement with a changing world. Members of LBC staff wrote for journals, such as *Third Way*, addressing socio-political matters. Several staff members were also active in the political arena in this period. Five joined the recently formed Social Democratic Party (SDP) in the early to mid-1980s and one, Tony Lane, stood twice as an SDP local council candidate in the Northwood ward. Subsequently, to the dismay of many of his colleagues, he underwent a political conversion and from 1989 became an active member of the Conservative Party. Among the students, Michael Hastings, who worked with the EA on unemployment issues, was politically involved. In 1989 the challenge of two million unemployed and of social deprivation led to the creation of Evangelical Enterprises, an initiative backed by what was then the West Indian Evangelical Alliance and the Department of Trade and Industry. Hastings became a presenter of the BBC's 'Around Westminster'. In the 1990s the rise of New Labour was to attract some former LBC students. Graham Dale (at LBC from 1983 to 1985) worked for the EA in public affairs and would later become director of the influential Christian Socialist Movement, to which several leading Labour figures belonged. Evangelicals were taking important roles in society.

---

[45] CNAA appraisal, July 1985.
[46] CNAA report, 2 Dec. 1987.

Yet tensions within the evangelical constituency remained. In 1988, when evangelical Anglicans gathered at Caister (twice as many were at Caister as had been at Nottingham in 1977), some of those present were concerned about what they saw as growing liberal influences within the constituency. It was this concern that led to the creation of the Proclamation Trust, based at St Helen's, Bishopsgate. From the EA perspective, Ian Coffey, who became EA field director in 1988 and a decade later took over the leadership of Spring Harvest, spoke of the need for a 'theology of diversity'. Joel Edwards affirmed the 'rich tapestry of our cultural, historical and theological diversity within an authentic, biblically defined unity'.[47] As the EA grew – from about one thousand individual members in 1983 to nearly twenty thousand in 1989 – it attempted to meet the challenge of diversity. EA offices were set up in Scotland, Wales and Northern Ireland – a development in which Gilbert Kirby was involved. But cultural traditions could generate tension. For example, when Peter Cotterell wrote an article suggesting that Protestant marches in Northern Ireland were a barrier to forgiveness,[48] an LBC student from the province (who said he was a great admirer of Dr Cotterell) was outraged at such 'appalling ignorance and lack of sensitivity'.[49]

Growth in the confidence and influence of the EA was a development that had implications for the British Evangelical Council and for the separatist constituency generally. Another factor affecting separatism was the death in 1981 of Martyn Lloyd-Jones, who had been easily the BEC's best-known advocate. Many separatists were Reformed in their theological convictions and in the 1980s this Reformed camp became increasingly divided over the charismatic movement. The result of these factors was a weakening of the Reformed and separatist bloc that had attracted so many adherents in the 1960s. Some LBC-trained ministers of this persuasion had formed the core of the opposition

---

[47] J. Edwards, 'The Evangelical Alliance: A National Phenomenon', 53.

[48] *Today* (Dec. 1986), 12.

[49] *Today* (Jan. 1987), 6.

to Gilbert Kirby in the 1970s, but in the same period Kirby played a crucial role in influencing future leaders whose sympathies would lie with inclusive evangelicalism. Of the students who were strongly Reformed in their thinking, Bob Sheehan helped in the development of the Evangelical Library and Graham Cheesman became principal of the Belfast Bible College, perhaps indicative of the general trend towards a more pan-evangelical outlook.

The fissures that opened up in the 1980s between Reformed leaders over the charismatic movement affected a number of leaders who had been at LBC. The monthly *Evangelical Times*, which had 16,500 subscribers, carried some articles in 1985–86, for example by Tony Sargent, which showed a degree of sympathy for charismatic renewal. The overall aim, given the deepening rift between charismatics and non-charismatics in Reformed circles, was to attempt to offer an even-handed appraisal.[50] In *Reformation Today*, edited by Erroll Hulse, the *Evangelical Times* was subjected to severe criticism. One contributor, John Palmer, trained at the London Theological Seminary, stated that it was not possible to wed the Reformed and charismatic systems.[51] Some of those with Reformed convictions, however, pointed to the way in which Martyn Lloyd-Jones had emphasized the baptism of the Spirit, and by the mid-1980s Peter Lewis, from the Lloyd-Jones circle, was one of those representing an identifiably Reformed *and* charismatic position. At a time of new confidence, evangelicals were experiencing new tensions.

Charismatic and Restorationist Movements

Issues connected with the place of charismatic gifts in the life of LBC confronted Michael Griffiths early on in his period as principal. There was an electric moment in a college chapel service when a new student spoke in tongues. Discussions took

---

[50] *Ev T* (Dec. 1985), 19.
[51] *Ref T* (Jan./Feb. 1986), 25–32.

place at the academic board in February 1981 about prophetic utterances and the 'exercising of spiritual gifts' within the framework of LBC's devotional life. It was recognized that 'there may well be a legitimate place for prophecy or speaking in tongues and interpretations', but it was agreed that 'guidance and leadership should be clearly given'. To ensure that there was such guidance, it was decided that 'if a person felt he had a message from the Lord, it should first be brought to appointed, recognised leaders, both Faculty and students, who would decide whether or not the message should be given'. Students were to be told that if there was a 'prophetic' message for the college as a whole this should normally be submitted to a group for evaluation and that a message in tongues should not be given unless someone was able to give an interpretation. Two faculty members and two students would serve on a 'spiritually discerning group'.[52]

At the March 1981 academic board meeting there was considerable discussion about the feedback that had been received from students on the subject of spiritual gifts. A further statement by the faculty was agreed, as follows: 'Where free participation has been invited by the leader of the meeting, and where an individual feels compelled by the Lord to deliver a word immediately, the leader should be free to either respond immediately to weigh the prophecy, or refer the content to the specified group.' Joe Kapolyo, who was student chairman, endorsed this statement.[53] Michael Griffiths himself was committed to the importance of 'weighing' prophecy, and on the question of speaking in tongues he favoured the idea that a speaker in tongues was actually using a known language and that a translation was by someone who knew that language.[54] He did, however, invite charismatics to speak at the college – among them Gerald Coates, the leader of what became the Pioneer network, which included Martin Scott and Steve Clifford, former LBC students.

[52] Minutes of academic board, 4 Feb. 1981.
[53] Minutes of academic board, 4 March 1981.
[54] Griffiths, *Betrothal Gifts*, 64–5.

From the early 1980s, in a development that would have massive implications for British charismatic emphases, two major leaders within the Anglican charismatic movement, David Watson, in York, and David Pytches, at St Andrew's, Chorleywood, gave their backing to the ministry in Britain of John Wimber, the leader of the Vineyard Christian Fellowship in Los Angeles. Wimber's approach also affected non-Anglicans. Roy Pointer, a student at LBC in the 1970s who was working for the Bible Society, contacted Douglas McBain in 1981 and suggested that Wimber might be invited to visit some British churches to talk about ministry in the power of the Holy Spirit. McBain responded, and a series of meetings took place in 1982. These were followed by an international conference in London in 1984 which McBain was instrumental in arranging. McBain and others who initially supported Wimber (such as Nigel Wright, who was on the staff at Spurgeon's College from 1987) were to become increasingly critical of claims made for power evangelism.[55] Ian Pritchard was one former LBC student who joined the Vineyard movement. In a review in 1986 of Wimber's *apologia* for divine healing, Peter Cotterell was glad that Wimber took the view that healing was not for everyone, but he described Wimber's use of Scripture as naïve and even absurd.[56]

Others on the LBC staff were evaluating the new movement. In a thorough examination of spiritual gifts published in *Vox Evangelica* in 1985, Max Turner combined scholarly investigation of the New Testament material with contemporary application. Turner took issue with J.I. Packer, who had argued that modern healings, tongues and prophecy could not be

---

[55] McBain, *Fire*, ch. 7; N. Wright, 'A Baptist Evaluation', in D. Pytches (ed.), *John Wimber: His Influence and Legacy* (Guildford: Eagle, 1998), 244–56. Wimber defined 'power evangelism' as 'a spontaneous, Spirit-inspired, empowered presentation of the gospel . . . which is preceded and undergirded by supernatural demonstrations of God's presence' (J. Wimber, *Power Evangelism* [London: Hodder & Stoughton, 1985]), 46.

[56] *Third Way* (Nov. 1986), 25.

identified with New Testament phenomena. On the question of healing, Turner referred to Wimber's 'Signs, Wonders and Church Growth' course at Fuller Theological Seminary, in which healings were being documented.[57] *Today* later published a popular article by Turner in which he reiterated that people using their critical faculties believed they were seeing phenomena which were parallel to some of those described in the New Testament.[58] The later 1980s saw the focus move from healing ministries to the question of prophecy. In an article in 1987 on the subject, Peter Cotterell stated that if a supposed prophecy was delivered and it was proved to be wrong, then the prophet was discredited.[59] Wimber himself was to team up with a group known as the 'Kansas City prophets'. In August 1989 Paul Cain, one of this group, gave a specific prediction about revival in England.[60] The fact that revival did not materialize was to give Wimber cause for reflection.

A further problematic area was the view being espoused by some that healing and even financial prosperity were available to all if claimed by faith. This was part of a wider theological tendency towards what was termed 'over-realized eschatology'. Cotterell, writing in 1986, was trenchant about this 'heresy'. It was partly because he knew the suffering church in Ethiopia that Cotterell felt so strongly about naïve triumphalism.[61] Neil Hudson, who trained at LBC in the 1980s and became a lecturer at Elim's college at Nantwich, was to speak of the dangers of triumphalism within Pentecostalism.[62] Several Pentecostal and charismatic students, however, felt that LBC was ultra-cautious about areas such as healing. A request from some that Wimber should speak at LBC was turned down. Hudson found the LBC

---

[57] M.B. Turner, 'Spiritual Gifts Then and Now'. A year later, however, Wimber's course at Fuller was no longer offered.

[58] *Today* (Oct. 1985), 18–20.

[59] *Leadership T* (Sept. 1987), 28–9.

[60] McBain, *Fire*, 101.

[61] *Today* (March 1986), 11–13.

[62] D.N. Hudson, '*Worship*', 196–7.

discerning group's approach 'alien and intimidating'.[63] Keith
Warrington, another former LBC student, joined the Nantwich
college staff, and since Julian Ward was dean of students there the
LBC influence within Elim's training was considerable. Ward
contributed to introducing the wider charismatic movement to
historical Pentecostalism. Colin Warner, at the Assemblies of
God College, Mattersey Hall, had also studied at LBC.
Warrington and Hudson were to obtain PhDs for their work in
areas of Pentecostal theology/history.

It was within the Restorationist movement that triumphalist
attitudes seemed particularly evident. The Dales Bible Week, first
held in 1976, was followed by the Downs Bible Week, launched in
1979 and led by Terry Virgo. Three thousand people went to the
Downs in 1980, and by 1987 attendance had risen to nine
thousand enthusiastic participants. It was estimated in 1985 that
fifty thousand people were attending Restorationist Bible
weeks.[64] The idea of a 'denominational ceiling', beyond which
further development was impossible for those in historic
denominations, was a favourite Restorationist concept.[65] Terry
Virgo indicated that, in his view, denominational leaders
overseeing churches would simply defend the status quo. He
spoke about safe denominational churches enjoying a little
renewal. By contrast, true (present-day) apostles would produce
mature churches.[66] Such views were sharply at variance with
LBC's pan-denominationalism. On questions of authority and
leadership, in 1980 one Restorationist figure, Dave Tomlinson,
who would study for an MA at LBC in the 1990s, defended
authority structures: husbands ruling their homes and churches
led by elders.[67] Tomlinson's views, as we will see in the next
chapter, were to broaden significantly.

---

[63] Neil Hudson to the author, 15 June 1999.
[64] Marc Europe had estimated 5,000 churches and 180,000 members,
Today (Sept. 1985), 6–8.
[65] *Crusade* (Jan. 1981), 22.
[66] *Restoration* (Nov./Dec. 1981), 9–12.
[67] D. Tomlinson, 'Is Discipling Biblical?' *Restoration* (July/Aug. 1980),
1–4.

College Leadership and Management

Against the background of such debates about Christian leadership, which were sometimes highly charged, and given the political context in which strong leadership was being advocated by Margaret Thatcher, it is not surprising that LBC found itself confronted by issues concerning styles of leadership and management. Michael Griffiths, with his ebullient approach, was keen to have enthusiastic people on the LBC board who could offer commitment and expertise. Derek Warren, board chairman until he retired in 1983, was highly supportive. Board members included a number of people who shared Griffiths' background in UCCF and/or in overseas mission. Among these were Susan Brown, who worked for the IFES and had been women's secretary of UCCF. Two other board members, Meg Foote and Vera Sinton, offered LBC missiological (both had responsibilities at All Nations) and educational insights. In turn, Valerie Griffiths was on the board of All Nations.[68] Nigel Sylvester, a long-time friend of Michael Griffiths, was another LBC governor. Missionary societies were represented by Arthur Pont and then by Don Ford, an LBC student in the 1950s. Others on the college's board had business experience, an academic background or experience as local pastors.

As a result of decisions made in this period expansion took place. A new student block was built and was opened, free of debt, in 1985. It incorporated leisure facilities and music rooms. A control room for video equipment and an extension to the library were also provided, by adapting a games room adjoining the library. Griffiths was determined to improve the student/staff ratio, and this was achieved. The faculty expanded to 18, which had, of course, cost implications for LBC. Denominationally, Baptists and Anglicans were well represented on the staff, but Griffiths was keen to ensure a broad denominational spectrum. Bob Letham, who taught theology at LBC from 1986

---

[68] Interview with Michael Griffiths, 5 Jan. 1999.

to 1989, was a Presbyterian pastor/academic in the USA. Distance learning continued to expand. Under David Huggett, who took responsibility for distance learning material, there were developments in the style of extension studies. As we will see in the next chapter, LBC made strategic investment in the growth of the church in Romania. Griffiths' vision was that through the growth of LBC more people could be trained to be effective disciples of Jesus Christ.[69]

To some extent, however, the practicalities of expanding training opportunities became obstacles to the practice of training. The first presenting problem was that of LBC's geographical situation. The cost of housing for staff and students in the Northwood area was a constant concern. It was difficult to attract staff unless help was provided to buy houses. With the average age of students now twenty-eight, a considerable number had family responsibilities and could not live in single accommodation in LBC. Robert Boyd, who followed Warren as board chairman in 1983, was convinced that a move of site was essential. Boyd, then in his late sixties, was a scientist who specialized in the field of radio astronomy. He had been a professor at University College, London, as well as founder and director of the Mullard Space Science laboratory. Like Warren, he was a member of the Brethren. With Boyd's encouragement, the finance and general purposes committee of LBC decided in September 1987 that it did not consider it practicable, due to social and economic factors and trends, for the college to stay on the present site for the next decade.[70] It seemed that a decision had been made which settled the future direction of the college.

This was not in fact the case. There were advantages associated with being near London, and at a meeting in October 1987 the governors, while accepting the resolution from the finance and general purposes committee, said that any move must take into account effects on academic training and the implications of

---

[69] Interview with Peggy Knight, 16 Jan. 1999.
[70] Minutes of finance and general purposes committee, 22 Sept. 1987.

leaving the strategically significant London area.[71] LBC had, for instance, links with many London churches and evangelical organizations. Transport was a factor: rail links throughout the country made it relatively easy for LBC to function as a national college. It was also recognized that a move might mean a diminution of the international awareness of LBC. Moving to another part of the country would also have serious implications for staff. With all these factors to weigh up, Griffiths was uncertain about the balance of the arguments for and against a move, and in the early part of 1988 he was taking soundings about the potential advantages and disadvantages. A number of options were being seriously considered, one being De La Salle College, which was seven miles from Manchester. It was a Roman Catholic college, run by a lay teaching order, and it had rooms for at least 300 resident students.

Inevitably, this was a worrying period for staff and an uncertain era for students. For Griffiths it was a time of crisis. At an extraordinary meeting of the finance and general purposes committee on 16 August 1988, it was agreed to propose to the board that the move to a new site would require a new person to oversee arrangements. A letter dated 17 August 1988 was sent to Griffiths outlining recommendations the finance and general purposes committee would be making to the board. These proposals included Griffiths' retirement as principal after two more years and the implementation of a search for a principal elect. The academic board, meeting on 5 October 1988, was similarly informed that at the board of governors meeting on 14 October 1988 it would be proposed that, in the event of a move to De La Salle College,

> ... we should look for a Principal Elect to take us into a new era at the new site. The Principal Elect would be primarily responsible for formulating plans to make appropriate use of the wider potential of the De La Salle site. It was envisaged that the present Principal would

---

[71] Minutes of board of governors, 9 Oct. 1987.

continue under the title of Principal Emeritus which would enable him to concentrate on the area of his most valuable contribution to the work of the College without being primarily responsible for management and administration.

Robert Boyd, as board chairman, had expressed 'his strong conviction of the need for such an arrangement'.[72]

Griffiths was devastated. He understood the meeting of 16 August 1988 as a vote of 'no confidence' in him. To an extent, this was true. Boyd seems to have believed that the principal needed to be a 'Chief Executive Officer'. For his part, Griffiths had always made clear that he saw his skills as lying in areas other than the administrative. He considered that he had served LBC in a way that was in tune with the outlook of the board. Boyd saw it as an important task of the board to see that the college was faithful to its doctrinal position,[73] and Griffiths could not be faulted in that respect. Moreover, his writings had kept LBC to the fore. The financial pressures were to a large extent a result of the college's position in Northwood, although the increase in faculty numbers during the period added to the difficulties. Financial and other problems were, of course, exacerbated because some students did not wish to come to LBC until its future was clear. The decision to move was one with which Griffiths struggled and in the event, after a visit by the faculty and others to De La Salle College in October 1988, LBC pulled out of the negotiations. For Griffiths, who left LBC in the following year, this period was the most miserable of his Christian service.[74]

Conclusion

In 1980, Michael Griffiths set out an agenda for LBC which, a decade later, was largely fulfilled. Applied theology became much

---

[72] Minutes of academic board, 5 Oct. 1988.
[73] *C Rev* (Autumn 1983), 5.
[74] Statement to board of governors, 14 Oct. 1988.

more central. New ideas about mission and culture were introduced. The staff/student ratio improved and LBC staff members were contributing to the academic world. LBC was also affecting the wider evangelical constituency. University affairs, which were important to Griffiths, were not so obviously influenced by LBC – although students such as Michael Totterdell became university lecturers. The successful LBC summer schools continued and theological study weeks at LBC were also popular. Yet the prospects for the college as a whole appeared to be mixed. The evangelical scene in Britain was going through a period of change, with new leaders – a number of whom had trained at LBC – promoting contemporary and innovative expressions of evangelicalism which could sometimes make existing evangelical institutions seem rather cautious. Such tensions affected LBC. In addition, Michael Griffiths struggled with the expectations of some regarding his position at LBC. The role of chief executive officer of LBC was not one that Griffiths wanted, and the need to manage the college in a time of financial strain put enormous pressure on him.[75] In his final message to the LBC board, Griffiths said that the hardest thing about moving was losing the opportunity to teach students.[76] In fact, he would be able to take this work up again, as professor of mission studies at Regent College, Vancouver, and in the meantime the vision for a more goal-orientated model of training would shape LBC into the future.

---

[75] Interview with Tony Lane, 16 Jan. 1999.
[76] Michael Griffiths' 'Final Message' to the board of governors, 6 July 1989.

10

'To Renew the Tradition' 1990–99

The leadership of LBC during the 1990s fell to two people, both of whom had considerable previous experience as staff members – by contrast with the first three principals. In fact, the search committee appointed to look for a replacement for Michael Griffiths considered initially that someone from outside LBC would be best equipped to rebuild confidence. After pursuing a number of lines of enquiry, however, the committee became convinced that Peter Cotterell was the person to undertake the task. He had been acting principal since September 1989 and in March 1990, at a special meeting of the board of governors, he was appointed LBC's fourth principal.

In 1995, when Peter Cotterell retired, Derek Tidball followed him, becoming the first LBC principal to have trained at the college. In the early 1990s Cotterell operated with a new executive group. The members were Nick Mercer, assistant principal from 1990; an accountant, Philip Taylor (followed in 1991 by Jo-Anne Lewis); David Bradley, who brought a new administrative approach; David Payne, the academic registrar; and Mark Greene. After Tim Buckley retired in 1990, having served LBC for forty years, Peter Cotterell appointed Greene, a leaving student with a decade of experience in advertising, as director of strategic planning and lecturer in communications.[1] After a thorough review of the college's finances and marketing strategy, it was decided in September 1990 that LBC should stay in London.

---

[1] Interview with Peter Cotterell, 10 Aug. 1998.

The issues facing Cotterell at LBC in the early 1990s were not primarily theological, although he continued to give attention to the ways in which theology should be communicated and was very well known for his terse saying: 'To communicate simply you must understand profoundly.' This was an insight which he applied to the whole of his leadership. He saw it as vital to bring into being a well-founded confidence about the future of the college. This involved being both visionary and practical. Under Cotterell's leadership there were many significant new course developments, LBC was put on a secure financial footing and the college transferred in 1993 from CNAA to nearby Brunel University as its accrediting body. When Cotterell came to retire in 1995, Brunel awarded him an honorary doctorate (DUniv) in recognition of the important part he had played in linking LBC with the university. On the occasion of Cotterell's retirement, Mark Greene spoke about his many gifts as a leader, a manager and a team player. There were now 345 students at LBC, which signalled a rate of growth not seen since the 1950s. In addition, the college premises had been refurbished to create a more contemporary ambience and new technology was now in use.[2]

An Agenda for the Future

Students already at LBC in 1990 knew Cotterell for his enthusiastic lectures on missiology. An article in the *LBC Review* quoted his maxim that mission became missiology when people started thinking about what they were doing.[3] Cotterell also made an important contribution in the field of linguistics, insisting on the importance of this discipline in interpreting the Bible. This conviction had roots in his mission experience, and found expression in his first academic paper, published in *African Language Studies* in 1964. In *Linguistics and Biblical Interpretation* (1989), which Cotterell wrote with Max Turner,

---

[2] *LBC Rev* (Autumn 1995), 11.
[3] *LBC Rev* (Summer 1990), 1.

the complexity of 'meaning' in linguistic terms was explored. The authors argued that the 'discourse meaning' of the biblical text had to be determined and interpreters could then attempt to understand the text's significance for their own world. The gulf of language, culture and presuppositions separating the contemporary world from the text had to be recognized, but those seeking to explicate the biblical message should not be deterred.[4] For Cotterell, concern for the biblical data owed something to his scientific training: he took a degree in physics and mathematics (then lectured in physics), as well as studying at Spurgeon's College. More importantly, his commitment to apply theology was shaped by his years in Ethiopia. He claimed that everything he knew that was worth knowing about Christian living he had learned from Ethiopian Christians.[5]

It was while he was in Ethiopia that Cotterell taught himself Hebrew and Greek and took his BD. In 1970 he gained his PhD, from the School of Oriental and African Studies. As a result of his unusually varied experience, he was in touch with a number of academic institutions. The most crucial of these relationships for LBC was his close association with CNAA. In the 1980s he saw himself as 'prodding' CNAA over religious studies.[6] He had been invited to join the CNAA's theological and religious studies board, and in that capacity he visited almost every CNAA-based college in England and Wales that offered theological studies. He was an adviser to several colleges as they made their first approaches to CNAA. Most of the joint visits to colleges were done by Jonathan Sacks, later chief rabbi; George Carey, later archbishop of Canterbury; David Jenkins, then bishop of Durham; and Cotterell. Jenkins was the chairman of the religious studies board. At a later stage Cotterell was invited to join the CNAA's humanities board, and in 1990 he was special adviser to CNAA on religious studies. He also became an external examiner

---

[4] F.P. Cotterell and M.M.B. Turner, *Linguistics and Biblical Interpretation*, 69–72.

[5] *LBC Rev* (Summer 1990), 1.

[6] Interview with Peter Cotterell, 10 Aug. 1998.

for London University in African languages and literature. This academic expertise was of great value to Cotterell in guiding LBC in a period of strategic change.

CNAA accreditation, which enabled the incorporation of pastoral theology and missiology into the college's BA, gave LBC the opportunity to introduce its Christian Life and Ministry (CLAM) course in 1991. The idea of the CLAM certificate and diploma courses in higher education, and later of the BTh (which extended CLAM to graduate level), was to offer vocational training which would 'provide informed, well-rounded, reflective and pastorally sensitive team-workers for church leadership, who can communicate and model the Christian faith to a post-modern generation'. The main areas to be covered were study of the Bible, Christian thought and living, understanding of the world, Christian responsibility, and Christian formation. The courses were also intended to provide an academic curriculum that would inform teaching at primary and secondary levels of education.[7] The review was undertaken in 1994–95 and published in 1998. The CLAM course modules operated with a tutorial system and there was stress on group work. It was a creative new development and owed much to huge investment of time and energy on the part of Mary Evans, together with Robert Willoughby, Lish Eves and Deryck Sheriffs. At an external examiners' meeting, R.T. France described CLAM as the most innovative course in theology of which he was aware.[8] A new part-time certificate course, following the CLAM curriculum, started in 1993. It gave people who could attend college only in the evening an opportunity to gain a certificate in two years.

In 1993, the year of LBC's jubilee celebrations, numbers of students had risen to 290. Two years before, when growth in student numbers was beginning, Cotterell stated: 'I don't want to hoist LBC onto a comfortable plateau, a little further up than we were, but going nowhere.' Cotterell's robust assessment of the

---

[7] 'LBC Major Review', 1998, 3. The review was undertaken in 1994–95 and published in 1998.
[8] D.J. Tidball to the author, 12 June 1999.

evangelical life of the previous four decades was that the 1950s and 1960s were 'soothing plateaus', the 1970s and 1980s 'froth and fancy, bouncy castle Christianity'. Cotterell looked for better times 'when we rediscover the Bible and match the enthusiasm now spent in blowing bubbles to a biblical concern for telling out Good News'. At that point he suggested that 1993 would see 280 students at LBC.[9] Resources would need to match students. 1993 saw the appointment of Alan Linfield as librarian. LBC's jubilee appeal had as a major focus the raising of money for one particular expansionary scheme: what was to be called the Guthrie Centre for Biblical Research and Islamic Studies. This was opened in 1995, after over £400,000 had been raised, and it became an important postgraduate biblical research facility and centre for Islamic studies and Muslim–Christian relations. Cotterell was keen that Islam should be studied, since he argued that it was a major ideological force with which Christians had to engage.[10]

The fact that LBC had an effective internal management structure was crucial to its ability to adapt to the changes in the 1990s. In addition, Cotterell was able to rely on the business advice of Sir Maurice Laing, who became college president in 1993 after the death of Donald Guthrie. Sir Maurice had wide-ranging experience as the chairman of John Laing PLC and as president of the British Employers' Federation. He was, naturally, concerned that LBC should take sound business decisions. Also in 1993, Denis Cole was elected chairman of the LBC board of governors, succeeding archdeacon Eddie Shirras, who had taken over from Robert Boyd. Cole was managing director of Vale Truck Corporation and chairman of the Shaftesbury Housing Association. A key member of the board was Derek Imrie, professor of physics and dean of the faculty of science at Brunel University. Imrie attended Ruislip Baptist Church, where Peter and Geraldine Cotterell worshipped and

---

[9] *LBC Rev* (Autumn 1991), 2.

[10] I am grateful to Mark Greene for this comment on Peter Cotterell's thinking.

where Geraldine was missionary secretary. The link with Brunel was a significant step. Given such constructive developments it is little wonder that Cotterell considered his time as LBC principal a high point in his Christian service.[11]

When Derek Tidball, who had been president of the BU in 1990–91 and then BU secretary for mission and evangelism, succeeded Cotterell in 1995, his starting point was the basis laid by his predecessor. He brought wide experience of the evangelical scene and the ability to reflect on developments in this larger context of evangelicalism. When Tidball spoke about the future in the spring of 1996, he outlined a number of ideas for the future of LBC which built on what Peter Cotterell had achieved. There were plans to offer the CLAM programme at degree level to equip students to meet contemporary challenges to the gospel; to increase the number of postgraduate students; to establish the recently opened Centre for Islamic Studies as a vital resource; to open a new department of music and worship; and to use new technology more extensively.[12] Underlying these moves was Tidball's belief, which was to influence LBC's development, that evangelicals were being called to seek a fresh understanding of Scripture, a fresh application of it to the contemporary world and a fresh appropriation of it in their spiritual experience. Every generation, said Tidball in an article in the college's *Review* in autumn 1995, is called to 'renew the tradition'.[13]

In this article Derek Tidball suggested that the central doctrines of the faith were often buried beneath the latest evangelical trend and ridden over by whichever preacher was on the circuit at the time. Evangelicalism of this sort might be entertaining, but it would not, he argued, stand the test. He continued,

In the past, evangelicalism has survived because evangelicals have known what they believe, and been able to explain and defend those

---

[11] Interview with Peter Cotterell, 10 Aug. 1998.

[12] *LBC Rev* (Spring 1996), 3.

[13] *LBC Rev* (Autumn 1995), 3.

beliefs. Evangelical belief has been an anchor which has prevented the church being blown off course by the gentle breeze of trivia, the seductive winds of compromise, the fierce squalls of suffering and the howling gales of heresy.

It was not that Tidball was proposing that a particular form of evangelicalism had to be preserved at all costs, without any alteration. Indeed, he insisted that with changes in culture and the onset of postmodernity (a concept examined below), renewal of the tradition was vital. He was adamant, however, that 'we dare not forget what has been inherited'.[14] This analysis offered LBC and evangelicalism an agenda for the future.

The World Church

In view of the way evangelicalism was – as he put it – 'in transition', Derek Tidball had been calling in the early 1990s for 'a fresh examination of the meaning of mission, a fresh appreciation of the oneness of the world church and a fresh look at what it means to respond to the call of God'.[15] For LBC, this reappraisal led to a concentration on seeking to meet some of the needs of the new, post-communist Europe. In 1990, surveying the dramatic changes in the former communist bloc, Harold Rowdon reported that LBC staff had been going to Romania before the revolution in December 1989 and that this involvement was increasing. The British directors of the Romanian Missionary Society, Les and Dot Tidball, had initiated links with LBC in 1988.[16] Not long before the overthrow of the Ceaușescu regime, Conrad Gempf was in Romania teaching New Testament courses to three groups of pastors. It was now the intention to invest more LBC resources in Romania. Those participating included Robert Willoughby, Harold Rowdon, and Mike and Sally Alsford, former students at

---

[14] *LBC Rev* (Autumn 1995), 3.
[15] Tidball, *Evangelicals?* 237.
[16] *LBC Rev* (Spring 1991), 2. Les and Derek Tidball are brothers.

LBC who joined the staff of the University of Greenwich. In addition to LBC staff travelling to Romania, it was also hoped to bring qualified Romanian students to LBC for postgraduate work. LBC saw itself as filling the gap while evangelical seminaries were established in Romania, Hungary and East Germany.[17]

Other colleges, such as Spurgeon's, also had connections with Romania.[18] Josef Tson, a Baptist leader in Romania, was well known within the wider evangelical world. Paul Negrut, pastor of the very large Second Baptist Church, Oradea, became a research student at LBC in 1990 and completed his PhD four years later. In spring 1991 Graham McFarlane, who had recently joined the LBC staff (having been an LBC student) and who was serving as LBC's project director for the partnership with the Romanian Missionary Society, reported on developments. Degree-level training was by then being offered to 36 Romanian pastors, most of whom were leading large churches. The Jerusalem Trust had conversations with Cotterell and offered sponsorship, which meant that each year, for three years, four students would have finance to come to LBC for the final year of a BA. At a European Church Growth conference held at LBC in March 1992, Negrut spoke about two possibilities: either that spiritual advance in Eastern Europe would affect the rest of Europe, or that secularism would penetrate eastern countries. He considered that Europe was at a crossroads, and that churches had a crucial part to play.[19]

The spring 1993 issue of the *LBC Review* carried a further analysis by Negrut of the scene in Eastern Europe. He outlined the immense task of working for the moral and spiritual regeneration of the eastern bloc. As president of the Romanian Evangelical Alliance, Negrut was in a position to assess whether there had been any co-ordination of the effort from the west, and in his view there had been none. There was also a danger that

---

[17] *LBC Rev* (Summer 1990), 5.

[18] C. Doubleday, *Then the Curtain Opened*, chs. 4, 5.

[19] P. Negrut, *Focus on Eastern Europe*, 6–7.

western-centred churches would be created.[20] Negrut took up the post of theological college principal at the Emmanuel Bible Institute, Oradea – a college recognized by the University of Oradea for awarding degrees. Other Romanian students who studied for PhDs at LBC in the later 1990s and assumed lecturing positions in Romania include Alex Neagoe and Octavian Baban, both in the New Testament field. A number of former LBC students, such as Silviu Rogobete and Daniel Bulzan, have been involved with the Areopagus Centre for Christian Studies and Contemporary Culture. This project has received support from some Orthodox Church leaders, politicians and academics.

Through its staff and former students, LBC was also involved in enterprises in many other areas in the 1990s. Jacob Ajetunmobi, who left LBC in 1980, became chaplain to Nigerians in Britain and well known in the world Anglican communion. In 1999 he was appointed a bishop in Ibadan, Nigeria. Former students such as Michael Dunn and Chris Wigram served with OMF. Dunn was OMF Indonesia director for a time. The 'In Contact' organization, led by Patrick and Rosemary Sookhdeo, changed its name in 1996 to Servants Fellowship International. Its aim is to research current trends in Islam and assist work in the Muslim world.[21] LBC was also eager to listen to theologians from other regions. The Laing lectures offered a more international perspective in the 1990s. The visiting Laing lecturers in the 1980s represented, on the whole, British evangelicalism – for example the Methodist statesman, Donald English, historians such as David Bebbington and David Wright, biblical scholars like Gordon Wenham, and missiologist Colin Chapman. In the 1990s British biblical scholars such as Tom Wright and Howard Marshall were still prominent, and David Cook, the ethicist, also delivered a lecture. But the field became more international, with papers from Alan Kreider (a leading American Mennonite), from Stanley Grenz (Canada), from Joseph Tson and from Kwame Bediako (Ghana).

---

[20] *LBC Rev* (Spring 1993), 10.
[21] P. Sookhdeo to the author, 24 June 1999.

Bediako's Laing lecture, 'Cry Jesus! Christian Theology and Presence in Modern Africa', delivered in 1993, was an outstanding example of the shift in the centre of gravity of the world church. The lecture referred to the fact that in 1900 about 80 per cent of the world's Christians lived in Europe and North America, whereas in the early 1990s about 60 per cent of the world's Christians were in Latin America, Asia and Africa. But the shift, Bediako suggested, was not only a demographic one. Rather, Africa – on which he concentrated – now offered 'quite distinctive opportunities for fresh reflection and for new understandings, for example, as to how the Gospel engages with culture'. He used as the core of his address prayers from a Ghanaian Christian woman, Afua Kuma, and argued that the Christology of these texts, celebrating 'Jesus of the deep forest', 'stands as a significant illustration of an African response to Jesus which bears the stamp of an authentic African religious experience and meditation'.[22] The audience at LBC gained a sense of the way in which theology was being done at grassroots level in the growing African churches. Cotterell saw the lecture as setting before theologians a new task – that of grappling with the pressing questions and emerging oral theologies of a world in agony.

Cotterell himself had been seeking to come to terms with these issues from the perspective of the missionary movement. His book *Mission and Meaninglessness*, published by SPCK in 1990, explored the themes of the good news in a world of suffering and disorder. Writing in *Theology*, Haddon Willmer described Cotterell as 'a leader in the tiny company of people in England who attempt to write the systematic theology of mission'.[23] One of the subjects with which Cotterell was wrestling was the question of those who had not heard the gospel. In 1988 he had stated: 'Although there is clear Bible testimony that salvation comes to us exclusively through Christ, that testimony does not

---

[22] K. Bediako, 'Cry Jesus! Christian Theology and Presence in Modern Africa'.

[23] *Th* (Nov./Dec. 1992), 469–70.

also require an overt knowledge of Christ.'[24] Through his continued reflections on this area in *Mission and Meaninglessness*, Cotterell challenged some evangelical assumptions. An editorial in *The Expository Times* in 1991, reviewing *Mission and Meaninglessness*, suggested that the 'decade of evangelism' would spawn many books, but that few were likely to be of more interest. The editor noted that Cotterell wrote from an evangelical but not a fundamentalist perspective and highlighted the section on the poor, commenting that 'it is of the greatest significance that a writer from the Evangelical camp should regard the church's attitude to the poor as of equal importance to the preaching of the gospel, or rather, as an essential part of that preaching'.[25]

In fact, as has been shown in earlier chapters, there was considerable evangelical concern for social justice. Those activists who were not evangelicals were no longer dismissed as 'social gospellers'. Trevor Huddleston, known for his consistent opposition to apartheid in South Africa, was warmly received at LBC and described as the conscience of a generation of Christians. Former students of LBC, such as Eddie Prest of SU, had shown a deep concern for mission and justice in South Africa and elsewhere. From LBC's African ranks, Alex Muge, who was at the college from 1979 to 1982, became one of the three bishops of the Anglican Church in Kenya who regularly pronounced on social and political issues. Tony Lane spent seven months at the Nairobi Evangelical Graduate School of Theology and was with Alex Muge not long before he was killed in a road accident in August 1990.[26] Because he spoke out about socio-political issues, Alex Muge's life had been threatened. It seemed very likely that the bishop, who had addressed injustice so vocally, had been summarily silenced. Tony Lane later offered an appreciative assessment of the bishop's life and work.[27]

---

[24] F.P. Cotterell, 'The Unevangelized: An Olive Branch from the Opposition', 134; cf. F.P. Cotterell, *Mission and Meaninglessness: The Good News in a World of Suffering and Disorder*.

[25] Editorial, *Expos T* 102.4 (1991), 97–9.

[26] A.N.S. Lane, 'Kenya's Turbulent Bishop'.

[27] Ibid.

As Peter Cotterell reflected in 1991 on the pain of the world, he spoke of wars in Sudan and Ethiopia; of how Somalia was torn apart and Liberia had gone up in flames; and of how the Baltic states were being brutalized and the Gulf was spending its nights in terror. An authentic theological response was required.[28] In the 1990s there was certainly evidence of the continued commitment by former LBC students to this task of missiological reflection going on within the British context and being applied to the world. In addition to those staff at missionary training colleges noted in previous chapters, Pam Bryan was a tutor at All Nations Christian College and later moved on to work in a strategic role for the Baptist Missionary Society (BMS) based in West Africa. Richard Briggs, an LBC student in the early 1990s, also joined the ANCC staff. After editing the monthly magazine *Christianity*, Simon Jones, from a slightly earlier era at LBC, became a BMS area representative. At Redcliffe College the lecturing staff included Robert Cook and Richard Johnson. In these and other situations there was a determination – as expressed by Cotterell – for people engaged in world mission to think theologically about what they were doing.

Academic Excellence

In order to achieve a broader range of theological reflection it was decided to expand the postgraduate research possibilities at LBC. In 1990–91 three students completed PhDs, which represented the result of a significantly increased investment in this area, and from 1991, due to the vision of Cotterell and the energy and efficiency of Turner, the research department grew rapidly. In 1994–95 an MTh was introduced, and in that year there were 12 continuing research students and 25 new enrolments. Tony Lane became director of research from 1996, with Turner now vice-principal for academic affairs. In March 1998 the research department numbered 66 students, of whom 28 were enrolled for

---

[28] *LBC Rev* (Spring 1991), 5.

PhDs. This represented a massive change from the 1960s, when the award of the occasional PhD at LBC was an historic event. By the 1990s the position of evangelicals as a whole within the world of academic theology had changed out of all recognition. There were, for example, several highly respected professors in theological faculties in British universities who were evangelicals. One of these, Hugh Williamson, regius professor in Oxford, became a member of the LBC board of governors in 1999. A year earlier one of LBC's own staff, Max Turner, was made professor of New Testament studies by the vice-chancellor of Brunel (through LBC's link with the university).

Turner's specialist field was New Testament pneumatology, together with Lukan studies. His two most substantial books *The Holy Spirit and Spiritual Gifts: Then and Now* and *Power from on High* (both published in 1996) established him, according to Howard Marshall of Aberdeen University, as 'the leading scholar in this field in this country, if not in the English-speaking world'.[29] Steve Motyer's PhD thesis on anti-Semitism and John's Gospel was published by Paternoster in 1997 as *Your Father the Devil? A New Approach to John and 'the Jews'*. Robert Willoughby was also working on John, spending two years in Cambridge for this purpose. Conrad Gempf edited Colin Hemer's study of Acts, and his major project at the end of the 1990s was heavy involvement with the six-volume *Acts in its First Century Setting*. Antony Billington, previously director of distance learning, became lecturer in hermeneutics from 1996 and established himself as a much-appreciated teacher. Edward Adams was half-time lecturer in Greek and New Testament. He moved from half-time to full-time at King's College, London, and was followed in 1999 at LBC by Stephen Walton, from St John's, Nottingham. Walton was writing the Word commentary on Acts. LBC thus had a strong claim to being at the forefront of international New Testament scholarship, especially in Luke–Acts.

A look at the students who went into the field of New Testament scholarship and teaching reveals the influence of

---

[29] *LBC Rev* (Autumn 1998), 5.

LBC's biblical studies department in the decades of the 1980s and 1990s. Richard Bell, who became senior lecturer in New Testament at Nottingham, spoke of his respect for LBC's biblical studies contribution.[30] Daniel Chae, who was at LBC for his undergraduate and PhD studies, was another example. His PhD thesis, published in 1997 as *Paul as Apostle to the Gentiles*, was commended by Howard Marshall, Martin Hengel, Don Carson and Ralph Martin for its importance. For Martin, the Asian perspective offered by Chae was important. Andrew Clark, Kevin Ellis, Mehrdad Fatehi, Thorsten Moritz, Peter Oakes, Andrew Perriman, Mohan Uddin and Matthias Wenk were among others who began to make their mark through writing and lecturing on New Testament issues. Most took positions in British institutions, either within the university sector or in bodies such as the Open Theological College or Oak Hill. Peter Head moved in 1999 from Oak Hill to Tyndale House. A number of LBC graduates continued to be involved in teaching and training overseas. Perriman was in Gabon, Hans Breekveldt in South America, and David Firth, whose field was Old Testament, in Australia.

A further indicator of influence was the extent to which members of the LBC faculty were engaged in writing books and academic articles. An extensive list of publications appeared each year in *Vox Evangelica*. A volume presented to Peter Cotterell, *Mission and Meaning* (1995), indicated some of the areas of expertise of the staff. In the section on biblical perspectives there were contributions by David Payne (mission in Isaiah 40–55), Deryck Sheriffs (Nebuchadnezzar's theology), Mary Evans (the prophethood of believers), Robert Willoughby (the Jubilee), Conrad Gempf (Paul and Barnabas in mission), Steve Motyer (Jesus and the marginalized), Antony Billington (the Paraclete and mission), Daniel Chae (Paul and Romans) and Max Turner ('unity' in Ephesians). It was stressed, in keeping with Cotterell's own position, that scholarship should be offered to the wider church. In particular, Motyer, in his treatment of Jesus and the marginalized in John, drew attention to how mission to the poor

---

[30] R. Bell to the author, 1 Jan. 1999.

had been a constant feature of Cotterell's ministry.[31] The section of the book on 'historical and theological' issues included essays by Michael Griffiths, then at Regent College, Vancouver, on Thomas Valpy French (a model missionary to Muslims), by Tony Lane on justification and sanctification, and by Graham McFarlane on Edward Irving. Graham McFarlane's work on Christology and the Holy Spirit would strengthen the teaching of systematic theology at LBC.[32]

Given that the biblical and classical theological areas had traditionally been at the heart of LBC's life, it was the remainder of the contributions in *Mission and Meaning* (mostly philosophical and contextual), that had special significance for the more recent emphases of the college. Two of these essays dealt with the world church. Lish Eves wrote a missiological appreciation of the struggles of an ethnic church in Indonesia, and Keith Ferdinando, a former research student under Cotterell and then lecturer at Bunia Theological Seminary, Zaire, discussed sickness and syncretism in the African context. Harold Rowdon, who had retired in 1991 after 37 years at LBC, explored the theme of 'living by faith'. Church history at LBC was by then being taught by Meic Pearse. Although Pearse's speciality was the Radical Reformation, his essay in *Mission and Meaning* was on conversion, and it illustrated work that he was doing in the contextual area. His brief at LBC included teaching students how to contextualize the gospel in contemporary society. The essays by Mark Greene, on Christians and work, by Peter Hicks (who had returned to the college in 1991), on issues of 'Truth',[33] by Nick Mercer, on postmodernity, and by Derek Tidball, on the mission of the people of God, were pointers to important future studies.

Derek Tidball was determined, as he put it in his essay, to affirm 'the indispensable role of the church in God's mission to

---

[31] A. Billington, A.N.S. Lane and M.B. Turner (eds.), *Mission and Meaning*, 70.
[32] See G.W.P. McFarlane, *Christ and the Spirit*.
[33] To be taken up more fully in P. Hicks, *Evangelicals and Truth*.

the world'. He was well aware, however, of the way in which the church, with its lack of authenticity, its cultural captivity and its spiritual poverty, could hinder mission. These were avoidable 'scandals', and Tidball, through his leadership from 1995, would seek to address them. There was a related evangelical scandal, to which Tidball referred in the *LBC Review* of autumn 1995. A tendency to evangelical anti-intellectualism, he said, was producing what the American historian Mark Noll had recently called 'the scandal of the evangelical mind'.[34] The rest of the church, Tidball continued, frequently regarded evangelicals as characterized by arrogance rather than humility. Moreover, the wider world often saw evangelism as apparently displaying more interest in hunting spiritual scalps than in channelling grace to a hurting planet.[35] Part of Tidball's concern for holistic training and mission was expressed in the BTh degree. Whereas the BA continued to pursue subjects in depth, providing training for different types of theological teaching ministries and access to research, the BTh was a wider vocational degree, although it retained LBC's central focus – a commitment to teach biblical and theological studies to a high level.[36]

In 1994–95, when the major review of the college and its future direction took place, the areas of college life were itemized as academic and practical training, character formation, pastoral care, administration and personnel development. The aim for 2005 was for LBC to provide excellent delivery in each of these areas. The college set the goal of having at least 35 teaching staff and a total student body of 500 in order to accomplish this.[37] There were also discussions about whether an institution of this size would be more likely to develop through partnership or even merging with other bodies, as had happened with the Northumbria and Glasgow Bible colleges, which merged to form the International Christian College. Evangelical bodies, however, have

---

[34] M.A. Noll, *The Scandal of the Evangelical Mind*.

[35] *LBC Rev* (Autumn 1995), 3.

[36] 'LBC Major Review', 1998, 2.

[37] 'LBC Major Review', 1998, 83.

tended to be independent in their thinking, and some exploratory discussions, in which LBC was involved, stalled. The more likely scenario was that LBC would continue to resource other bodies. Tony Lane was chairman of the Tyndale Fellowship doctrine group, and David Searle (who left LBC in 1961) became warden of Rutherford House, a centre for theological study in Edinburgh. When Steve Brady became principal of Moorlands College in 1999 he joined other college principals with LBC connections such as Richard Massey (Birmingham Bible Institute), Graham Cheesman (Belfast Bible College), Tony Sargent (International Christian College), Ken Roxburgh (Scottish Baptist College) and William Atkinson (Regents Theological College, Nantwich).

Mission in the Market Place

Derek Tidball's conviction was that the teaching of the Bible had to be shown to be relevant to contemporary issues and had to equip people for ministry, for mission and for the market place. To achieve this aim a variety of in-depth training was required. LBC's expectation was that many of 'tomorrow's leaders' would be ordained, but many would not; many would be women; many would not be full-time religious professionals but would earn their living outside the church; many would be deeply affected by postmodern culture; many would not have deep Christian foundations before they started training; and many would be in specialized ministries. Students would be affected by wider sociological trends such as individualism and non-denominationalism. Referring to 'Generation X', Tidball argued that because of 'the hang-ups, yearnings, passions and dissatisfactions which that generation can muster, character formation must rise up our agendas'. Although he had done some of his own studies through distance learning and valued that option – and LBC was a founding member of the Open Theological College – he was adamant about the limitations of the internet as a tool for formation.[38]

---

[38] *Christianity* (Jan. 1998), 28–34.

Mark Greene, as vice-principal (community) and lecturer in communications, had a vision for LBC and other such colleges to be at the leading edge of thinking about engagement with culture. He was not aware of any full-time lecturer in communications in any evangelical theological college in Britain. There was also, he argued, an urgent need for colleges to help equip people for the whole of life.[39] The tasks ahead were to provide an academically credible evangelical theological education, to enable students to develop gifts and skills, and to help them grow in character and spiritual maturity. In 1994 Greene's widely read book, *Thank God It's Monday*, was published. As a preview to the book, Greene wrote an article in the *LBC Review* (spring 1994) in which he considered Christian responsibility in the workplace. This emphasis was – through the influence of Bill Allen – a feature of vocation training at Spurgeon's College, and it had been high-lighted in a Methodist report.[40] Greene had undertaken research which indicated that 50 per cent of evangelicals had never heard a sermon on work. Christians, Greene argued, were not being equipped for life.[41] LBC teaching staff were determined to seek to make relevant connections in their lectures.

What was being argued by a number of people by the later 1990s – at LBC and elsewhere – was that the contribution of individual Christians to the local church was being valued, but that their wider contribution to the kingdom of Christ through their work had been marginalized. In the light of this critique, the college was determined to seek to contribute in new ways to the concept Greene called wisdom for life. In 1998 LBC launched a video under its *God@Work project* entitled 'A Vision for Work-place Ministry'. This production featured Greene and also David Prior, director of the Centre for Workplace Theology in the city of London. Talks on workplace issues were also produced under the title 'Wisdom for Workplace'. Speakers included Jill Garrett,

---

[39] Interview with Mark Greene, 14 June 1999.

[40] *The Ministry of the People of God in the World: Report to Conference, 1990* (Peterborough, 1990).

[41] *LBC Rev* (Spring 1994), 4.

managing director of Gallup UK, and Michael Schluter, associated with the Jubilee Centre in Cambridge. Mark Greene reported in autumn 1998 on the fact that the college had mounted five workplace conferences. He referred also to various initiatives connected with Christians in the workplace, such as the project led by Richard Higginson and associated with the Anglican Ridley Hall, Cambridge.[42] LBC, with others, was fully involved in a conference on leadership held in Sheffield in 1998, sponsored by Spring Harvest. This pioneering event attracted one thousand people, many of them holding responsible positions in the wider world.

An understanding of wider possibilities affected LBC's course development. A one-year course in music and worship was launched, and in 1998 this was extended to a diploma and degree in 'Theology, Music and Worship'. The vision was for an integrated training, with in-depth interaction between these three areas. Within the LBC story, music had always been important. Tim Buckley and Owen Thomas had led college choirs and Thomas gave lectures on music in worship.[43] In 1998 Graham Kendrick, by then widely regarded as Britain's leading contemporary hymn-writer, spoke in the *LBC Review* of the increased interest in traditional liturgical forms of worship, in newer developments such as dance and multimedia, and in Celtic and Taizé music. He considered that theological reflection such as was offered in the LBC course was essential, and he referred to the danger of 'historical amnesia' which ignored the past. Kendrick was not aware of any similar training opportunities in Europe.[44] David Peacock, head of the new music department, had wide experience in teaching, had been full-time director of music at Upton Vale Baptist Church, Torquay, and had edited several music books. Chris Redgate, a lecturer with Peacock, was a professional musician with wide experience.

---

[42] *LBC Rev* (Autumn 1998), 2, 9.
[43] Notes from Owen Thomas, 20 May 1999.
[44] *LBC Rev* (Spring 1998), 2.

A number of other new initiatives marked the 1990s. Gill Dallow joined the faculty in 1991 as director of training, having been RE adviser in the diocese of Bath and Wells. In that year Jack Ramsbottom retired and Sheena Gillies joined the pastoral staff at All Souls, Langham Place. A year later LBC launched, with Scripture Union, the first nationally validated course, to diploma level, to provide training for children's workers. Dallow was course leader. In 1993 LBC and Latin Link began an experiment using a certificate course to train students for cross-cultural mission, with Mary Evans as course leader. This involved two terms of study at LBC – following the CLAM course – and then nine months in South America, combined with supervised study. Missiological concerns also led to the appointment of Cecil McSparron as the first OMF teaching fellow at LBC. A further initiative was an integrated course in theology and counselling. This was introduced as a one-year certificate in 1998.[45] LBC worked in conjunction with Crusade for World Revival (CWR), based at Waverley Abbey House. CWR's founder, Selwyn Hughes, was strongly committed to the venture, which involved recognition by the Association of Christian Counsellors and the British Association for Counselling.

LBC also continued to serve those who did not attend the courses run at the college but who were distance learners or who came to conferences at LBC. In addition to her work with over three thousand distance learners, Alison le Cornu, director of Open Learning (from 1996), who had an MSc in adult education, was responsible for plans to introduce the part-time CLAM course at certificate level and an MA by distance learning. Study weekends and conference events also took place. Val Edwards, the LBC conference manager, noted that about nine hundred people were at LBC over the course of a summer vacation period. Some summer conferences acted as refreshers and opportunities for reskilling for ministers and leaders. Derek Tidball, in reflecting on the 're-tooling' of seminaries, stressed that there must be encouragement to ask hard questions in the light of changing

---

[45] *LBC Rev* (Spring 1998), 3.

times. He also insisted, however, that the introduction of a variety
of courses and modes of learning at LBC did not mean pragmatic
approaches ruled. 'An understanding of the Bible from a textual,
theological and historical viewpoint is crucial', he stated in 1998,
'and, if abandoned, will set the church adrift on a sea of nihilism.'
He insisted, too, that colleges could only offer part of the
necessary whole life training.[46]

Postmodernism and Post-Evangelicals

Those formulating training at LBC were acutely aware that what
was offered and was relevant at a certain stage could quickly
become dated. In a series of articles, Tidball spoke about the
implications of postmodernity, which he saw as bound up with a
loss of confidence in modernity's belief in progress, reason,
science, industrialization and liberal democracy. The influence of
postmodernity was to be felt in the challenge to comprehensive
pictures (or 'big stories'), in social fragmentation, in consumer-
ism, in the blurring of image and reality, in approaches to the
sacred, in the questioning of gender distinctions, in the rise of
mass culture and in loss of hope. He argued that Christians should
welcome certain trends: the deposing of arrogant rationalism, a
rediscovery of the spiritual, openness to tradition and an
emphasis on listening to others' stories. On the other hand,
Christianity itself was essentially a metanarrative, a big story.
Tidball's assessment was that the 'collapse of truth and
objectivity, the merging of image and reality, the worship of
pluralism and relativism and the strength of the gods of consum-
erism' made mission more difficult. He referred to the suggestion
of Graham Cray, principal of Ridley Hall, that the themes of
community, journey and spirituality were relevant for evangelism
in postmodern contexts.[47]

---

[46] *Christianity* (Jan. 1998), 28–34.
[47] D.J. Tidball in *Mainstream* (Jan. 1996), 11–18.

In the early 1990s Nick Mercer, who was assistant principal at LBC until he moved into Anglican ministry in 1995, also contributed to this reflection. Writing in the *LBC Review* in autumn 1994, he spoke about there being increased contact points for those sharing the Christian faith. At the same time it was harder, he believed, to live with the grey areas: the roles of women and men; divorce and remarriage; the way that Christians 'do church'. Yet this, he argued, was part of the painful process of deciding how to remain faithful to the authority of Scripture within a particular culture. Mercer, who was always keen to connect with new thinking, referred to a Christian fellowship led by Dave Tomlinson, called Holy Joe's, meeting in a South London pub. Tomlinson had recently preached at LBC on the 'freedom' passages in Galatians 5, suggesting that many evangelicals saw no room for imagination or creative licence.[48]

Partly in response to this idea, Mercer argued that in the light of postmodernity the task of theology and biblical interpretation was more important than ever. It was essential to know clearly what things were non-negotiable and what could be left to personal taste. Since the 1980s Mercer, a Baptist minister, had been aesthetically an Anglo-Catholic.[49] Given his appreciation of wider spiritual influences, he wished to respond positively to fresh thinking about the gospel and culture. Mercer spoke of God the Holy Trinity as community, and he suggested that in this community of love people could find their identity in the postmodern sea of shifting images and personal fragmentation. A vibrant corporate spiritual life, he contended, pointed to the transcendence which postmodernity denied but which humanity's image-of-Godness yearned after. The church should challenge others not by promoting a dull Christian counter-culture but by confronting society with godly living. 'We should', said Mercer in 1994, 'receive with thanksgiving all the exciting experiences that

---

[48] *LBC Rev* (Autumn 1994), 5.
[49] N. Mercer, 'Living Intimately with Strangers – A Post-Evangelical Pilgrimage?' ch. 4 in G. Cray et al. (eds.), *The Post-Evangelical Debate*.

postmodernity brings us, while demonstrating that we are primarily citizens of heaven with a greater hope.'[50]

In the following year, Dave Tomlinson, then studying for an MA at LBC, came to a measure of fame with his book *The Post-Evangelical*. At the 1995 Greenbelt festival there was considerable discussion of *The Post-Evangelical*, a book which was being seen as articulating the concerns of some who felt that evangelicalism had become stranded on the reefs of a past culture. Tomlinson was being praised in these circles for encouraging evangelicals to think for themselves, rather than accepting inherited views. As defined by Tomlinson, to be post-evangelical was 'to take as given many of the assumptions of evangelical faith, while at the same time moving beyond its perceived limitations'. He spoke about conflicts some were feeling. 'I have suffered twenty years of religious and theological censorship', one person had exclaimed. 'I have been warned about this and told to keep away from that. I've had enough of it. It's time for me to make up my own mind.'[51] In a review in *Third Way* of *The Post-Evangelical*, Nick Mercer noted growing concerns about 'the cultural and theological constraints that seem to be part and parcel of British evangelicalism, about the relief many voice when you dare to express doubt and agnosticism in public meetings'.[52]

The issues raised were taken up in a number of articles and in a book of essays entitled *The Post-Evangelical Debate* (1997). Some evangelicals were sympathetic to Tomlinson's case. Pete Ward, the Archbishop of Canterbury's adviser for youth ministry, felt that Tomlinson had identified important shortcomings in the charismatic brand of evangelicalism. Ward referred to a critique of Tomlinson by Alister McGrath, in which McGrath described *The Post-Evangelical* as 'one of the most superficial and inadequate treatments of the contemporary state of evangelicalism that I have read'.[53] For Ward, this critique – which, he said,

---

[50] *LBC Rev* (Autumn 1994), 5.

[51] D. Tomlinson, *The Post-Evangelical*, 3.

[52] *Third Way* (Sept. 1995), 30.

[53] *Alpha* (Aug. 1996), 28.

read rather like 'a pretty tough treatment of a lacklustre student's extended essay by a testy Oxford academic' – missed the point. While Ward accepted that Tomlinson's work was a little naïve, it was a pointer to the fact that a charismatic subculture was passing its sell-by date.[54] While Mercer had reservations about some of Tomlinson's arguments, he was, like Tomlinson, attracted to symbol in worship. By 1996, having left LBC and Baptist ministry, he had become an Anglo-Catholic priest, serving first at St Edmund the King, Northwood Hills. He said that he could no longer call himself a conservative evangelical.[55]

Other contributors to *The Post-Evangelical Debate* offered a more rigorous appraisal of post-evangelical thinking. Michael Saward, a prebendary of St Paul's Cathedral, argued that Tomlinson's criticisms were being made against the background of 'the ghetto-mindedness of his own brand of evangelicalism'. Saward saw two evangelical strands. One of these strands took the view that agreement with 'my interpretation' was essential for church unity – the Brethren and the house churches, to which Tomlinson had belonged, had exemplified this attitude. The other strand (Saward's own) wished to affirm catholicity and the importance of keeping the whole diverse church together.[56] Nigel Wright, who had been tutor in doctrine at Spurgeon's College, took the view that post-evangelicalism was a term which offered no constructive way forward. Like Tidball, he wanted a renewed commitment to evangelical faith and the development of forms of evangelicalism that would take account of valid criticisms while maintaining continuity with the tradition.[57] In a more extended analysis of postmodernism, *Picking Up the Pieces* (1997), David Hilborn, who was to take up the post of theological secretary of

---

[54] P. Ward, 'The Tribes of Evangelicalism', in *Post-Evangelical Debate*, 25, 32.

[55] N. Mercer, in *Post-Evangelical Debate*.

[56] M. Saward, 'At Root, It's a Matter of Theology', ch. 5 in *Post-Evangelical Debate*.

[57] N. Wright, 'Re-imagining Evangelicalism', 109 in *Post-Evangelical Debate*.

the EA, mounted what Tidball called serious and legitimate challenges for post-evangelicalism.[58]

LBC hosted a number of conferences on postmodernism. One of these, Val Edwards noted, was attended by 90 men and three women. It seemed that the new thinking did not always break down gender barriers. Dialogue took place at the London Institute of Contemporary Christianity between Tidball and Tomlinson, and their differing perspectives were featured in 1996 in the *New Christian Herald*. Tomlinson reiterated his concern to give people space to grow in ways that many found difficult, or impossible, in the average evangelical church. Tidball argued that post-evangelicalism had little positive to say. Nor did it appreciate evangelical history. 'Evangelicalism', Tidball suggested, 'has always been dynamic and made sensitive adaptations to the cultural currents in which it found itself.' At the same time evangelicals were committed to the claim of truth as universal and revealed in Jesus Christ. For their part, post-evangelicals seemed to Tidball to be shy of the concept of truth. He sympathized with those who had been hurt by judgemental attitudes on the part of evangelicals, but he felt that a movement was being created out of the pain of a few individuals. While welcoming post-evangelicalism's pastoral heart and missionary agenda, he did not see in it an adequate gospel.[59]

Spirituality and Culture

A serious claim being increasingly made in the 1990s was that many evangelicals did not have an adequate spirituality. In 1988 Alister McGrath had highlighted the paucity of evangelical institutions and journals dedicated to promoting evangelical spirituality. Regent College, Vancouver, where Iain Provan, a former LBC student, was a professor, had two chairs of 'spiritual theology'. James Houston and Eugene Peterson, whose books

---

[58] *LBC Rev* (Autumn 1997), 10; cf. D. Hilborn, *Picking up the Pieces*.
[59] *New Chr H* (16 Oct. 1996), 10–11.

became highly influential in Britain in the 1990s, occupied these chairs. All too often, McGrath suggested, the area of spirituality was a massive blind spot for evangelicals. This served to devalue the tradition of evangelical devotion. He spoke about the rich strands of the tradition: the Reformation, the Puritan era, evangelical revivals of the eighteenth century, the holiness movements and charismatic renewal.[60] At LBC, spirituality was taught by Nick Mercer until 1995 and then by Chris Jack, who was appointed as college chaplain and lecturer in applied theology. Chris Jack was previously the principal of Romsey House, a theological training college in Cambridge. His aim was to explore the evangelical tradition and also to introduce students to other streams of Christian experience.

In the 1950s the predominant influences on the spiritual ethos at LBC had been Reformed theology and Keswick. From the 1960s there was an increasing interest in the charismatic movement, an interest that reflected changes going on in wider evangelicalism. LBC was, however, always committed to reflecting the evangelical spectrum of thinking. In the 1970s and 1980s there were, as we have seen, worries about aspects of charismatic renewal. One group from the college had set up a relatively short-lived charismatic community in Wales. Weighing of prophetic words had been an issue highlighted by Michael Griffiths, and there was much discussion about the way in which John Wimber, the Vineyard movement's leader, promoted 'prophetic' ministries. Wimber later commented: 'I turned my brain off for a couple of years.'[61] Douglas McBain, who had supported Wimber for a time, suggested that proper evaluation of renewal was more likely to happen within respected Christian traditions than in new networks. There was, he argued in 1997, an imperative need to anchor charismatic life within 'established denominations, with their deeper roots, experience and lines of accountability'.[62]

---

[60] A.E. McGrath, *Evangelicalism and the Future of Christianity*, 137–8.
[61] *Chr T* (14 July 1997), 47.
[62] D. McBain, 'Mainstream Charismatics', 58.

This was a perspective with which Derek Tidball had considerable sympathy. During the 1980s many Baptist members had
moved to Restorationist churches, impressed by statements from
figures such as Arthur Wallis who said that the leaders of the
charismatic movement within the historic denominations did not
want radical reformation.[63] In 1986 Terry Virgo had launched
New Frontiers International, and several Baptist churches
identified with this group. For Tidball, much Restorationist spirituality was biblically naïve. Often the Bible was read without any
recognition of the cultural divides created by the intervening
centuries. He instanced the strong teaching being given by some
on the subordination of women. In addition, the movement
tended to be historically innocent, seeing the story of the church in
terms of a nose-dive after the apostolic period followed by a
gradual climb in altitude since the Reformation. There were,
Tidball, believed, elements within this of cultural snobbery, and
also an assumption that it was possible to measure the work of the
Spirit. In addition, some Restorationists believed that they would
maintain 'pristine purity', unlike other groups that had (in their
view) become 'institutionally bound, motivationally mixed,
lethargic and impure'.[64]

Equally, Derek Tidball maintained, there was no room for
complacency about the quality of existing evangelical spirituality.
He was concerned for renewal, deeper commitment, reality in
worship and a way of life free from the restrictions of
over-institutionalization. It seemed, in the early 1990s, that after
thirty years of charismatic renewal the movement itself was
becoming 'routinised'. Charismatic evangelical circles were jolted
by what became known as 'the Toronto Blessing', which originated at the Vineyard church near the Toronto airport and arrived
in Britain, at Holy Trinity, Brompton (HTB), in May 1994. The
fact that people in such a prominent, upper-class church began to
'laugh in the Spirit' and exhibit physical contortions and other

---

[63] *Restoration* (July/Aug. 1981), 11–14.
[64] D.J. Tidball, 'The Challenge of Restorationism: A Critique', *Fraternal*
(Jan. 1988), 18–19.

phenomena aroused the interest of the national press. HTB attracted two thousand people to its services every Sunday at the peak of the 'Blessing'. By June 1995 over three hundred thousand different people – including significant numbers from Britain – had attended the Toronto Vineyard to participate in the experience. There was a desire for release from inhibitions and perhaps also nostalgia for an earlier phase of the charismatic movement when freedom was more evident.[65] Martyn Percy spoke of Toronto's 'playfulness in a post-modern setting'.[66]

Within LBC, the Toronto Blessing had an influence in the autumn of 1994. Early in the term, Gerald Coates, leader of the Pioneer churches, was invited by some students to hold a Toronto-style meeting in the college's student centre. LBC's Meic Pearse (who described himself as from the Roger Forster/Gerald Coates end of the house church spectrum) considered that the college term that followed saw a greatly heightened spiritual awareness. He did not, however, necessarily see Toronto and the college's spiritually charged atmosphere as being in direct causal relationship.[67] Andrew Walker was one of those monitoring and writing on the Toronto Blessing and reactions to it. He said that Graham McFarlane at LBC (who had visited the Toronto Vineyard) was someone whose judgement he valued and he noted that McFarlane felt that Toronto, 'although a mixed blessing', had more to recommend it than Walker himself could see.[68] John Wimber, however, was to withdraw endorsement of the Toronto Vineyard. Along with HTB, St Andrew's, Chorleywood, which attracted many thousands to its New Wine weeks in the 1990s, was an influential centre associated with the Toronto Blessing, and after Max Turner returned from Aberdeen he attended St Andrew's, which is near LBC.

---

[65] S.E. Porter and P.J. Richter (eds.), *The Toronto Blessing – or Is It?* 22–3.
[66] M. Percy, *Words, Wonders and Power*, 153.
[67] Conversation with Meic Pearse, 14 June 1999.
[68] A. Walker, 'Thoroughly Modern', 41, footnote 59.

In other circles, ways of worship were changing even more dramatically. A report in the *LBC Review* in 1992 on Greenbelt, written by David George, a student who would become a reporter with West Country Television, described an alternative outdoor service led by Chris Brain, leader of the Nine O'clock Service (NOS) in Sheffield. George commented that rave worship of the NOS variety was in its infancy. It should not, he argued, be rejected out of hand, but without theological content the gospel could be emasculated.[69] This warning seemed to be amply justified when (from 1993) Matthew Fox's Creation Spirituality began to become a dominating influence within NOS. The leaders moved away from their evangelical/charismatic roots, which had been nurtured in St Thomas Crookes, Sheffield. In 1994, Brian Draper, then a student at LBC, talked about the tendency – against the background of the collapse of overarching belief structures – to make up 'truth' and pick and mix a spiritual formula for living, and he discussed the way NOS was recreating symbolism from all eras of Christianity. For Draper there was a legitimate challenge to become ecologically aware, to offer community and to provide people with identity in a fast fragmenting city-culture.[70] August 1995, however, saw stories of abuse at NOS emerging, and by 1996, after a welter of publicity, NOS had collapsed.[71]

The demise of NOS, although a blow to those, such as Draper, committed to exploring alternative worship, did not mean that all such new expressions were discredited. Dave Tomlinson was right in thinking that there were evangelicals looking for a renewal of spirituality through the older contemplative streams of the church. Although Tomlinson did not explain the Ignatian tradition in any depth, he spoke about the helpfulness of its use of the imagination. The riches of this tradition, with its emphasis on the whole person 'indwelling' Scripture, were being discovered increasingly

---

[69] *LBC Rev* (Autumn 1992), 5.

[70] *LBC Rev* (Autumn 1994), 4.

[71] R. Howard, *The Rise and Fall of the Nine O'clock Service*.

by evangelicals.[72] Pete Ward was among those who considered that 'modern' worship was beginning to seem a little weary. He suggested that 'guitars, choruses and informality . . . in the 1990s appear to be yesterday's style'.[73] Brian Draper, who was review editor of *Third Way* from 1995 to 1997 as well as a part-time LBC research student, and who in 1998 became *Third Way's* managing editor, was co-ordinator of an alternative worship service, Live on Planet Earth, in Cranbrook, Kent. He had a particular interest in ecclesiology and postmodernity.[74] In 1999 Meic Pearse, in a book which he co-authored, warned against church worship 'absolutising the cultural forms of a past generation'.[75]

Conclusion

The 1990s constituted a period of considerable advance for LBC. The healthy state of the college by the middle of the decade was due in no small measure to Peter Cotterell's leadership. Not only was he a gifted teacher in such fields as biblical interpretation and missiology, but he was also a highly effective team leader.[76] Staff appointed in the 1970s, especially Max Turner and Tony Lane, were by the 1990s respected figures in the world of scholarship. The college experienced normal staff turnover in this period, losing David Payne, Jack Ramsbottom, Sheena Gillies, Ian Macnair and Nick Mercer, who had been appointed in the 1980s, and Gill Dallow and Cecil McSparron, who joined the staff in the early 1990s. But a strong teaching team, which offered expertise in the academic and practical areas, remained at the core of the

---

[72] For example, A. Netherwood, *The Voice of This Calling: An Evangelical Encounters the Spiritual Exercises of Saint Ignatius* (London: SPCK, 1990).

[73] P. Ward, in *Post-Evangelical Debate*, 25, 32.

[74] *Third Way* (June 1997), 29.

[75] M. Pearse and C. Matthews, *We Must Stop Meeting Like This*, 142.

[76] *LBC Rev* (Autumn 1995), 11.

college. Derek Tidball was determined to capitalize on these strengths and to push LBC forward so that it could meet the challenges of the next millennium. As we will see in the concluding chapter, the college had achieved an enormous amount, including training a wide range of evangelical leaders. But Tidball and others were aware that in the 1990s a new generation of leaders had to emerge. Rob Warner, who worked with Clive Calver in offering reflections on evangelicalism, emphasized that as leaders died or neared retirement there was a need to hand over the reins.[77] A major task, not only for charismatics but also for evangelicals as a whole, was to renew the tradition. The concluding chapter explores the evangelical tradition and the future.

---

[77] *Renewal* (Nov. 1994), 10.

11

'Greater Options Available'

In a consideration of evangelical unity and diversity in *Who are the Evangelicals?* (1994), Derek Tidball spoke about concerns regarding the fragmentation of evangelicalism. He argued that there had always been diversity within the movement. As we have seen, this had certainly been a factor affecting the ethos of LBC from the college's early days. Tidball also accepted, however, that the evangelicalism of the 1990s was mirroring the 'greater options available' within society generally.[1] David Bebbington spoke in *Evangelicalism in Modern Britain* of the 'kaleidoscope of Evangelicalism', but he suggested that as the end of the twentieth century approached, the movement, although more fragmented than it had been, still had an underlying unity. His view was that evangelicalism had, perhaps especially in the 1970s and 1980s, come into 'a broad place'. It was also, he said, 'likely to occupy a more salient position within British Christianity in the twenty-first century than in the twentieth'.[2] This concluding chapter examines four areas of importance for British evangelicals and for LBC: evangelical theology, British churches, pan-denominationalism, and mission and society. Some challenges for LBC are included. Finally, some comments are made about the extent to which LBC has mirrored its context and to what extent it has affected the development of this broader evangelicalism, especially in Britain, from the 1940s to the 1990s.

---

[1] Tidball, *Evangelicals?* 220.
[2] Bebbington, *Evangelicalism*, 270.

LBC and Evangelical Theology

In the inter-war period, when discussions began about the formation of LBC, the theological standing of evangelicalism was low in
terms of broader acceptance of the movement. Evangelicalism, as
Adrian Hastings points out with reference to the 1920s, was 'in
no state of health to do battle effectively with the Anglo-Catholics
for England's Protestant heritage'.[3] The reasons for conservative
evangelical weakness given by Oliver Barclay, an analyst writing
from within the IVF strand of the movement, were mainly related
to theology. A basic problem, as Barclay saw it, was that conservatives neglected theological education. As a result, many
thinking people moved away from conservative evangelical
positions. A further consequence, he suggested, was that the task
of evangelical leadership was often taken up by people with little
doctrinal depth. Indeed, some were anti-intellectual. There was
also a strong strain of negativity.[4] LBC was not the only body set
up in the 1940s to seek to address these weaknesses. Tyndale
House and the Tyndale Fellowship, both of which date from the
mid-1940s, were to be central to the retheologizing of evangelicalism. There were also denominational theological colleges that
would rise to this challenge. But LBC led the way in offering, to
the evangelical constituency as a whole, degree-level courses that
involved serious evangelical engagement with biblical and theological issues.

This process was exhilarating, although not without occasions
of pain. The first casualty at LBC was H.L. Ellison, whose
comments on the inspiration of Scripture would have raised very
few theological eyebrows in the 1990s, but who was edged out of
his teaching post after his article on this topic in *The Evangelical
Quarterly* in 1954. Ernest Kevan wanted to have scholars of
Ellison's calibre on the LBC staff, but he could not hope to
influence the evangelical community of the time if he alienated
some of its most significant leaders – which he felt he would have

[3] Hastings, *History of English Christianity*, 202.
[4] Barclay, *Evangelicalism*, 42–3.

done had Ellison remained on the LBC staff. Despite the setback over Ellison, Kevan carried on with appointing younger members of staff who, he believed, would offer theological stimulus to the students. In 1961 Donald Guthrie, who had been appointed in 1949, was awarded his doctorate, and he went on to become the leading biblical scholar on the LBC faculty. His *New Testament Introduction* attained a huge circulation as a basic textbook. The *Festschrift* awarded him in 1982 to mark his retirement conveyed the indebtedness felt to him by LBC and by the wider scholarly world. For another member of staff, Ralph Martin, who would also become a major writer in the New Testament field, LBC did not prove to be so congenial. Having been appointed in 1959, and having established himself as a highly popular teacher, Martin upset a few of the leaders of the Reformed constituency of the early 1960s. For a second time Kevan lost a gifted member of staff whose theological position proved to be too broad for some evangelicals.

Despite these losses, LBC's faculty members were achieving their goals of educating a new generation of evangelical leaders. Gifted staff such as Ellison and Martin, although they left LBC after relatively short periods of time, had, nonetheless, a lasting impact on their students. Other faculty members appointed by Kevan were to remain at least until the 1970s. These included the vice-principal, Dermot McDonald, Harold Rowdon, Leslie Allen and Arthur Cundall, all of whom would make important contributions in their fields. McDonald, in particular, was a prolific author. Leslie Allen, although a respected academic, found himself coming under adverse scrutiny from some former LBC students in the later 1970s. But by this time LBC was in a stronger position than had been the case in previous decades. It was, therefore, able to weather theological storms more successfully. Allen continued as a member of staff. The hostility he had encountered, however, made him deeply aware of what Ellison – a fellow member of the Brethren – had suffered. Allen's commentary on Ezekiel 20–48, published in 1990, was dedicated quite pointedly to the memory of H.L. Ellison, 'whose torch as an Old Testament teacher I proudly strive to bear'.[5] The commentary was in the Word Biblical Commentary series and Ralph Martin was the series' New Testament editor.

Students who emerged from LBC were to help to change the face of evangelical scholarship. Tony Thiselton, professor of Christian theology in the University of Nottingham (and canon theologian of Leicester Cathedral), is an outstanding example. His two major books *The Two Horizons* (1980) and *New Horizons in Hermeneutics* (1982), both dealing with the perspectives of biblical text and reader, are, as Peter Hicks has noted, widely regarded as magisterial.[6] Thiselton also attempted to wrestle with the issues of postmodernity in *Interpreting God and the Postmodern Self* (1995). It is a book which has been widely acclaimed. Jürgen Moltmann, for instance, commented that it was an enormously rich and influential work, which demonstrated that Thiselton, in Moltmann's view, was a theologian who was leading theology convincingly into the postmodern age. Another former LBC student, David Wells, who became professor of systematic theology and academic dean at Gordon-Conwell Theological Seminary (Charlotte), USA, has been less sanguine about the state of evangelical theological endeavour in the 1990s, as seen in his *No Place for Truth, or Whatever Happened to Evangelical Theology?* (1993). Certainly LBC has contributed more to biblical scholarship than to systematic theology, but the writings of the faculty in the later 1990s represented both biblical and theological disciplines.

What might the challenges be in this area for the future of LBC? In an essay in 1996 on evangelical theological education, Richard Mouw, president of Fuller Theological Seminary, suggested that at the same time as theological seminaries respond to increasing diversity of demand – the greater options – and offer new courses, they should also 'continue to preserve a solid foundation in the study of the Scriptures, systematic theology and church history'.[7]

---

[5] L.C. Allen, *Ezekiel 20–48*; L. Allen to the author, 4 Feb. 1999.

[6] Hicks, *Evangelicals*, 117ff.

[7] R. Mouw, 'The Challenge of Evangelical Theological Education', 288.

In seeking to fulfil this vision, LBC can draw from its tradition in at least two significant ways. The college's unique international links mean that it is superbly placed to be a meeting point of western and non-western thought. It can, therefore, be a leader in enabling western theology to listen seriously to non-western evangelical theologians. In 1998, a remarkable 51 per cent of postgraduate LBC entrants were from overseas. The second area of traditional strength is the college's commitment to theology that is taken into the 'secular' market place. In his discussion of the idea of Christian scholarship, George Marsden has argued for the importance of Christian perspectives in the broader academic disciplines.[8] LBC's undergraduate and postgraduate courses can inform those who will take positions of scholarly influence not only in university theological faculties but also in other areas of academic life.

LBC and the British Churches

A similar breadth of pan-evangelical experience has been present in the story of LBC and its relationship to denominationalism. Although Ernest Kevan's own interdenominational experience when he was appointed principal was limited, his thinking was denominationally broad. Gilbert Kirby, during his principalship, built on the foundation that had already been laid. Kevan quite happily recruited Baptists, Anglicans, Methodists and members of the Brethren to the LBC staff. He showed considerable independence of mind in not allowing the college to be squeezed into a separatist mould when fissures opened up between the more inclusive and exclusive sections of evangelicalism. The student body, although always predominantly Free Church, was mixed. Among the Anglican students from Kevan's era were Michael Baughen, who became Bishop of Chester, David Wheaton, who became principal of Oak Hill, and Joyce Baldwin, who was principal of Trinity College, Bristol, for a year. One

---

[8] G.M. Marsden, *The Outrageous Idea of Christian Scholarship*, 22.

Anglican theologian, Paul Avis, who had been an LBC student, did not stay in the evangelical camp but contributed to ecumenical conversations a perspective which owed much to his evangelical heritage. As he argued in *Ecumenical Theology* (1986) and elaborated in *Christians in Communion* (1990), the aim of ecumenical theology was to liberate and mobilize the dynamic of Christian existence in the church.[9]

By the late 1980s there were reckoned to be at least seven evangelical bishops in the Church of England.[10] This evangelical episcopal presence was to grow, as was the evangelical influence among clergy and laity. In 1995 the elections to the Church of England's general synod meant that evangelicals, representing 41 per cent of those elected, were the biggest grouping.[11] LBC had contacts at various levels within Anglicanism, not only in England but also overseas. Cyril Okorocha, for example, who was at LBC in the mid-1970s, later became director of mission and evangelism for the Anglican Communion. At the highest level, George Carey, who had studied for both his MTh and PhD through LBC, represented something of the broadening of evangelicalism from the 1960s to the 1990s. He recalled that, at the time when Dermot McDonald was his MTh supervisor, he also came to know Eric Mascall, then at King's College, London, who was able to help Carey with the work he was undertaking on patristic theology. Carey found himself increasingly influenced by wider spirituality through his research, and for him this was enriching. His growing appreciation of patristic thought led him to take an interest in ecumenical theology.[12] Carey came to LBC in 1996 to address the students and in a subsequent interview spoke of the strength of evangelicalism as being its commitment to mission – based on the uniqueness of Christ and the finality of his revelation – and its affirmation of personal conversion to Christ. Evangelicalism's

---

[9] P. Avis, *Christians in Communion*, vii.

[10] *Leadership T* (May 1988), 18–21.

[11] J. Martin, *Gospel People? Evangelicals and the Future of Anglicanism*, 15.

[12] Martin, *Gospel People?* 51.

weaknesses, he suggested, were often its doctrines of church and sacraments.[13]

For some evangelicals in the Church of England, the outlook represented by Carey was too broad. At the 1993 Anglican Evangelical Assembly there was a presentation about a new Anglican movement, called Reform. Reform claimed that evangelicalism had become theologically woolly and morally flabby. Tony Higton, who had studied at LBC, was at that stage a leading member of Reform.[14] Because of the threat to evangelical unity which appeared to be emerging, Richard Bewes of All Souls, Langham Place, worked hard to bring those with differing views together. A conference called by the evangelical bishops in 1995 attracted 1,500 lay people and clergy. The major issue for Reform became the ordination of practising homosexuals.[15] *Strangers and Friends*, by Michael Vasey, a tutor at Cranmer Hall, Durham, asked for a reconsideration of the traditional Christian position of opposition to homosexual practice. At the 1996 Evangelical Anglican Leaders' Conference the conservatives were largely absent. There was much discussion at that conference of hermeneutics. It was evident that evangelical Anglicans were becoming increasingly divided over a number of issues. LBC had links with leaders within the various groups and with those, like John Stott, who transcended the divisions. Through LBC, Stott received a Brunel University DD. At the DD ceremony Derek Tidball spoke of Stott's possibly unmatched contribution to worldwide evangelicalism.

LBC has also trained those who have become leaders within the Baptist denomination. The autumn 1991 *LBC Review* noted that three former LBC students had taken up, or were about to take up, new positions with the BU. Derek Tidball would be secretary for mission and evangelism, Malcolm Goodspeed secretary for ministry, and Eric Westwood, who had been with

---

[13] Steer, *Church on Fire*, 328–9.

[14] In 1999 Tony Higton became general director of the Church's Ministry Amongst Jewish People.

[15] Martin, *Gospel People?* 80–1.

the Baptist Missionary Society in Brazil and missioner for the Northern Baptist Association, would be the BU's president. Indeed, during the 1990s three LBC-trained Baptist ministers became president of the BU – a remarkable record for an interdenominational college. Among LBC's student body, Baptists remained the largest group, as they had been from the beginning. A denominational survey in 1996 showed that 94 students were Baptist, followed by 64 Anglicans, 33 independent evangelicals and 25 classical Pentecostals.

The obvious challenge here is to attract students from other de-nominational backgrounds. LBC has come a long way, since its initial uncertainty over Pentecostal and charismatic questions, to-wards achieving the vision of spiritual unity encouraged by Gilbert Kirby. The challenge inherent in such a legacy is to con-tinue thoughtfully to seek ways to draw movements of renewal more fully into the life of the institution. A significant area of net-working could be the Black majority churches. An article in *Christianity* in 1999 estimated that at least 25 per cent of Britain's one million-strong Black population could be found in a church on an average Sunday.[16]

Most of the rapidly growing churches in the London area in the 1990s were Black majority churches. A number of classical Pente-costals have, as has been noted, taken advantage of the training offered at LBC. It remains to be seen to what extent the newer charismatic churches will wish to train their own leaders and to what extent they will be prepared to allow them to reflect more widely. In 1996 there were only sixteen students from newer churches at LBC. Andrew Walker's 1998 revision of *Restoring the Kingdom* suggested that at this point the main new church networks had about 50,000 people between them.[17] The first thesis produced from within these networks that offered critical reflection on aspects of Restorationist theology was an LBC MTh thesis by Martin Scott of Pioneer, who examined the eschatology

---

[16] *Christianity* (June 1999), 25.
[17] Walker, *Kingdom*, 324, 342, 383.

of the new churches.[18] Meic Pearse was an academic moderator for much of Pioneer's training and Max Turner saw signs of some newer churches wanting to engage theologically.[19]

Pan-Denominationalism and LBC

From its beginnings, LBC had links with the main pan-denominational evangelical organizations in Britain, such as the IVF, SU and the EA. The rapid growth of the EA under the leadership of Clive Calver, with his LBC connections, meant that several former LBC students became central figures within the Alliance. In 1991 Joel Edwards and Ian Coffey were appointed as LBC governors. Both were working for the EA – Edwards as general secretary of the African Caribbean EA, and Coffey as Alliance field director. By the early 1990s the EA could fairly be said to represent most aspects of evangelical church life in Britain. In 1995 EA membership included 2,778 individual churches and 707 organizations. To that could be added 14 whole affiliated denominations, totalling about five thousand member churches. It was a substantial constituency. The EA was, therefore, the leading pan-evangelical organization in Britain, acting as a facilitator of evangelical unity and a resourcing agency.[20] In terms of both general and council EA membership, Anglicans and Baptists predominate. Anglicans and Baptists together account for over 60 per cent of EA membership – a figure not dissimilar to the proportion of these denominations at LBC.

Other developments, in addition to the growth of the EA, have helped to create a more developed sense of pan-denominational evangelical identity. From its relatively small beginnings, Spring Harvest grew to eighty thousand people. LBC has regularly provided speakers for Spring Harvest platforms. Numerous

---

[18] J.M. Scott, 'The Theology of the So-called "New Church" Movement: An Analysis of its Eschatology'.
[19] Interview with Max Turner, 16 Jan. 1999.
[20] Edwards, 'Evangelical Alliance'.

similar events, organized by evangelicals within or outside the main denominations, bring together many tens of thousands of people each year. By the early 1990s, praise walks called 'March for Jesus' were attracting a quarter of a million people in Britain. Steve Clifford, a former LBC student, was one of those deeply involved. LBC's relationship with the IVF/UCCF was not as strong by the 1990s as it had been in the college's earlier period, but there was still considerable common ground, especially through the Tyndale Fellowship. The 1980s had seen the UCCF launch the Whitefield Institute in Oxford to train people in theology, ethics and religious education, and Tony Lane was on the institute's council. Within the EA there was a concern to sharpen theological work and a decision was made in 1994 to set up ACUTE – the Alliance Commission on Unity and Truth among Evangelicals. Max Turner was a member of its steering group. LBC has continued its long-standing links with SU – through John Grayston, a former student, as head of Bible Ministries – and with Christians in education – for example through Trevor and Margaret Cooling, directors of the Education Centre at Stapleford, Nottinghamshire.

There were, of course, those evangelicals in the 1990s who had serious reservations about having fellowship with anyone belonging to a body connected with the ecumenical movement, and the British Evangelical Council provided for such a viewpoint. It, too, had LBC connections, with Alan Gibson as its general secretary until his retirement in 1999. There were still tensions within evangelicalism over ecumenism, and the division of 1966 cast a long shadow, but older divisions over issues such as interpretations of Calvinism were becoming less relevant for a new generation of evangelicals. The Reformed camp had been divided in the mid-1980s over attitudes to charismatics.[21] From that point on there were two papers, the *Evangelical Times* and the more open *Evangelicals Now*, largely serving independent churches. The dominant trend, however, was towards flexibility over ecclesiastical allegiance. Individual LBC faculty members

---

[21] Bebbington, *Evangelicalism*, 268.

were more willing by the 1980s and 1990s to move across denominational boundaries. Yet in many cases denominational convictions are deeply held by teaching staff. One, Conrad Gempf, remains a committed Lutheran.

The year 1996 marked 150 years of the EA, and as well as celebrations throughout the country a volume of essays was produced – For Such a Time as This – as a tribute to Gilbert Kirby. An EA national assembly held in Bournemouth in that year attracted three thousand church leaders. Joel Edwards, who was then UK director of the EA and heavily involved in the arrangements, would soon take over from Clive Calver as general director. Calver was to move to a new post in the USA as president of World Relief. The 1996 EA gathering was the first formal assembly since 1966, and it was held against the background of questions about the Toronto Blessing and post-evangelicalism. The EA approached LBC about producing material for a presentation on contemporary society, and a multimedia presentation exploring life in Britain in the 1990s was produced. Martyn Eden, of the EA, Mark Greene, and students from LBC became heavily involved in this project. Edwards described how platform addresses, worship and seminars enabled reflection on the postmodern context, evangelical diversity and engagement with society.[22] At the end of the assembly, a declaration was produced which covered crucial areas of belief and practice. The focus was on Christ, Scripture and unity; the church and mission; and church and society. It was an agenda that had relevance not only for those present but also for the future vision of LBC.

Derek Tidball's view was that in a changing evangelical scene there were two possible responses that he considered unwise. The first was to resist change and to seek to retain past ways of thinking, while the other was to be overly accommodating. One 'resistant' approach analysed by Tidball was separatism – the attempt by evangelical movements to insulate themselves from the mainstream of the church. Theologically, Tidball argued, this

---

[22] Edwards, Lord, Make us One, 73–4. The LBC video was entitled The Hero.

view of the church was questionable – especially in view of the New Testament teaching about 'the unity and catholicity of the church and freedom brought about by the gospel'.[23] There was still a tendency in the 1990s for some groups to operate in a more insular way. The Stoneleigh Bible Week, for example, which twenty thousand people were attending in the mid-1990s (in the wake of the excitement about Toronto), had a platform line-up drawn almost entirely from its own New Frontiers leadership.[24] The network with which Dave Tomlinson had been associated, however, had been given a 'prophetic word' that the 'house church movement' was over. This word was taken to mean that new churches had no future as a movement distinguished from the mainline churches.[25] LBC, with its commitment both to evangelism and to strengthening pan-denominational links, has a natural role to play within the wider stream of evangelical renewal.

Mission, Society and LBC

LBC would not have grown as rapidly as it did in the 1950s had it not been for the Billy Graham crusades. These crusades continued to have an influence on British thinking about evangelism. But decline in churchgoing continued and approaches to mission began to change. Alpha, a course introducing the Christian faith, has become widely used. By 1996 around five thousand courses were being run all over the world, attended by approximately a quarter of a million people. Alpha courses provide a non-threatening setting – including a meal – in which people are introduced to the Christian faith. Although evangelism was becoming a more low-key affair, however, there was still a

---

[23] Tidball, *Evangelicals?*, 224–8.

[24] T. Virgo, *A People Prepared*, 17.

[25] N. Wright, 'The Nature and Variety of Restorationism and the "House Church" Movement', 71–2.

concern for evangelistic challenge.[26] LBC also wished to emphasize the communication of the gospel – not only through small groups but also through the more traditional preaching ministry. In addition to writing commentaries, Tidball produced books such as *Skilful Shepherds* (1997) and *Builders and Fools* (1999), dealing with issues of ministry. Mark Greene wrote *The Three-Eared Preacher*, a feedback tool for busy ministers. It was vital, as he saw it, for preachers to 'think about what people are thinking'. The transdenominational mix at LBC presented, in Greene's view, an opportunity for different models of ministry and mission to be explored.[27]

A number of staff at LBC have had specific mission responsibilities. Mary Evans, for example, as the UK chair of the Sudan Interior Mission and Chris Jack on the international council of the European Christian Mission (ECM) and as chairman of the ECM's British council. Mark Greene was UK chairman of Jews for Jesus, and was embroiled in controversy in the early 1990s about an advertisement that the organization had placed which critics called 'insulting' and 'insensitive'. In response, Peter Cotterell defended evangelism directed towards the Jews. Sigmund Sternberg, of the Council of Christians and Jews, said that it was impossible to be a Jew and a Christian. Greene replied that it was possible to be a Jew by race and a Christian by belief.[28] Cotterell's own particular interest was the Islamic world, and LBC appointed Peter Riddell, an Islamic specialist, to its Centre for Islamic Studies. Riddell's PhD, from the Australian National University, was in Islamic studies and linguistics, and he taught at an Indonesian university before doing postdoctoral research at the Hebrew University of Jerusalem. As well as undertaking university teaching in Australia, Riddell worked for the international development programme of Australian universities. His experience was strongly multicultural.

---

[26] Hilborn, *Pieces*, 210–14.
[27] I am indebted to Mark Greene for his reflections.
[28] *LBC Rev* (Spring 1992), 4–5.

Mission in a multicultural and multifaith environment was clearly a more controversial matter in the 1990s than it had been earlier in the century. An important aspect of multi-ethnic mission in Britain, already noted, was the growth of the Black churches. Joel Edwards, general secretary of the EA, was the most prominent Black evangelical in Britain at the end of the 1990s. A post Edwards held previously, general secretary of the African Caribbean Evangelical Alliance, was later taken by Mark Sturge, an LBC student from 1992 to 1995. In 1998, there were 38 nationalities represented at LBC. Even more emphasis is likely to be placed in the future on the inappropriateness of any concept of Christian mission as an exportation of White, western thinking. Allegations could easily have been made in the past, and indeed were made with justification in some instances, about Christian imperialism and triumphalism. Peter Cotterell was deeply suspicious of any simplistic views of God's purposes as seen from a comfortable western perspective. There was a sense, for him, in which God was *not* on the throne since much was not according to the divine will.[29] More theology in the future is likely to come from the 'underside of history', from non-western viewpoints, and LBC has a continuing and vital role in expressing the diversity of evangelicalism worldwide.

A further factor affecting mission and ministry is likely to be the role of women. Within the Church of England, a measure was passed by the general synod in 1986 which laid the groundwork for women being admitted to the diaconate, and this in turn led to them being accepted as priests. By 1997, a tenth of the Church of England's clergy were women.[30] In parallel to this, evangelical events such as Spring Harvest gave greater prominence to women. In 1985 Faith Forster was the first woman to preach from the main platform at Spring Harvest. At LBC, women had been on the staff since Kevan's era, and 1996 saw the publication of *The Study Bible for Women: The New Testament*, edited by Mary Evans, with Catherine Clark Kroeger and Elaine Storkey. This

---

[29] *LBC Rev* (Spring 1991), 5.
[30] Steer, *Church on Fire*, 330.

volume was seeking to allow the perspective of women to be heard. Women who had connections with LBC were well represented – ten were contributors – and Mary Evans spoke of the progress LBC had made in the training of women. She added that much remained to be done.[31] In 1998, 44 per cent of the students beginning undergraduate courses at LBC were women, but at postgraduate level the figure was only 16 per cent. Gill Dallow moved from LBC to become children's ministry adviser to the Leicester diocese and a local parish minister, and in 1999 Jane Rennie was appointed to the LBC staff. In the same year Dianne Tidball, who had studied at LBC and who had subsequently married Derek, became a Baptist minister. She had been a secondary school teacher.

Mission in the 1990s was also even more closely associated with social and political action. The trend in overseas mission was towards increasing support for relief and development work. Issues such as the burden of debt crippling many Third World countries were being addressed. It was Mark Greene, who moved to become director of Christian Impact in 1999, who suggested the slogan 'Drop the Debt'. This slogan was used very successfully by the Jubilee 2000 campaign in its huge demonstrations throughout Europe in 1999. The ideas which took shape in Jubilee 2000 stemmed from talks among a small group in the mid-1990s. A pivotal moment was when Greene gave this group a presentation in which he sketched out a strategy for achieving its aims. TEAR Fund, Christian Aid, Catholic Fund for Overseas Development (CAFOD) and the World Development Movement ranged themselves behind the campaign. From small beginnings, 90 organizations joined the campaign, and following the meeting of the leaders of the world economic community in May 1998 (when seventy thousand people formed a human chain in Birmingham) the British government called for a fundamental review of debt relief at meetings of the World Bank.[32] Commitment by evangelicals to such issues was in tune with LBC's vision of mission involving the whole of life.

---

[31] *LBC Rev* (Spring 1996), 4–5.
[32] *Baptist T* (24 June 1999).

This vision affected thinking about evangelical life in the context of British society. Graham Dale, who left LBC in the 1980s, reflected on the political role of the EA's Whitefield Associates, of which he was project consultant. For him it was a mark of political maturity to realize that evangelicals lived in the world alongside others who did not share their faith but with whom they could work for the common good and to achieve socio-political objectives.[33] LBC was pleased, in 1991, that Paul Cattermole, who had been at LBC in the 1960s, was awarded an MBE for service as a senior army chaplain in Northern Ireland. Paul Carter, another former LBC student, was also a chaplain in the forces. In 1996–97 Julia Jaeger was the second woman to become chair of the LBC old students' association. She was a sergeant in the Metropolitan Police. By the mid-1990s there were, as Clive Calver pointed out, nationally known social projects run by Baptist minister and television presenter, Steve Chalke; Christian Action Networks that had been encouraged by Sir Fred Catherwood; AIDS Concern for Education and Training; and publications such as *Westminster Watch*. All of these ventures were pointing to evangelical influence in society.[34]

A final factor in the mission of the church at the turn of the millennium is the emphasis on spirituality. At a time when evangelicals were exploring streams of spirituality, Derek Tidball drew from the writings of Richard Foster, an American evangelical Quaker, who wrote seminal books such as *Celebration of Discipline* (1978). Tidball found, on becoming LBC principal, that the existing fellowship groups at LBC had, in most cases, ceased to function effectively. He replaced these with 'Renovaré Groups' (a title taken from Foster), which were small committed prayer cells. Involvement in small groups increased from 50 per cent of the student body to over 90 per cent. The college was ready to learn from wider Christian tradition, and the Orthodox Metropolitan Anthony Bloom, for example, had led a

---

[33] Hilborn, *Pieces*, 258–9.
[34] C. Calver, 'Afterword', 198–210.

quiet day in the 1980s. Deryck Sheriffs wrote a significant book on Old Testament spirituality entitled *The Friendship of the Lord*. It set out a world-engaging spirituality based on solid academic research and concern to be true to the text of Scripture. Tidball wrote:

> It is easy in today's world to come up with a hybrid spirituality which is no longer evangelical or to transform the evangelical tradition so much that it ceases to be evangelical. The challenge then is so to breathe life into tradition that it does, as it can, answer the deepest inner searches of the contemporary seeker.[35]

This was an important agenda for mission.

Derek Tidball's words here also reveal another crucial overall change to which LBC has contributed in post-World War II Britain – in the area of evangelical attitudes to tradition and catholicity. Although Tidball speaks quite matter-of-factly about 'tradition', it was something that most British evangelicals in the 1940s rejected almost by definition. There was a widespread supposition that evangelicals, alone among so-called Christians, possessed the truth; indeed, they could virtually be equated with Christians. The views of people and movements associated with LBC demonstrate that by the end of the 1990s this was decidedly not the assumption that was generally being made. Over the previous decades many evangelicals had come to understand that they were part of the wider church, rather than believing that they constituted the whole of the church visible.[36] This insight further equipped evangelicals for the massive task of mission in the new millennium.

Conclusion

Inevitably, LBC has been affected by trends in evangelicalism and in wider society. Its story, however, is also one of

---

[35] Tidball, *Evangelicals?* 224–8.

[36] I am indebted to David Bebbington for these insights.

innovation. In the 1940s and 1950s it was a pioneer of academic evangelical theology in an interdenominational British setting. Those who studied at LBC under Ernest Kevan and his team went on to affect evangelical theological education in many parts of the world. At times the college struggled to decide where the theological boundary lines should be drawn, but it refused to be bound to a narrow expression of evangelical faith and LBC's influence helped to shape a more reflective form of evangelical life. Having weathered some of the evangelical divisions of the 1960s, the decade of the 1970s, under the leadership of Gilbert Kirby, saw the college sending out many who would become significant leaders of the 1980s. The college had difficulty in coming to terms with some of the issues raised by charismatic renewal, and it did not initially give a theological lead in this area, although Max Turner later compensated for that lack. LBC did, however, succeed in creating a type of theological training that was properly 'applied'. These concerns were shared, and were worked out in various ways, by Michael Griffiths, Peter Cotterell and Derek Tidball in the 1980s and 1990s.

Surveys in the second half of the 1990s show that almost half of those leaving LBC normally go into pastoral ministry and into mission in Britain or elsewhere. About a quarter go on to further study. The remainder enter teaching or other professions. It is clear that very many denominational and transdenominational bodies have been strengthened by those who have trained at the college and all the signs are that this will continue to be the case. Former students have taken many strategic positions in churches, colleges, hospitals, schools and mission agencies throughout the world. Greater choices for study and training are now available to larger numbers of students. Among these options are new ideas for equipping people theologically in relation to areas such as worship and counselling. A major challenge for the college in the next century may be to maintain its traditionally high standards of academic scholarship and its commitment to training for ministry while at the same time responding to a culture very different from that of fifty years ago. Evangelicals will be called to provide what Tidball described as 'a clear but humble pathway through the supermarket variety of spiritualities on offer'. LBC's future task, which is in continuity with its past, will be to educate evangelicals who will effectively communicate the Christian gospel in a rapidly changing market place of ideas.

Bibliography

Allen, L.C., *The Books of Joel, Obadiah, Jonah and Micah* (Grand Rapids: Eerdmans, 1976).

——, *Ezekiel 20–48* (Word Biblical Commentary, 29; Dallas: Word, 1990).

——, 'Personal Reminiscences', in M.J. Wilkins and T. Paige (eds.), *Worship, Theology and Ministry in the Early Church: Essays in Honor of Ralph P. Martin* (Sheffield: JSOT Press, 1992), 33–6.

Avis, P., *The Church in the Theology of the Reformers* (Atlanta: John Knox Press, 1981).

——, *Ecumenical Theology and the Elusiveness of Doctrine* (London: SPCK, 1986).

——, *Christians in Communion* (London: Chapman Mowbray, 1990).

Barclay, O., *Evangelicalism in Britain, 1935–1995* (Leicester: IVP, 1997).

Bebbington, D.W., *Evangelicalism in Modern Britain: A History from the 1730s to the 1980s* (London: Unwin Hyman, 1989).

——, 'Evangelicalism in its Settings: The British and American Movements since 1940', in M.A. Noll, D.W. Bebbington and G.A. Rawlyk (eds.), *Evangelicalism: Comparative Studies of Popular Protestantism in North America, the British Isles and Beyond, 1700–1990* (Oxford: Oxford University Press, 1994), 365–88.

Bediako, K., *Theology and Identity* (Oxford: Regnum, 1992).

——, 'Cry Jesus! Christian Theology and Presence in Modern Africa', *Vox Evangelica* 23 (1993), 7–25.

Billington, A., A.N.S. Lane and M.M.B. Turner (eds.), *Mission and Meaning* (Carlisle: Paternoster, 1995).

Bowers, P., 'Evangelical Theology in Africa: Byang Kato's Legacy', *Evangelical Review of Theology* 5.1 (April 1981), 35–9.

Boyd, A. *Baroness Cox: A Voice for the Voiceless* (Oxford: Lion, 1998).

Brady, S., 'Gilbert Kirby, an Evangelical Statesman: A Tribute and a Profile', in S. Brady and H.H. Rowdon, *For Such a Time as This* (London: Scripture Union, 1996), 1–20.

Bruce, F.F., *In Retrospect: Remembrance of Things Past* (London: Pickering & Inglis, 1980).

Buchanan, C., 'Anglican Evangelicalism: The State of the "Party" ', *Anvil* 1.1 (1984), 10–12.

——, *Is the Church of England Biblical?* (London: Darton, Longman & Todd, 1998).

Calver, C., 'Afterword', in J. Wolffe (ed.), *Evangelical Faith and Public Zeal* (London: SPCK, 1995), 198–210.

Carey, G., *The Gate of Glory* (London: Hodder & Stoughton, rev. edn, 1992).

Catherwood, H.F.R., *The Christian in Industrial Society* (London: Tyndale Press, 1966).

——, 'An Interview', in C. Catherwood (ed.), *Martyn Lloyd-Jones: Chosen by God* (Crowborough: Highland Books, 1986).

——, *At the Cutting Edge* (London: Hodder & Stoughton, 1995).

Chadwick, O., *Michael Ramsey: A Life* (London: SCM Press, 1990).

Chae, D.J.-S., *Paul as Apostle to the Gentiles* (Carlisle: Paternoster, 1997).

Chester, T., *Awakening to a World of Need* (Leicester: IVP, 1993).

Clements, K.W., *Lovers of Discord: Twentieth-Century Theological Controversies in England* (London: SPCK, 1988).

Coad, F.R., *A History of the Brethren Movement* (Exeter: Paternoster, 1976).

——, *Laing: The Biography of Sir John W. Laing, C.B.E. (1879–1978)* (London: Hodder & Stoughton, 1979).

Coates, G., *An Intelligent Fire* (Eastbourne: Kingsway, 1991).

Cooke, G., 'Why Women at London Bible College?' *Areopagus* (Spring 1972).

Costas, O., *The Church and its Mission: A Shattering Critique from the Third World* (Wheaton, IL: Tyndale House Publishers, 1974).

Cotterell, F.P., 'The Unevangelized: An Olive Branch from the Opposition', *International Review of Mission* 77 (Jan. 1988), 131–35.

——, *Cry Ethiopia* (Eastbourne: MARC, 1988).

——, *Mission and Meaninglessness: The Good News in a World of Suffering and Disorder* (London: SPCK, 1990).

Cotterell, F.P., and M.M.B. Turner, *Linguistics and Biblical Interpretation* (London: SPCK, 1989).

Cray, G., et al. (eds.), *The Post-Evangelical Debate* (London: Triangle, 1997).

Doubleday, C., *Then the Curtain Opened* (Leicester: IVP, 1998).

Dudley-Smith, T., *John Stott: A Comprehensive Bibliography* (Downers Grove, IL: IVP, 1995).

——, *John Stott: The Making of a Leader* (Leicester: IVP, 1999).

Eastman, M., with P. Cousins (eds.), *The Bible and the Open Approach in Religious Education* (London: Tyndale Press, 1968).

Eddison, J., *A Study in Spiritual Power* (Crowborough: Highland Books, 1992).

Edwards, B., *Revival: A People Saturated with God* (Darlington: Evangelical Press, 1990).

Edwards, J., 'The Evangelical Alliance: A National Phenomenon', in S. Brady and H.H. Rowdon (eds.), *For Such a Time as This* (London: Scripture Union, 1996), ch. 5.

——, *Lord, Make us One – But not all the Same!* (London: Hodder & Stoughton, 1999).

Ellison, H.L., 'Some Thoughts on Inspiration', *Evangelical Quarterly* 26.4 (1954), 213–14.

——, *From Tragedy to Triumph: The Message of the Book of Job* (London: Paternoster, 1958).

Evans, M.J., *Woman in the Bible* (Exeter: Paternoster, 1983).

——, *1 and 2 Samuel* (NIBC OT; Peabody, MA: Hendrickson, 1999).

Evans, M.J., C. Kroeger and E. Storkey (eds.), *The Study Bible for Women: The New Testament* (Grand Rapids: Baker Book House, 1995).

Fiedler, K., *The Story of Faith Missions* (Oxford: Regnum, 1994).

Field-Bibb, J., *Women towards Priesthood: Ministerial Politics and Feminist Praxis* (Cambridge: Cambridge University Press, 1991).

Gill, D.W.J., and C. Gempf, *The Book of Acts in its First Century Setting*, II: *The Book of Acts in its Graeco-Roman Setting* (Grand Rapids: Eerdmans / Carlisle: Paternoster, 1994).

Gillett, D.K., *Trust and Obey: Explorations in Evangelical Spirituality* (London: Darton, Longman & Todd, 1993).

Gillies, D., *Unity in the Dark* (London: Banner of Truth Trust, 1964).

Green, M., 'Christ's Sacrifice and Ours: Relating Holy Communion to the Cross', in J.I. Packer (ed.), *Guidelines: Anglican Evangelicals Face the Future* (London: Church Pastoral Aid Society, 1967), 87–117.

Greene, M., *Thank God it's Monday: Ministry in the Workplace* (Bletchley: Scripture Union, 1994).

Griffiths, M., *Give up your Small Ambitions* (Chicago: Moody, 1971).

——, *Cinderella with Amnesia: A Restatement in Contemporary Terms of the Biblical Doctrine of the Church* (London: IVP, 1975).

——, *Cinderella's Betrothal Gifts* (Sevenoaks: OMF, 1978).

——, *Shaking the Sleeping Beauty: Arousing the Church to its Mission* (Leicester: IVP, 1980).

——, *What on Earth are you Doing? Jesus' Call to World Mission* (Leicester: IVP, 1983).

——, *Tinker, Tailor, Missionary? Options in a Changing World* (Leicester: IVP, 1992).

Guinness, O., *The Dust of Death* (Downers Grove, IL: IVP, 1972).

Guthrie, D., *New Testament Introduction* (3 vols.; London: Tyndale Press, 1961–65).

——, 'Recent Literature on the Acts of the Apostles', *Vox Evangelica* (London: Epworth Press, 1963), 33–49.

——, *Galatians* (New Century Bible; London: Nelson, 1969).

——, *New Testament Theology* (Leicester: IVP, 1990[4]).

——, *The Pastoral Epistles: An Introduction and Commentary* (Tyndale NT Commentary Series, 14; Leicester: IVP, 1990).

——, *I Stand for Truth* (London, 1992).

Harper, M.C., *As at the Beginning: The Twentieth-Century Pentecostal Movement* (London: Hodder & Stoughton, 1965).

——, *The True Light* (London: Hodder & Stoughton, 1997).

Harris, H.A., *Fundamentalism and Evangelicals* (Oxford: Oxford University Press, 1998).

Hastings, A., *A History of English Christianity, 1920–1990* (London: SCM Press, 1991).

Hebert, G., *Fundamentalism and the Church of God* (London: SCM Press, 1957).

Henry, C.F.H. (ed.), *Revelation and the Bible* (London: Tyndale Press, 1959).

——, *Frontiers in Modern Theology* (Chicago: Moody, 1965).

Hicks, P., *Evangelicals and Truth* (Leicester: IVP, 1998).

Higton, T. (ed.), *Sexuality and the Church* (Eastbourne: Kingsway, 1987).

Higton T., and G.W. Kirby, *The Challenge of the Housechurches* (Oxford: Latimer House, 1988).

Hilborn, D., *Picking up the Pieces* (London: Hodder & Stoughton, 1997).

Hocken, P., *Streams of Renewal* (Carlisle: Paternoster, 1997).

Howard, D.M., *The Dream That Would Not Die* (Exeter: Paternoster, 1986).

Howard, R., *The Rise and Fall of the Nine O'clock Service: A Cult within the Church* (London: Mowbray, 1996).

Hudson, D.N., 'Worship', in K. Warrington (ed.), *Pentecostal Perspectives* (Carlisle: Paternoster, 1998), 177–203.

Hulse, E., *Billy Graham: The Pastor's Dilemma* (Hounslow, Middlesex: M. Allen, 1966).

Hylson-Smith, K., *Evangelicals in the Church of England, 1734–1984* (Edinburgh: T. & T. Clark, 1988).

——, *The Churches in England from Elizabeth I to Elizabeth II*, III: *1833–1998* (London: SCM Press, 1998).

Johnson, D., *Contending for Faith: A History of the Evangelical Movement in the Universities and Colleges* (Leicester: IVP, 1979).

Jones, H.R., *Unity in Truth* (Darlington: Evangelical Press, 1991).

Kato, B., *Theological Pitfalls in Africa* (Kisumu, Kenya: Evangelical Publishing House, 1975).

Kay, W.K., *Inside Story* (Mattersey: AOG, 1990).

Kevan, E.F., 'The Principles of Interpretation', in C.F.H. Henry (ed.), *Revelation and the Bible* (London: Tyndale Press, 1959), 283–98.

——, 'Legalism: An Essay on the Views of Dr Emil Brunner', in R.P. Martin (ed.), *Vox Evangelica*, II: *Biblical and Historical Essays by Members of the Faculty of the London Bible College* (London: Epworth Press, 1963), 50–57.

——, *Salvation* (Grand Rapids: Baker Book House, 1963).

——, *The Grace of Law: A Study in Puritan Theology* (London: Carey Kingsgate Press, 1964).

Kirby, G.W., 'What of the Future?' in H.H. Rowdon, *London Bible College: The First Twenty-Five Years* (Worthing: Walter, 1968), 138–40.

——, *Ernest Kevan: Pastor and Principal* (Eastbourne: Kingsway, 1968).

——, 'An Age of Ferment', an unpublished paper reviewing the 1970s.

——, *Too Hot to Handle* (Lakeland: Marshall, Morgan & Scott, 1978).

——, 'Social Trends in the 1980s', an unpublished paper.

Kuhrt, G.W., 'Principled Comprehensiveness', in A.F. Gibson (ed.), *The Church and its Unity* (Leicester: IVP, 1992).

Laird, J., *No Mere Chance* (London: Hodder & Stoughton, 1981).

Lane, A.N.S., 'Kenya's Turbulent Bishop', *Evangelical Review of Theology* 16.1 (1992), 66–81.

Lewis, P., *The Genius of Puritanism* (Haywards Heath: Carey Publications, 1975).

——, 'The Doctor as a Preacher', in C. Catherwood (ed.), *Martyn Lloyd-Jones: Chosen by God* (Crowborough: Highland Books, 1986).

Lindsell, H., *The Battle for the Bible* (Grand Rapids: Zondervan, 1976).

Lloyd-Jones, D.M., 'Christ our Sanctification', in D.M. Blair et al., *Christ our Freedom* (London: IVF, 1939), 54–78.

——, *Preaching and Preachers* (London: Hodder & Stoughton, 1971).

——, *Training for the Ministry Today* (London: LTS, 1977).

Lundin, R., A.C. Thiselton, and C. Walhout, *The Promise of Hermeneutics* (Grand Rapids: Eerdmans / Carlisle: Paternoster, 1999).

Marsden, G.M., *Fundamentalism and American Culture: The Shaping of Twentieth-Century Evangelicalism, 1870–1925* (Oxford: Oxford University Press, 1980).

——, *Reforming Fundamentalism: Fuller Seminary and the New Evangelicalism* (Grand Rapids: Eerdmans, 1987).

——, *The Outrageous Idea of Christian Scholarship* (New York: Oxford University Press, 1997).

Martin, J., *Gospel People? Evangelicals and the Future of Anglicanism* (London: SPCK, 1997).

Martin, R.P., *Carmen Christi: Philippians ii. 5–11 in Recent Interpretation and in the Setting of Early Christian Worship* (London: Cambridge University Press, 1967).

Martin, W., *The Billy Graham Story: A Prophet with Honour* (London: Hutchinson, 1992).

McBain, D., 'Mainstream Charismatics', in S. Hunt, M. Hamilton and T. Walter (eds.), *Charismatic Christianity: Sociological Perspectives* (Basingstoke: Macmillan, 1997), 43–59.

——, *Fire over the Waters: Renewal among Baptists and Others from the 1960s to the 1990s* (London: Darton, Longman & Todd, 1997).

McDonald, H.D., *Theories of Revelation: An Historical Study, 1860–1960* (London: Allen & Unwin, 1963).

——, 'What is Meant by Religious Experience?' *Vox Evangelica* II (London: Epworth Press, 1963), 58–70.

——, 'The Changing Emphasis in the Doctrine of Providence', *Vox Evangelica* III (London: Epworth Press, 1964), 58–75.

——, *Jesus, Human and Divine: An Introduction to New Testament Christology* (Lanham, MD: University Press of America, 1989).

——, *The New Testament Concept of Atonement: The Gospel of the Calvary Event* (Cambridge: Lutterworth Press, 1994).

McFarlane, G.W.P., *Christ and the Spirit* (Carlisle: Paternoster, 1996).

——, *Why Do You Believe What You Believe About the Holy Spirit?* (Carlisle: Paternoster, 1998).

McGrath, A.E., 'Evangelical Anglicanism: A Contradiction in Terms?' in R.T. France and A.E. McGrath (eds.), *Evangelical Anglicans: Their Role and Influence in the Church Today* (London: SPCK, 1993), 10–21.

——, *Evangelicalism and the Future of Christianity* (London: Hodder & Stoughton, 1994).

——, *To Know and Serve God: A Biography of James I. Packer* (London: Hodder & Stoughton, 1997).

Mitchell, G., *Comfy Glasgow* (Fearn: Christian Focus Publications, 1999).

Motyer, S., *Your Father the Devil? A New Approach to John and 'the Jews'* (Carlisle: Paternoster, 1997).

Mouw, R., 'The Challenge of Evangelical Theological Education', in D.G. Hart and R.A. Mohler (eds.), *Theological Education in the Evangelical Tradition* (Grand Rapids: Baker Book House, 1996), 16:284–9.

Murray, I.H., *D. Martyn Lloyd-Jones: The Fight of Faith, 1939–1981* (Edinburgh: Banner of Truth Trust, 1990).

Negrut, P., *Focus on Eastern Europe* (Bedford, 1992).

Noll, M.A., *The Scandal of the Evangelical Mind* (Grand Rapids: Eerdmans, 1994).

Packer, J.I., ' "Keswick" and the Reformed Doctrine of Sanctification', *Evangelical Quarterly* 27.3 (1955), 153–67.

——, *Evangelism and the Sovereignty of God* (Downers Grove, IL: IVP, 1961).

——, *Keep in Step with the Spirit* (Leicester: IVP, 1984).

Parsons, G., 'Contrasts and Continuities: The Traditional Christian Churches in Britain since 1945', in G. Parsons (ed.), *The Growth of Religious Diversity: Britain from 1945*, I: *Traditions* (London: Routledge, 1993), 23–94.

Pearse, M., *The Great Restoration: The Religious Radicals of the Sixteenth and Seventeenth Centuries* (Carlisle: Paternoster, 1998).

Pearse, M., and C. Matthews, *We Must Stop Meeting Like This* (Eastbourne: Kingsway, 1999).

Percy, M., *Words, Wonders and Power* (London: SPCK, 1996).

Pollock, J.C., *A Cambridge Movement* (London: J. Murray, 1953).

——, *The Good Seed: The Story of the Children's Special Service Mission and the Scripture Union* (London: Hodder & Stoughton, 1959).

Poole-Connor, E.J., *The Apostasy of English Non-Conformity* (London: Thyne & Co., 1933).

Porter, S.E., and P.J. Richter (eds.), *The Toronto Blessing – or Is It?* (London: Darton, Longman & Todd, 1995).

Randall, I.M., 'Spiritual Renewal and Social Reform: Attempts to Develop Social Awareness in the Early Keswick Movement', *Vox Evangelica* 23 (1993), 67–86.

——, 'Conservative Constructionist: The Early Influence of Billy Graham in Britain', *Evangelical Quarterly* 67.4 (1995), 309–33.

——, 'Schism and Unity: 1905–1966', in S. Brady and H.H. Rowdon, *For Such a Time as This* (London: Scripture Union, 1996), 163–77.

——, *Evangelical Experiences: A Study in the Spirituality of English Evangelicalism, 1918–1939* (Carlisle: Paternoster, 1999).

Robinson, J.A.T., *Honest to God* (London: SCM Press, 1964).

Robinson, J.A.T and D.L. Edwards, *The Honest to God Debate* (London: SCM Press, 1963).

Rowdon, H.H., *The Origins of the Brethren, 1825–1850* (London: Pickering & Inglis, 1967).

——, *London Bible College: The First Twenty-Five Years* (Worthing: Henry E. Walton, 1968).

——, 'Donald Guthrie: An Appreciation', in H.H. Rowdon (ed.), *Christ the Lord* (Leicester: IVP, 1982), ix–xi.

Sargent, T., *The Sacred Anointing: The Preaching of Dr Martyn Lloyd-Jones* (London: Hodder & Stoughton, 1994).

Saunders, T., and H. Sansom, *David Watson* (London: Hodder & Stoughton, 1992).

Saward, M., *The Anglican Church Today: Evangelicals on the Move* (Oxford: Mowbray 1987).

——, *A Faint Streak of Humility: An Autobiography* (Carlisle: Paternoster, 1999).

Scott, J.M., 'The Theology of the So-called "New Church" Movement: An Analysis of its Eschatology' (Brunel University MTh, 1997).

Sheriffs, D., *The Friendship of the Lord: An Old Testament Spirituality* (Carlisle: Paternoster, 1996).

Silk, M., 'The Rise of the "New Evangelicalism": Shock and Adjustment', in W.R. Hutchison (ed.), *Between the Times: The Travail of the Protestant Establishment in America, 1900–1960* (Cambridge: Cambridge University Press, 1989).

Smith, D.W., *Transforming the World?* (Carlisle: Paternoster, 1998).

Sookhdeo, P., (ed.), *All One in Christ* (London: Marshall, Morgan & Scott, 1974).

——, (ed.), *Jesus Christ the Only Way: Christian Responsibility in a Multicultural Society* (Exeter: Paternoster, 1978).

——, 'Race in Britain – A Challenge to the Church', *Christian Graduate* 33.2 (1980), 2–5.

Steer, R., *Church on Fire: The Story of Anglican Evangelicals* (London: Hodder & Stoughton, 1998).

Stone, J.R., *On the Boundaries of American Evangelicalism* (Basingstoke: Macmillan, 1997).

Stott, J.R.W., *Fundamentalism and Evangelism* (London: EA, 1955).

——, 'Evangelism in the Student World', *Christian Graduate* 12.1 (1959).

——, *Your Mind Matters: The Place of the Mind in the Christian Life* (London: IVP, 1972).

——, *New Issues Facing Christians Today* (London: Marshall Pickering, 1999).

Thiselton, A.C., *Two Horizons: New Testament Hermeneutics and Philosophical Description* (Grand Rapids: Eerdmans / Carlisle: Paternoster, 1980).

——, *New Horizons in Hermeneutics: The Theory and Practice of Transforming Biblical Reading* (London: Marshall Pickering, 1992).

Thomas, O., 'Irresistible Grace', in D. Guthrie (ed.), *Vox Evangelica* (London: Epworth Press, 1965), 55–64.

Thompson, P., *Climbing on Track: A Biography of Fred Mitchell* (London: China Inland Mission, 1953).

Tidball, D.J., *Contemporary Evangelical Social Thinking – A Review* (Nottingham: Shaftesbury Project, 1977).

——, *An Introduction to the Sociology of the New Testament* (Carlisle: Paternoster, 1983; republished under the title *The Social Context of the New Testament* [1997]).

——, *Skilful Shepherds: An Introduction to Pastoral Theology* (Leicester: IVP, 1986).

——, *Builders and Fools* (Leicester: IVP, 1999).

——, *Who are the Evangelicals? Tracing the Roots of Modern Movements* (London: Marshall Pickering, 1994).

——, *Crossway Bible Guides – Leviticus* (Leicester: Crossway, 1996).

Tomlinson, D., *The Post-Evangelical* (London: Triangle, 1995).

Turner, M.M.B., 'Spiritual Gifts Then and Now', *Vox Evangelica* 15 (1985), 7–64.

——, *Power From on High: The Spirit in Israel's Restoration and Witness in Luke–Acts* (Sheffield: Sheffield Academic Press, 1996).

——, *The Holy Spirit and Spiritual Gifts: Then and Now* (Carlisle: Paternoster, 1996; updated and reprinted in 1999).

Tyler, H., 'The Encourager', in C. Catherwood (ed.), *Martyn Lloyd-Jones: Chosen by God* (Crowborough: Highland Books, 1986).

Virgo, T., *A People Prepared* (Eastbourne: Kingsway, 1996).

Walford, J.D., *Yesterday and Today* (St Albans: Crusaders, 1995).

Walker, A., 'Thoroughly Modern', in S. Hunt, M. Hamilton and T. Walter (eds.), *Charismatic Christianity: Sociological Perspectives* (Basingstoke: Macmillan, 1997).

——, *Restoring the Kingdom: The Radical Christianity of the House Church Movement* (Guildford: Eagle, 1998).

Wells, D., *No Place for Truth* (Leicester: IVP, 1993).

Welsby, P.A., *A History of the Church of England, 1945–1980* (Oxford: Oxford University Press, 1984).

Wenham, J., *Facing Hell: An Autobiography, 1913–1996* (Carlisle: Paternoster, 1998).

West, W.M.S., *To be a Pilgrim: A Memoir of Ernest A. Payne* (Guildford: Lutterworth Press, 1983).

Wright, N., 'The Nature and Variety of Restorationism and the "House Church" Movement', in S. Hunt, M. Hamilton and T. Walter (eds.), *Charismatic Christianity: Sociological Perspectives* (Basingstoke: Macmillan, 1997), 60–76.

Appendix 1

Doctrinal Basis

The London Bible College accepts and proclaims the historic truths of Christian faith and conduct, including the following:

a) *God and the Human Race*

We believe that the Lord our God is eternally one God:
    Father, Son and Holy Spirit,
    and that he fulfils the sovereign purposes of his providence
    – in creation, revelation, redemption, judgement,
    and the coming of his kingdom –
    calling out from the world a people,
    united to himself and to each other in love.

We acknowledge that though God made humanity
    in his own likeness and image,
    conferring on us dignity and worth
    and enabling us to respond to himself,
    we are now members of a fallen race,
    who have sinned and come short of his glory.

We believe that the Father's holy love is shown supremely
   in that he gave Jesus Christ, his only Son, for us
   when, through our sinfulness and guilt, we were subject
   to his wrath and condemnation;
   and that his grace is shown supremely
   by his putting sinners right with himself
   when they place their trust in his Son.

We confess Jesus Christ
   as Lord and God, the eternal Son of the Father;
   as truly human, born of the virgin Mary;
   as Servant, sinless, full of grace and truth;
   as only Mediator and Saviour of the whole world,
   dying on the cross in our place,
   representing us to God,
   redeeming us from the grip, guilt and punishment of sin;
   as the Second Adam, the head of a new humanity,
   living a life of perfect obedience,
   overcoming death and decay,
   rising from the dead with a glorious body,
   being taken up to be with the Father,
   one day returning personally in glory and judgement
   to bring eternal life to the redeemed and eternal death to the
   lost,
   to establish a new heaven and a new earth, the home of
   righteousness,
   where there will be no more evil, suffering or death;
   as Victor over Satan and all his forces,
   rescuing us from the dominion of darkness, and
   bringing us into his own kingdom;
   as the Word who makes God known.

We believe in the Holy Spirit
   who with the Father and the Son is worthy of our worship,
   who convicts the world of guilt in regard to sin, righteousness
   and judgement,
   who makes the death of Christ effective to sinners,

enabling them to turn to God in repentance
and directing their trust towards the Lord Jesus Christ;
who through the new birth unites us with Christ,
who is present within all believers;
and makes us partake in Christ's risen life,
pointing us to Jesus,
freeing us from slavery to sin,
producing in us his fruit,
granting to us his gifts, and
empowering us for service in the world.

b) The Scriptures

We believe that the Old and New Testament Scriptures
are God-breathed since their writers spoke from God
as they were moved by the Holy Spirit;
hence, they are fully trustworthy in all that they affirm;
and as the written Word of God they are our supreme authority
for faith and conduct.

We acknowledge the need for the Scriptures to be rightly
interpreted
under the guidance of the Holy Spirit and
using the gifts of understanding and scholarship that God has
given to his people.

c) The Church and its Mission

We recognise the Church
as the body of Christ, of which he is the head,
held together and growing up in him through the one Spirit;
both as a total fellowship throughout the world, and
as local congregations in which believers gather to worship
God,
growing in grace through Word, prayer and sacrament.

We acknowledge the commission of Christ

to proclaim the Good News to all people,
making them disciples, baptising them, and
teaching them to obey him.

We acknowledge the command of Christ
to love our neighbours,
resulting in service to the Church and to society,
in seeking reconciliation for all with God and their fellows,
in proclaiming liberty from every kind of oppression; and
in spreading Christ's justice in an unjust world

. . . until he comes again.

February 1998

Appendix 2

Leadership of London Bible College 1943–99

Presidents
Rev W.H. Aldis 1946–48
Montague Goodman 1949–58
Sir John Laing 1959–78
Sir Eric Richardson 1978–89
Dr Donald Guthrie 1989–92
Sir Maurice Laing 1993–99
The Baroness Cox 1999–

Vice-Presidents
Bishop H. Gough 1949–59
Rev J. Russell Howden 1952–59
Philip Henman 1970–80
E.G.A. Bartlett 1975–80
Sir Eric Richardson 1976–78
Derek Warren 1986–99

Chairmen
Rev W.H. Aldis 1943–46
Montague Goodman 1946–58
Rev J. Russell Howden 1948–51
Philip Henman 1958–70
Sir Eric Richardson 1970–77
Derek Warren 1977–83

Prof Sir Robert Boyd 1983–90
Ven Eddie Shirras 1990–93
Denis Cole OBE 1993–99
James Armstrong 1999–

Vice-Chairman
Dr Martyn Lloyd-Jones 1943–56

Principals
Dr W.G. Scroggie (Director) 1943
Fred Mitchell (Director) 1943–46
Dr E.F. Kevan 1946–65
Rev Gilbert W. Kirby 1966–80
Dr Michael Griffiths 1980–89
Dr E. Peter Cotterell 1990–95
Dr Derek J. Tidball 1995–

Vice-Principals
Dr H. Dermot McDonald 1958–75
Dr Donald Guthrie 1978–83
Dr R.T. France 1983–88
Rev Nick Mercer (Assistant) 1990–95
Mark Greene (Community) 1995–99
Professor Max Turner (Academic) 1995–

Appendix 3

LONDON BIBLE COLLEGE

Full-Time Members of the London Bible College Academic Staff

E.F. Kevan
  Principal 1946–65

J.H. Stringer 1946–53
H. Dermot McDonald
    1948–75
  (Vice-Principal 1958–75)
E.W. Hadwen 1948–49
P.G. Eyers 1948–53
D. Guthrie 1949–83
  (Vice-Principal 1978–83)
H.L. Ellison 1949–55
T.J. Buckley 1950–90
R.N. Ash 1951–57
O.J. Thomas 1951–76
J.C. Connell 1953–78
H.H. Rowdon 1954–91
J.C.J. Waite 1955–61

Miss R. Parker 1955–61
H.C. Oakley 1957–64
Mrs M. Dannatt 1958–62
R.P. Martin 1959–65
L.C. Allen 1960–83
Miss M. Manton 1961–67
A.E. Cundall 1961–80
G.W. Grogan 1965–69

G.W. Kirby
  Principal 1966–80

D. Jackson 1967–75
Miss E. Knight 1967–88
D. Carnegie 1968–70
J.F. Balchin 1972–85
A.N.S. Lane 1973–

M.M.B. Turner 1974–86;
  1991–
  (Vice-Principal 1995–)
D.R. de Lacey 1975–81
R.L. Sturch 1975–79
E.P. Cotterell 1976–95
  Principal 1990–95

D.J. Tidball 1977–85
  (p/t from 1972)
  Principal 1995–

Miss M.J. Evans 1978–

M.C. Griffiths
  Principal 1980–89

P.G.A. Caley 1981–83
R.L. Gordon 1981–82
R.T. France 1981–88
  (Vice-Principal 1983–88)
I.H. Cory 1981–85
P.A. Hicks 1981–85; 1991–
D.C.T. Sheriffs 1982–
J.F. Webb 1982–94
J.-M. Heimerdinger 1983–
I.M. Macnair 1983–97
Miss S.M. Gillies 1984–91
A.J. Bishop 1984–85

R.F. Willoughby 1984–
M. Parsons 1984–88
D.F. Payne 1985–96
R.W.A. Letham 1986–89
N.S. Mercer 1986–95
  (Assistant-Principal
  1990–95)
C. Caragounis 1986–87
J. Ramsbottom 1986–91
S. Motyer 1987–
Miss A.F. Eves 1988–
M. Van Hamersveld 1989–90
C.H. Gempf 1989–
M. Greene 1990–99
  (Vice-Principal 1995–99)
G.W.P. McFarlane 1990–
Mrs G. Dallow 1991–98
A. Billington 1991–
C. McSparron 1991–97
A. Linfield (Librarian) 1993–
M.T. Pearse 1994–
P.G. Riddell 1995–
Miss A. Le Cornu 1996–
C. Jack 1997–
E. Adams 1997–99
C. Redgate 1997–
D. Peacock 1997–
Mrs J. Rennie 1999–
S.J. Walton 1999–

Name Index

Adams, Edward 254
Aeropagus 10, 142, 161, 180, 199
Africa Inland Mission (AIM) 34, 77–8, 114, 132, 137
Aldis, W.H. 12, 16, 21–5, 31, 34, 38, 76, 149
All Nations [Christian] College (ANCC) 20, 34, 38, 182, 213
    also All Nations Missionary College
Allen, Leslie 123, 132, 141, 170, 205–6, 207, 225–6, 275
Ash, R.N. 65
Atkinson, David 217

Balchin, John 92, 183, 202, 214–5, 220, 224
Baldwin, Joyce 48, 81, 224, 277
Bamber, Theo 44, 61, 65, 72, 105, 139
Barth, Karl 54, 125–9, 138
Bartlett, E.G.A. 65
Baughen, Michael 87, 277
Beasley-Murray, George 36, 39–40, 49, 61, 107, 129, 176, 220

Bediako, Kwame 1, 168, 179, 221, 250–1
Begg, Alistair 178, 200
Bible Training Institute (BTI) 15, 79, 81, 108, 124, 170, 178, 224
Billington, Antony 254–5
Bonhoeffer, Dietrich 117, 118, 127–8
Boyd, Robert 238, 240, 246
Brady, Steve 78–9, 206, 258
British Council of Churches 67, 130, 133
British Evangelical Council (BEC) 84, 92, 151–3, 155, 213, 231, 282
British Youth for Christ (BYFC, YFC) 58, 60, 176
Bruce, F.F. 17, 18, 25, 26, 76, 85–6, 125, 129, 203, 227
Brunel University 243–4, 246, 279
Brunner, Emil 54, 119, 125
Buckley, Tim 65, 79, 81, 93, 97, 105, 108, 110, 139, 151, 225, 242, 260
Bush, Elizabeth 222

Author Index